KT-431-854

Cases in Organisational Behaviour

SHREWSBURY COLLEGE OF ARTS & TECHNOLOGY
MAIN CAMPUS, LONDON RD.

Telephone 01743 342354

To Renew Book Quote No:
and last date stamped.

020333

Cases in Organisational Behaviour

**Derek Adam-Smith and
Alan Peacock**

University of Portsmouth

PITMAN PUBLISHING
128 Long Acre, London WC2E 9AN

A Division of Longman Group UK Limited

First published in 1994

A CIP catalogue record for this book can be obtained from the British Library.

ISBN 0 273 60390 6

Typeset by PanTek Arts, Maidstone, Kent
Printed and bound in Great Britain by Bell & Bain, Glasgow

The Publishers' policy is to use paper manufactured from sustainable forests.

CONTENTS

ACKNOWLEDGEMENTS

The compilation of an edited work such as this volume would not have been possible without the co-operation of the contributors on whose research and experience the cases are based. Our thanks to them for providing an interesting and challenging set of cases.

The framework for the order of the cases is based upon that used by our colleague at Portsmouth, Laurie Mullins, in the current edition of his book, *Management and Organisational Behaviour*. We are grateful to Laurie for the interest and enthusiasm he has shown in our work. Thanks also to another of our colleagues at Portsmouth, David Goss, for his comments on the Introduction.

Our special thanks to Mandy McCartney for her patience, good humour and diligence in typing the drafts of the publication and to Penelope Woolf, our publisher at Pitman, for her support and encouragement.

Derek Adam-Smith
Alan Peacock

NOTES ON THE EDITORS AND CONTRIBUTORS

EDITORS

Derek Adam-Smith B.Tech., M.A., Cert. Ed., M.I.T.D., is a Senior Lecturer in Human Resource Management at Portsmouth Business School where he teaches on both undergraduate and postgraduate courses. Derek has also worked as a consultant to a wide range of organisations in both the public and private sectors on a number of human resource management issues.

Alan Peacock M.Sc., D.M.S., M.I.P.M., M.M.S., is Head of Department of Human Resource Management at the University of Portsmouth Business School. He was employed for many years as a personnel specialist in both public and private sector organisations. He is a director of an employers' organisation and regularly presents cases to industrial tribunals.

CONTRIBUTORS

Gary Akehurst B.Sc. (Econ.), M.Sc. (Econ.) Retail Management, University of Wales, Cert. Ed. University of Manchester, Fellow of the Tourism Society and Member of the Institute of Management. He is currently Professor of Marketing and Head of Research in the Management Division of Southampton Institute Business School. Previously a senior management consultant with a leading firm of management consultants based in London; prior to this he worked in five university business schools and two international firms of chartered accountants.

Joanna Brewis B.Sc., is a Lecturer in Organisational Behaviour/Human Resource Management at the University of Portsmouth. She is currently working on her doctoral thesis which centres on a Foucauldian analysis of sexual harassment. She has an honours degree in Management Science and two years teaching experience in Organisational Behaviour.

Tony Callen D. Phil., is a Principal Lecturer in the School of Languages and Area Studies at the University of Portsmouth.

Marjorie Corbridge B.A., M.I.P.M., is a Senior Lecturer in Human Resource Management at Portsmouth Business School. She has many years practical personnel management experience in the National Health Service throughout the Wessex Region. Her main area of interest is the effective use of information technology to support HRM decision making.

Per Darmer Ph.D., M.Sc., is Assistant Professor in Organisational Behaviour at the Southern Denmark Business School, Sonderborg, where he teaches on undergraduate and masters programmes including international aspects of organisational behaviour on the School's International BA degree. His primary research interest is in organisational culture.

Tony Emerson B.Sc., M.Phil., is a Senior Lecturer in Management in the Business School, South Bank University. Within the University, he is responsible for the Research Unit in the M.Sc. in Human Resource Development programme, and is Course Director for the Co-operative Business & Management Skills Programme. He has been active in the 'new' co-operative sector since its emergence in the mid-1970s. His experience also includes serving as Chair of a local authority Economic Development Sub-Committee, and management training for voluntary and public sector organisations.

Pernille Eskerod M.Sc., B.A., is a doctoral candidate at the Southern Denmark Business School, Sonderborg. Her thesis explores the organisational behaviour aspects of project organisations and much of her research has been undertaken at Oticon. She also teaches project management and leadership on masters courses at the Business School.

David Farnham is Professor of Employment Relations at the University of Portsmouth. His publications include *Personnel in Context, The Corporate Environment, Employee Relations* (Institute of Personnel Management), *Understanding Industrial Relations* with J. Pilmott and *Public Administration in the UK* with M. McVicar (Cassell). He has also edited, with S. Horton, *Managing the New Public Services* (MacMillan).

Peter Gal Diploma in Pedogogics, Komensky University, Czechoslovakia. Postgraduate student in School of Business, Australian Catholic University. Peter is currently employed in the hospitality industry in Australia after a career of 20 years in the electronics industry in Czechoslovakia.

David Goss B.A., Ph.D., is a Reader in Organisational Behaviour at the University of Portsmouth Business School. He is the author of books on small business and human resource management and has written numerous articles in the areas of industrial sociology and HRM. He is currently researching the workplace implications of HIV/AIDS.

Sarah L. Henson B.A. (Hons) Business Studies, M.A. Industrial Relations is a graduate of the Institute of Personnel Management and is currently lecturing in Organisational Behaviour at the University of Portsmouth Business School.

Dr Henner Hentze is Professor of Personnel Management at the Fachhochschule Münster. He has several years experience as a middle manager in the personnel and training department of a tyre company and is a consultant in personnel and organisational issues and has a particular interest in medium-sized companies.

Dr Linda Hicks is a Principal Lecturer at the Portsmouth Business School. She is Course Manager of the Business Studies degree programme and has taught organisational behaviour to undergraduate and postgraduate students. A Chartered Occupational Psychologist Linda has experience as a practitioner and consultant. She has a particular, but not an exclusive, interest in gender and culture issues and is committed to workplace equality.

Robert Jones B.Sc. (Econ.), M.Sc. (Lond.), Ph.D. (Wits.), Senior Lecturer, School of Business, Australian Catholic University. He is a consultant with a range of Australian companies on workplace reform and Total Quality Management.

Linda Keen M.A. Social Work, B.A. Sociology, M.B.A., Ph.D. (expected completion date summer 1994). Research and Development Officer at Canterbury Business School. Linda has lectured for many years on a wide variety of management training/development programmes, mainly on Human Resource Management and Organisation Behaviour; her particular interest is in Public Sector Management. She was a District Councillor for 8 years.

Alex Littlewood B.Sc., M.A., M.I.P.M., is the Personnel Manager of a medium-sized company in the service sector. Her role covers the full range of personnel services for managers and employees and her particular areas of interest include job satisfaction, organisational culture and employment law.

Brian Aubrey McCormack gained an honours degree in Physics from Sheffield University and a Masters degree in Manpower Studies from Westminster University. He is a Fellow of the Institute of Personnel Management. As Partnership Executive of the HRD Partnership he is currently involved in a Learning Network of organisations defining competence-based change agent skills.

Linda McCormack gained an honours degree in Geography/Economic History at the University of Sheffield and is a fellow of the Institute of Personnel Management. After many years as a practising Personnel Manager, Linda was previously Course Director of the Personnel Management course at the Portsmouth Business School and is currently the Commercial Manager for the University of Portsmouth Enterprise Limited (UPEL). Linda sits on the IPM's National Quality Assurance Panel and lectures on Employee Development on the School's M.A. in Manpower Studies.

Tom McEwan B.A., M.B.A., Ph.D., is the Faculty Co-ordinator for International Development at Portsmouth Business School. He has carried out attitude surveys and various consultancies in the Hotel and Aeronautics industries and the NHS on the problems of introducing change in these organisations.

Karen Meudell M.B.A., D.M.S., M.I.P.M., M.I.T.D., M.B.I.M., is a Senior Lecturer in Organisational Behaviour, University of Portsmouth Business School. She has 17 years experience as a Human Resource Management practitioner and consultant in a variety of industries and eight years teaching experience in human resource management and organisational behaviour.

Laurie J. Mullins M.A., F.C.I.S., M.I.Mgt., D.M.S., M.Inst.A.M., is a Principal Lecturer at the Business School, University of Portsmouth. He has undertaken a range of consultancy work, and is an advisor and examiner for a number of educational bodies. Laurie is a regular contributor to a variety of journals and author of *Management and Organisational Behaviour* and *Hospitality Management: A Human Resources Approach*.

Roger Edward Page Ph.D, C.Eng., F.I. Chem.E., B.Tech., is Technical Director at Pall Europe Limited. Dr Page read Chemical Engineering at Bradford and Cambridge. After several years in Switzerland with a large pharmaceutical company in Production Development and Strategic Planning, he returned to the UK to join Pall Europe. He set up a new manufacturing plant in Ilfracombe (Devon) and managed this multimillion pound turnover plant with 200 people until promoted to Technical Director, where he manages Research and Development and, in a matrix organisation, the technical standards of Pall throughout Europe.

Stephen Pilbeam holds a Diploma in Personnel Management and is a Fellow of Institute of Personnel Management. He is a Senior Lecturer in Human Resource Management at Portsmouth Business School. Stephen has 15 years management experience including positions as a Training Officer, Personnel Manager and in General Management with a major national retailing organisation.

K. Alan Rutter B.A. (Hons), D.B.A., is a Secior Lecturer at Portsmouth Business School where he is currently researching strategic management problems using action research and cognitive mapping methods. Formerly, he held senior management positions in both large and medium-sized multinational firms.

Tony Strike D.M.S., M.I.P.M., is Assistant Director of Human Resources for Portsmouth NHS Trust.

Dr Dolores Thomson Yong B.A. (Hons), M.A., Ph.D., M.B.I.M., is a Senior Lecturer in International Economics (Hogeschool voor Economische Studies, Rotterdam) and Senior Research Fellow (EUR-ASIAN Institute for Organisation and Economics, Erasmus University, Rotterdam). Born in Malaysia, Dolores has worked at the former Anglian Regional Management Centre and the National University of Singapore. Currently she is pursuing her interest in international management in Holland.

Frederick William Turner holds a Diploma in Municipal Administration and is a Fellow of the Institute of Housing. He worked in local government for 38 years including posts as Director of Housing of the London Borough of Merton, Director at Clacton UDC and Directorships at Hove B.C. (Sussex). In these posts he held full membership of the Chief Officer's Management Team.

Jeff Watling B.Pharm., M.R.Pharms, M.B.A., M.C.P.P., is pharmaceutical advisor to Wessex Regional Health Authority and is also the pharmaceutical services manager for Portsmouth Hospitals NHS Trust.

Irene Watson M.I.P.M., is a Human Resources Consultant and partner in I & I Consulting. Irene has significant experience as a Personnel and Training Manager in both the public and private sectors and, more recently, as an independent HR consultant. Throughout her career, she has been closely involved with management education and training as a visiting lecturer, course tutor and external examiner.

Ian White B.A., is an honours graduate of the Business School, University of Portsmouth where his specialist interests included Organisational Analysis and Management of Personnel. Ian has undertaken a number of business assignments and has a particular interest in research investigations into improved organisational performance.

David Young B.Sc., M.Sc., Dip. ITD., is currently Training Resources Manager at London Co-operative Training Limited, a regional co-operative federation representing local co-operative enterprise development agencies throughout London and South-East England. He also works as an independent consultant, and as an Associate Lecturer in the Business School, South Bank University. Formerly a co-operative training and development worker at Ealing Co-operative Development Agency Ltd, he has been active in the 'new' co-operative sector since 1979, and he has been involved in the setting up and co-management of several common ownership co-operative businesses.

PREFACE

The case study method is now well established in the teaching of business and management studies. The aim of this book is to provide suitable material which explores issues relating to managerial knowledge, skills and competencies through exercises, role play and discussion groups and which is intended to support texts that deal with concepts and ideas relating to organisational behaviour. It provides material which is up to date and firmly grounded in real life organisations. Organisations that have agreed to be identified by name have approved the text and the use of detailed information. Some organisations, however, prefer to remain anonymous and in these cases the authors have changed some facts and names without distorting the main organisational issues and outcomes.

The growing 'internationalisation' of business and management, particularly where companies operate on a trans-European basis, has provided new challenges for the teaching of organisational behaviour. The inclusion of case studies which either directly deal with European issues or provide opportunities for cross-cultural analysis provides a necessary dimension which the editors consider to be an essential requirement for the text.

Tutors are increasingly acting as facilitators, developing student competence through discovery learning, critical questioning, and problem solving, and encouraging students to improve social and communication skills. Many of the contributions in this text can be used in a variety of ways to facilitate the learning process and can be additionally used as a form of assessment on both undergraduate and postgraduate programmes of study. This is particularly useful on modular courses which feature both core units and options. The cases suggest a range of activities that can be adapted to the particular needs of tutors and students.

As indicated above, the particular focus of this collection is the consideration of a managerial approach to organisational behaviour and the cases seek to provide a basis on which to formulate a critical appraisal of different perspectives on the structure, operation, and management of organisations and interactions among people who work in them. The book, it is hoped, will allow students to assess the relevance and value of organisational behaviour theories to an understanding of the behaviour of people at work. The underlying theme is to provide illustrations of the role of management as an integrating activity. This focus links with Laurie Mullin's book *The Management of Organisational Behaviour*, also published by Pitman Publishing, which is highly regarded by tutors of the subject and whose 'encyclopedic' approach provides opportunities to develop a wide range of case studies which explore various aspects of the subject and where relevant reading for students is contained in one text. It is therefore expected that this volume of case studies will be seen as complementary to this book. The cases can also be used to develop students' understanding where their knowledge has been gained from other reading.

A separate Lecturer's Guide is available to tutors to support their use of the cases.

INTRODUCTION

Organisational behaviour is a field of study concerned with attempts to understand the behaviour of people, individually and in groups, in relation to an organisational context. The subject area seeks to integrate contributions from the social sciences, particularly psychology, social psychology, sociology, political science and anthropology, and can provide managers with a systematic approach to the explanation and prediction of peoples' behaviour. Indeed, it is in the understanding of the 'human side' of work that organisational behaviour makes its unique contribution to management. The purpose of this book is to present cases containing practical problems whose solutions may be found through the application of social/behavioural theories. This is not to deny the value of the case material for other purposes but the primary aim is to allow readers to evaluate the utility of these theories in relation to the management of people in work organisations.

This chapter begins with a brief review of some current issues facing managers and of developments in the study of organisational behaviour before assessing the more specific use of the subject to managers. Against this background, consideration is given to how cases in the book can help managers in their understanding of people's behaviour at work. The framework used to group cases in each part of the book is presented and the chapter concludes with a brief introduction on how to tackle case studies.

WHY MANAGERS NEED ORGANISATIONAL BEHAVIOUR

The value of organisational behaviour to the work of management can be considered both in the light of the issues currently facing organisations and some of the key developments in the subject itself. Managers are faced by increasingly complex demands originating both from within their organisations and the environments within which they operate. Many of these demands are linked to the increasingly rapid pace of change that now characterises social and organisational life.

Political, economic, social and technological changes over the past decade have significant implications for the management of organisations. The election of right-wing governments in European countries, such as the

United Kingdom, France and Sweden, has resulted in a greater emphasis upon market forces as the key determinant of economic and social policies. In the UK this philosophy has led to the abandonment of the post-war consensus between government, employers and trade unions on the management of the economy and the emergence of individualism rather than collectivism as the focus for employee relations.

Despite the United Kingdom's reservations concerning the content of the Social Chapter of the Maastricht Treaty the influence of the European Community on employment legislation is likely to continue. Significant amongst these are measures to widen equality of opportunity. While the United Kingdom has an established body of anti-discrimination legislation, the groups covered and the detailed actions which are determined to be discriminatory continue to expand beyond those envisaged by the drafters of the original Acts of Parliament.

Economic change is reflected in the growth in international competition and the widened market for goods and services. Internationally, the increased competitiveness of the Pacific Rim economies has tested the ability of companies in Western industrialised countries to match, if not better, the price, quality, delivery and service offered by companies in the newly industrialised nations. In Europe the establishment of the Single Market and the consequential free flow of goods, services, capital and labour has provided difficulties and opportunities for companies operating in this market place. While the absence of trade tariffs can facilitate movement of goods and services between member states, unstable exchange rates – following the near collapse of the Exchange Rate Mechanism – mean that this avenue to price advantage cannot be relied upon. The challenge is to identify and implement other strategies to achieve competitive advantage, in particular the more innovative, flexible and imaginative use of human skills and potential (Best, 1990).

Social and technological change have implications for the labour market. Towards the end of the 1980s commentators in the United Kingdom were heralding the effects on organisations of the demographic 'time-bomb'(see, for example, Atkinson (1989)). Particularly important, it was suggested, was the reduction in the number of young people joining the labour market and of the lack of skills in the workforce. While the recession has cut the size of the labour force, thereby masking the impact of the demographic trough, limited recruitment is producing a workforce with an older average age. Significantly, society now contains a substantial number of young people who have had little or no formal work experience. If there is a significant upturn in demand and this pool of potential recruits called upon, the attitudes and perceptions of these young people will create a new set of challenges for managers.

The issues relating to an inadequately trained labour force can be cast alongside the technologically induced shifts in employment from manufacturing to the service sector. The manufacturing base is arguably comprised of more automated plant requiring greater technical competence in its operation and maintenance. The implications for employment are a decline in the number of semi-skilled and unskilled jobs traditionally associated with this sector of employment. Concurrently, the expansion of the service sector has resulted in the growth of jobs typically requiring lower levels of skill, highlighting the difficulties associated in motivating employees undertaking routine tasks in comparatively low paid occupations.

Similarly the authority of management is no longer as secure as it was; conflict over managerial decisions may arise along a number of fault lines. Economic inequality has been a traditional cause of discontent in work organisations but emerging sources can also be identified reflecting developments in the wider society. Gender and sexual divisions, and race and ethnicity are now firmly placed on the management agenda (Liff and Aitkenhead, 1992). An understanding of the attitudes, feelings and aspirations of those who may perceive discriminatory treatment is needed by managers in order that they may seek a resolution of the conflict engendered by such tensions.

There is evidence to suggest that the business environment is becoming increasingly international. The development of trading blocks like the European Community and the rise of the Pacific economies are two of the factors already cited that support this view. To these can be added the growth of multinational companies adopting global marketing and production strategies facilitated by sophisticated international communication systems and 'globalised' markets. In addition, the collapse of communist regimes in Eastern Europe offer tantalising but challenging new trading opportunities. Managers are increasingly likely therefore to find themselves working for companies that have sales and/or production operations in other countries. An understanding of how far, and in what ways, behaviour is influenced by differences in national culture is a pertinent question for those managers in such positions.

The increasingly competitive market place has led organisations to adopt strategies intended to ensure their survival and growth both during the economic boom of the 1980s and the recession of the early 1990s. The implementation of initiatives such as total quality management, just-in-time and computer-aided manufacture present managers with new systems of thought and practice which affect their working lives directly. They are being called upon to contribute to organisational attempts to foster the commitment of employees to the goals of the organisation, embrace the concept of an 'empowered' workforce and accept greater responsibility for the 'people side' of management. These developments can be located within the idea of 'soft' models of Human Resource Management (HRM) which themselves propose a changing role for managers where, for example, they may be more appropriately viewed as 'teamleaders' or 'cell co-ordinators'.

The changing demands faced by managers pose major questions concerning the behaviour of people, the answers to which are complex. Organisational behaviour offers managers a means of grasping these issues clearly and analysing them in relation to their individual, organisational and environmental implications.

DEVELOPMENTS IN ORGANISATIONAL BEHAVIOUR

A key element of organisational behaviour is the attempt to define the structure of organisations and the role of management in their operation. *Classical theory* postulated a set of universal principles which should guide the design of an organisation irrespective of its purpose, size or the people working within it. These logically determined, rational principles emphasised a hierarchy of management and highly formalised organisational relationships (see, for example, Fayol (1949)).

The classical view held that the economic efficiency of organisations could be enhanced by a clear division of labour and that a subordinate should have only one superior to whom he or she was responsible. From this it followed that the authority relationship inside organisations should pass along a chain of command from the top down with each manager having the right to direct the work of subordinates while simultaneously subject to the direction of his or her own manager. The number of employees for whom each manager was responsible – the span of control – should be small. While the actual number varied a figure of under ten was considered appropriate if the manager was to be able to maintain effective control of the employees' work activities. A further component of the classical view was that co-ordination of activities produced through a division of labour should be achieved through grouping them into specialised departments, functionally, geographically or product determined.

As these principles indicate, a central pillar of classical theory was the prescribed role for management in organisations, namely being charged with co-ordinating the activities of employees to ensure that organisational objectives are achieved. Typically, management was seen as divided into four functions:

- Planning – defining the organisation's goals, developing plans to achieve these goals and establishing methods to co-ordinate the necessary activities.
- Organising – deciding the structure of the organisation, determining the tasks to be done, who is to do them and establishing internal relationships.
- Leading – unifying and harmonising efforts within the organisation and obtaining maximum return from those employed.
- Controlling – establishing measures of performance and monitoring work progress against plans and taking corrective action when necessary.

Major criticisms have been levelled against the classical view of organisations. The values that underpin it held that for an efficient organisation there needed to be a unity of effort and this was seen to underestimate the creativity of employees and their capacity to cope with uncertainty. Similarly, the classical view fails to take into account sufficiently the impact of conflict on organisational life, particularly when the right of managers to manage is questioned. It is also clear that the work of managers is highly fragmented and does not fall into discrete packets labelled planning, organising, leading or controlling. Despite these criticisms the legacy of classical theory is such that many companies are organised and managed in a way which reflects its propositions.

The limitations of the classical theory of organisations have been recognised. While the environment within which organisations operated was relatively stable the search for the most appropriate structure and systems guided management thinking. But as the environment became more competitive it also became clear that there was no one best, universal structure for organisations. What emerged was a *contingency approach* recognising that there are a number of variables including environment, size, technology and workforce characteristics which will influence organisational design and the role of management. In addition the work of Hofstede (1980 and 1985) and Porter (1990) suggested that effective organisational form and management style are influenced by national cultures.

Thus the principles of the classical theorists were re-evaluated and different ideas postulated: the rigid adherence to the division of labour was seen to produce human diseconomies; boredom, poor quality, increased absenteeism and high labour turnover exceeded the economic advantages. Alternative forms of job design were encouraged which sought to widen rather than narrow job functions. Job enrichment schemes and autonomous work groups were held to result in increased productivity and improved quality in contrast to the restrictions inherent in the logic of the division of labour. The order which the unity of command principle sought to bring to reporting relationships was challenged by the benefits gained from different organisational forms like the matrix structure where employees report to different superiors for different parts of their work. The right to manage inherent in the person's formal position within the authority hierarchy of the organisation was increasingly called into question. New systems of work organisation; participation, teamworking and empowerment called upon managers to play a supportive, enabling role quite different to that of issuing instructions and expecting them to be followed without question. Better trained and more experienced staff responsible for determining their own level of output and working to specified quality standards suggested that the narrow span of control conceived by classical theory was no longer appropriate. In addition 'delayering' of management, with its consequential increasing span of control, can be identified as a deliberate strategy in many organisations. While 'departmentalisation' of activities remains a major component in the structure of organisations it is increasingly common for this to be arranged on a customer basis and there is a growing trend in the creation of work teams which cross traditional departmental lines.

In their review of the evolution of organisations and management Evans, Doz and Laurant (1989) argue that the environment is now more turbulent, highly competitive and complex than ever and that even the contingency model carries a level of rigidity that necessitates a search for new forms of organisation. This, they argue, can be conceptualised through the *dualistic organisation*. Rather than choosing between polar opposites (centralisation –decentralisation, formal–informal, individuality–teamwork etc.), organisations can gain competitive advantage by balancing these opposites in response to pressures in the environment. Dualistic organisations therefore recognise that while decentralising business units may produce enhanced performance, there is still a need to integrate their role into the overall organisation. The creativity encouraged by informality has to be channelled through a formal system if the ideas generated are to be turned into profitable ventures for the organisation. Individual capabilities need to be developed but these contributions can be maximised by effective teamwork.

The role of management in dualistic organisations becomes one of maintaining a dynamic balance between these binary opposites, i.e. managing in a constant tension. The successful organisation in the current complex environment is one that recognises such dualities as opportunities not irreconcilable contradictions.

> Dualities should not be viewed as threats to consistency and coherence, but as opportunities for creative organisation development, for gaining competitive advantage, for organisation learning and renewal.
>
> *Evans, Doz and Laurant (1989), p.224*

ORGANISATIONAL BEHAVIOUR AND MANAGEMENT

The complexity of the environment within which organisations operate and their responses to them have created a situation where the effective management of people becomes a prime requisite if organisations are to successfully achieve their goals. Organisational behaviour offers managers a means of understanding self and others, interpersonal relations and group working, and organisational and environmental dynamics.

Organisational behaviour is typically characterised as operating at three levels of analysis – individual, group and organisational. The application of these theories offer a number of options concerning the way in which organisations may be structured and managed. Studies of personality, attitudes, learning theories and the process of perception provide insights into the ways in which individuals differ and the implications for such issues as motivation and job satisfaction. At the next level, an analysis of group dynamics, communication networks and leadership theories are often complemented by attempts to understand the nature of power and politics, and the causes and resolution of conflict. An understanding of the impact upon behaviour of the structural design of organisations and its internal culture assist in the understanding of the way in which organisations may be developed and how change may be managed.

However, as the previous sections have tried to indicate, organisations are significantly influenced by the environment within which they operate. The complex interaction between internal and external pressures, where change can be seen as normality, is a major determinant of the performance of the organisation and its members. The result of this interweaving of factors can be usefully understood by viewing the organisation as an open system. Open system theory suggests that organisations take inputs from the environment including capital, people and materials and transform them into outputs such as products or services and return them to the environment. It also proposes that the organisation receives information about its performance through feedback loops. This information can then be analysed and any necessary adjustments attempted. In this sense the open system approach proposed here is a significant departure from traditional systems theory which views the organisation as a 'closed system' governed by either rigid environmental determinism or a self-governed tendency towards structural equilibrium (Whittington, 1989).

The open systems approach highlights the fact that the organisation is in continuous interaction with its environment and that it needs to respond to changes in that environment. In doing so, it proposes that organisations and the people who compose them possess a degree of self-regulation and choice, and are flexible and adaptable. Managers must, therefore, assess the implications of environmental change on the organisation and the people working within it. Organisational behaviour offers them theories which may help explain how people may react to strategies designed to cope with such changes.

CASES IN ORGANISATIONAL BEHAVIOUR

The impact on organisations, managers and their subordinates of internal and external changes is a theme reflected throughout the cases presented in this book. The body of knowledge offered by organisational behaviour can be explored in the analysis of the implications of these changes for managers concerned with the effective performance of people in the achievement of organisational objectives. Few real-life incidents deal with a single issue and this section explores a number of the key threads which are woven through the cases.

International aspects of organisational behaviour

The 'globalisation' of the business environment suggests a need for an international perspective of the study of organisational behaviour to allow an assessment of the extent to which theories about people's behaviour are transferable from one country to another. The increasing likelihood of managers having to deal with behavioural issues in organisations outside their own country is recognised through the inclusion of cases drawn from across Europe and beyond. Two concern companies located in Denmark (Cases 5 an 9), one in France (Case 25) and one which deals with a Franco-German company (Case 6). Wider international aspects are reflected in cases located in companies operating in Australia (Case 7) and Singapore (Case 2). In particular, the cases examine the value of theories developed in Western industrialised nations to managers operating in an industrialising Eastern culture (Case 2) and how a manager trained in a style of management appropriate to his own national culture may need to adjust when working in a foreign subsidiary (Case 6). Similarly, the success of a merger between companies based in different countries may be influenced by managements' sensitivity to national cultural differences and their implication for work behaviour (Case 5).

Organisation design

Organisational responses to opportunities or threats identified in the external environment may necessitate new or modified forms of structure. This may result in a radical approach to win competitive advantage (Case 9), to increase formalisation in a climate of rapid expansion (Case 2), or be aimed at integrating business units following a take–over (Case 11). Changes in the environment may produce high levels of uncertainty such that managers may need to explore new approaches to the development of their organisation's strategy (Case 10). In any event, structures are not neutral: they will have an impact upon the behaviour of those working in the organisation, while at the same time this behaviour influences the structure. This may involve changes in the work roles of middle managers (Case 13) or the impact upon manager–employee and employee–employee relationships (Cases 3 and 8). The extent to which managers apply principles of organisation theory is explored in Case 1.

Developments in the public sector

The British Conservative Government's approach over the last decade has caused radical changes in the structure and function of the public sector; most notable, perhaps, has been the introduction of market forces as the prime driver for increasing efficiency. In local government the implications for managers of traditional political tensions (Case 8) have been overlaid with complexities arising from the Compulsory Competitive Tendering for services and a move towards a more consumer-oriented management of service provision with consequential changes to organisational structure and new responsibilities for middle managers (Case 13). Similar pressures can be identified in the National Health Service. These changes have highlighted such issues as accountability, budgetary control and working arrangements (Cases 12 and 19) as well as the changing role of support services inside these organisations (Cases 19 and 24).

Mergers and acquisitions

In the private sector the growth of companies through mergers, acquisitions and diversification continues with consequential implications for organisation structure and management control systems (Cases 11 and 17). The extent to which separate business units are integrated into the overall structure will vary and may be influenced by the style of the holding company, the commercial success of the subsidiary and its geographical location. Where units have been allowed substantial autonomy the planning and management of later attempts at closer working relationships pose an interesting challenge for managers (Cases 5, 6 and 23).

Organisational culture

Recent attention in the study of organisations has been given to viewing organisations in terms of cultures (see, for example, Deal and Kennedy (1989) and Handy (1985)) and attempting to explain the impact of this on behaviour. The growing interest is reflected in its representation in the cases which explore the operation of culture in a number of aspects of organisational life. Issues relating to organisational culture can arise in the aftermath of a take-over where the subsidiary's culture is markedly different to that of the parent company (Case 17) such that management are faced with major problems of achieving an appropriate balance between integration and differentiation. Organisations may attempt to create new cultures as part of a strategy for survival and growth (Case 26) but it appears that such initiatives need to take account of the nature of the organisation and may be closely related to the prevalent management style (Cases 7, 15 and 25). Cultures, it is proposed, have direct impact upon the performance of the organisation (Case 14) and upon the behaviour of individuals within it (Case 3).

Leadership

The role of the manager as a leader and explanations of the attributes of a 'good' leader occupy a significant proportion of organisation behaviour literature. At one level the impact on a firm of a transformational/charismatic leadership style, typically associated with business founders and senior executives, is often closely related to attempts to establish and maintain an appropriate organisational culture as a means of enhancing a company's fortunes (Cases 7, 15, 25 and 27). A change in senior management which results in a modified approach to the style in which the organisation is run and in shifts in priorities can be important influences on the behaviour of employees (Cases 10 and 23). Where managers have been successful in turning round a loss-making company and have created a positive commitment amongst employees they may face difficulties when pressures in the environment necessitate the introduction of strategies which appear to undermine management credibility in the eyes of the workforce (Case 5). At the department level the leadership role of the manager can be influential in the performance of the team of employees (Case 26) and is subject to the prevailing pressures and tensions within the organisation as a whole (Case 8). There is interest in the extent to which a leadership style developed through training and experience in one national culture can be applied to other countries (see, for example, Hofstede (1980) and (1985), Smith (1992), and Cases 2 and 6).

Job satisfaction and motivation

The concern of managers for improved productivity and reduced labour turnover and absenteeism has led to considerable interest being shown in those factors that influence attitudes to work and levels of motivation amongst employees. The concept of job satisfaction, that is, an employee's attitude towards his or her job, is inherently complex and multifaceted (Cases 7 and 14). The nature of interpersonal relationships at work, the way in which these may flourish inside different types of organisation structure and the extent to which they meet employee's expectations may, it is suggested, influence levels of satisfaction at work (Case 3). Co-operative ventures are typically portrayed as ones in which motivation and morale are likely to be higher than is found in traditional work organisations. It seems, however, that this is only likely to be the case if the company is able to build upon a commitment amongst its members to the co-operative ethos (Case 16). While a number of factors can be cited as significant in determining an employee's motivation, leadership style and the methods of management control utilised by the organisation are particular features which are argued to be relevant (Cases 5 and 17). Maintaining levels of motivation following key interventions in the employment policies the organisation pursues is a key task for managers. For example, a continued employee interest in, and enthusiasm for, quality improvement schemes is vital if such initiatives are to achieve long-term benefits envisaged by the company (Case 15). In contrast, managers also need to consider the impact upon the morale of the remaining employees of a redundancy programme which has resulted in job losses amongst their work colleagues (Case 21).

Equal opportunities

Whether legal enactment, both in Britain and through European Community measures, has reduced discrimination and provided genuine equality of opportunity can be questioned. None the less, these measures and the pressures resulting from a greater awareness in society of gender, disability, ethnicity and sex differences challenge the attitudes and behaviour of those in work organisations. Stereotypes of women can impede their progress into managerial positions even in organisations which may be perceived as potentially female empowering (Case 4) while the structure of relationships can lead to incidents of sexual harassment (Case 3). Discriminatory behaviour can also be seen against those with specific sexual orientations particularly where these are perceived to pose a threat to co-workers (Case 18). The need for equitable treatment of employees with a disability provides an additional element in the management decision-making process (Cases 20 and 21). A related issue is how applicants with limited work experience, for example, young people who have found difficulty obtaining employment after leaving school, or who have gaps in their employment, for example women returning to the labour market, may be credited with knowledge and skills gained from undertaking other activities (Case 22).

Employment law

Attempts to use legal measures to change behaviour, particularly that of managers, in employment matters has been a developing trend over the past two decades. The influence of employment law can be seen in relation to conduct of the dismissal of an employee (Case 20) and handling staff reductions in attempts to maintain the viability of an enterprise (Case 21). The limited aspects of employment covered by the law and whether those matters not covered can be left to voluntary initiatives remains a feature of the debate in employment practice (Case 18). These cases also provide opportunities to consider the ethical and moral responsibilities owed to staff by managers in their dealings with them and thereby connects with some of the issues related to the social responsibilities of management.

Training and development

A regular criticism levelled against industry, particularly in Britain, is that it fails to invest adequately in the training and development of the workforce. A series of government schemes have been launched, with varying degrees of success, over the past 30 years which have been designed to encourage employers to increase the resources devoted to training; the latest being the Investors in People initiative (Case 27). The definition of competence needed to perform specific work roles is an emerging approach to the identification of employees' training needs (Case 22) on which the recently established British National Council for Vocational Qualifications initiative is based. It is suggested that training and development has a role to play in developing managers and employees' abilities to cope with organisational change strategies resulting from financial and market pressures (Cases 12 and 23). In some cases the approach marks a radical shift in the way learning and training are conceptualised to the extent that it can encourage the emergence of a new culture within the organisation (Case 26). Conversely, the prevailing male-dominated culture in some industries is sufficiently pervasive to raise important questions about women's access to management development programmes and how this relates to equal opportunities at work (Case 4).

Power and politics in organisations

There is a growing realisation that such central themes in organisational behaviour as structure, leadership and motivation are unable fully to explain people's behaviour. The recognition that other forces may be at work has led to a growing interest in the study of the influence of power relationships on behaviour. The concept of power aids in the explanation of the sources and possible means of resolving conflict at work and how power bases may be utilised in political networking by individuals. The particular significance of power as an factor in behaviour can be seen in those organisations where there is an overt Political Party involvement in their establishment and functioning (Cases 8 and 16). Power is also a major influence in interpersonal relations, particularly where the power base arises through a manager–employee relationship (Case 3). Organisational politics can have a bearing on leadership style (Cases 6, 10 and 27), while informal networks inside organisations appear to be an important factor in an individual's chances of promotion, particularly if there are barriers to them joining such networks (Case 4). Perceptions of the nature of power and means of resolving differences have been related regularly to a person's Frame of Reference (see Fox (1974) and Cases 17 and 19). National cultural differences in how conflict is viewed has, it is suggested, important implications for cross-cultural management (Case 2).

The search for an understanding of the complex variables that influence people's behaviour at work provides a major challenge to managers. The cases which follow provide an opportunity for managers to evaluate the utility of organisational behaviour theories as a guide to their search.

USING THE CASE STUDIES

The collection contains twenty-seven cases grouped in six parts which broadly follow the structure of Mullins' book (1993). These are:

- Management and organisational behaviour
- The individual, groups and leadership
- Context of the organisation
- Organisational processes
- The personnel function
- Improving organisational performance

Individual case studies follow a common structure commencing with background information to set the context of the problem. This is followed by the facts relevant to the issue, the behaviour of the people concerned, and a set of specific questions or activity brief for students. Recommended reading, which should be readily available to students, is given for each case.

It is recognised that while each case will have a particular topic and focus, there may well be other themes included in the case. In order to help tutors identify appropriate cases, an index, in the form of a matrix, is shown in Figure I. 1 which for each case, identifies the major topic covered and possible links with other aspects of organisational behaviour.

TACKLING CASE STUDIES

The main objective behind the use of case studies is usually the application of theoretical knowledge to practical situations. The following cases have been collected to provide suitable material that will enable participants to demonstrate analytical ability, logical thinking, judgement, creative skills, social skills, persuasiveness, communication skills and skills in self-analysis. They should also provide an interesting vehicle for reinforcing basic concepts and skills and can be used for individual or group assessments. The traditional approach promoted by the Harvard Business School to case study analysis is the use of open discussion amongst group members. However this can be restrictive and consideration should be given to alternatives such as formal presentations and role play. The activities suggested at the end of each case should therefore be used as a guide but the material should be adapted and used to meet the needs of tutors and their groups.

It should be recognised that the case study method is very different from traditional teaching methods such as the lecture, seminar and tutorial. To avoid possible problems in the transfer of learning it should be realised that students often find difficulty in defining problems and dealing with ambiguous problems particularly in the area of organisational behaviour where there is no *right* answer. Traditional study skills that are often appropriate to

Case number	1	2	3	4	5	6	7	8	9	10	11	12	13	14	15	16	17	18	19	20	21	22	23	24	25	26	27
PART 1 Management and Organisational Behaviour	●	●	●			O	O		O	O						O	O										
PART 2 The Individual Groups & Leadership		O	O	●	●	●	●	●						O				O	O		O						
PART 3 Context of The Organisation	O	O							●	●	●	●	●			O											O
PART 4 Organisational Processes					O						O		O	●	●	●	●			O	O		O		O		
PART 5 The Personnel Function				O														●	●	●	●	●	O	O		O	O
PART 6 Improving Organisational Performance			O	O			O	O		O		O			O							O	●	●	●	●	●
Suitable for role play activities		✔			✔								✔	✔	✔				✔	✔	✔	✔		✔			

Key: ● Main topic   O Supporting topic

Fig I.1 Matrix showing relationship of cases to organisational behaviour topics

lectures are not easily applicable to the case study approach. After a lecture a student can reflect on facts learnt and can often reinforce these by reference to books or lecture notes. After a case discussion a student may feel that progress through the case study process is slow and seemingly inefficient. However the true benefit of the case study method is to provide a vehicle for developing skills which are essential to managers who are required to make decisions on organisational behaviour issues. In addition, since it can be argued that there is little at stake, students and tutors are free to experiment in the learning process.

In order to assist students to cope with complex and uncertain situations it is useful to provide guidance on how to deal effectively with case study analysis. *This guidance should not imply mechanical procedures and production of standard answers but rather be used to promote broad and flexible guidelines which will allow students to develop their own personal case study style.*

Easton (1982) provides an excellent step-by-step approach to case study analysis. He promotes a seven-step process which is summarised below:

- **Understand the situation** – Spend time reading the case and getting a 'feel' for the main issues. Organise the information and consider which is not valid, precise or relevant and what is missing. What is fact and what is opinion.
- **Diagnose the problem area** – The difference between what is (or will be) and what we would like the situation to be. Easton warns that this is often difficult as some problems are symptoms of more fundamental problems. It is often necessary to unravel complex relationships and distinguish between cause and effect and then determine which problems are high priority and why.
- **Generate alternative solutions** – Understand the nature of alternative solutions before using a variety of methods to link them up. Be as creative as possible in formulating solutions. Consider the use of appropriate creative techniques such as brainstorming. List and organise solutions using evaluation cycles or solution trees.
- **Use solutions to predict outcomes** – Predict all possible outcomes and realise that not all outcomes are likely to occur. Again, techniques can be used for listing and estimating the probability of likely outcomes.
- **Evaluate alternatives** – List the pros and cons of each and subsequently elaborate, qualify and quantify to allow direct comparisons to be made, then make the choice.
- **Round out the analysis** – Review the two previous stages and decide how much information to include. Provide a contingency plan to cope with the possibility of events not turning out as you expect.
- **Communicate the results** – Plan how best to communicate the result and consider the original requirements of the case study brief. Use appropriate communication methods and provide clear links between problems and solutions.

RECOMMENDED READING

The following readings provide more detailed guidance on the use and analysis of case studies.

Easton, G. (1992). *Learning from Case Studies*, Second Edition, London: Prentice Hall.
Mullins, L. J. (1984). 'Tackling Case Studies', *Student Administrator*, Vol 1, No 5.
Reynolds, J. I. (1980). *Case Study Method in Management Development*, Geneva: International Labour Office.
Tyson, S. and Kakabadse, A. (1987). *Case Studies in Human Resource Management*, London: Heinemann.

REFERENCES

Atkinson, J. (1989). 'Four Stages of Adjustment to the Demographic Downturn', *Personnel Management*, August.
Best, M. (1990). *The New Competition: Institutions of Industrial Restructuring*, Cambridge: Polity.
Deal, T. and Kennedy, A. (1989). *Corporate Cultures*, Harmondsworth: Penguin Books.
Easton, G. (1992). *Learning from Case Studies*, Second Edition, London: Prentice Hall.
Evans, P., Doz, Y. and Laurant, A. (1989). *Human Resource Management in International Firms: change, globalization, innovation*, London: MacMillan.
Fayol, H. (1949). *General and Industrial Management*, London: Pitman.
Fox, A. (1974). *Beyond Contract: Work, Power and Trust Relations*, London: Faber and Faber.
Handy, C. (1985). *Understanding Organizations*, Third Edition, Harmondsworth: Penguin Books.
Hofstede, G. (1980). *Culture's Consequences; International Differences in Work-Related Values*, London: Sage.
Hofstede, G. (1985). 'The Interaction Between National and Organizational Value System', *Journal of Management Studies*, 22:4.
Liff, S. and Aitkinhead, M. (1992). 'Equal Opportunities: an Attempt to Restructure Employment Relations', in J. Hartley and G. Stephenson (eds) *Employment Relations*, Oxford: Blackwell.
Porter, M. (1990). *The Competitive Advantage of Nations*, London: MacMillan.
Mullins L. (1993). *Management and Organisational Behaviour*, London: Pitman.
Smith, P. B. (1992). 'Organizational Behaviour and National Culture, *British Journal of Management*, Volume 3, Number 1.
Whittington, R. (1989). *Corporate Strategies in Recession: social structure and strategic choice*, London: Unwin Hyman.

PART 1

Management and organisational behaviour

Part 1 introduces three case studies that provide a general view of the nature of organisational behaviour, consider differing approaches to organisations and management and explore outcomes resulting from decisions and actions of management in different organisational settings. The opening case deals with an issue in a modern commercial organisation located in England. The title *'Application of organisation theory in Helgaton Limited'* captures the essence of the issues explored which result from an empirical investigation into the extent to which organisational theory can assist managers to cope with change.

In contrast, the second case *'Sentosa Engineering – managing in an eastern culture'* provides a view of formal organisational structures in a rapidly expanding organisation located in Singapore. The context provides an interesting view of issues associated with the management of a multi-ethnic workforce, with attitudes and value systems of the workforce spanning both Eastern and Western cultures.

The final contribution *'The role of intimacy at work: Interactions and relationships in the modern organisation'* compares and contrasts the culture and resulting interpersonal relationships within two organisations in the British University system. The views and values of staff in each organisation promote different outcomes that affect individuals and organisational processes. In particular, the case focuses on managerial decision making and the role of intimacy at work.

CASE 1

Applications of organisation theory in Helgaton Limited

Laurie Mullins and Ian White

Ideas on organisations, and their structure and management can be traced back for thousands of years. The Industrial Revolution and ensuing factory systems, however, challenged many of these traditional ideas. Since that time there have been many developments in management thinking intended to meet these challenges and focusing on a whole range of organisational issues. As a result a recognised body of theory has evolved which provides a number of contrasting approaches to improving organisational performance and effectiveness (for example Mullins, 1993).

The wide range of elements which make up any one organisational study and the divergence of perspectives adopted by authors means that it is difficult to provide one all-embracing definition of organisation theory. However, one convenient definition is: 'organization theory can be defined as the study of the structure, functioning and performance of organizations, and the behaviour of groups and individuals within them' (Pugh, 1990, p.ix).

It is often argued, however, that theories have only limited validity in the explanations or predictions they offer and little relevance to real-life situations (for example Lee, 1990). This case study presents the results of an empirical investigation that attempts to assess the extent to which organisation theory has any practical applications for managers in a modern commercial organisation.

BACKGROUND

The overall mission of Helgaton Ltd is to deliver quality business products and systems throughout the UK and Ireland. The company employs more than 4,000 people in nearly 50 locations. In order to help in the drive to fulfil the mission there are four stated 'Common Goals' related to customers, quality, profitability, and employees. These Common Goals are intended to provide central direction and focus for departments and the individuals within them.

Emphasis on quality

The continuing desire of Helgaton Ltd to become a Total Quality Company is the embodiment of corporate values. Quality is a basic business principle and means providing customers with innovative products and services that fully satisfy their negotiated requirements. This philosophy is reflected for example in terms of the BS 5750 status awarded to Helgaton Ltd by the British Standards Institute.

Tasks, Goals and Objectives

In consideration of the overall mission of Helgaton Ltd, the corporate plans are embodied within a series of functional Tasks, Goals and Objectives (TGO). Each individual employee receives a TGO which is a translation from the functional level into the targets and actions which are relevant for the individual job role.

Restructuring

Helgaton Ltd is also a change-oriented company. During 1992 a major restructuring process was undertaken. In order to provide a more customer responsive structure a whole layer of middle management was removed from the customer service division. Attention was also focused on developing closer teamworking among sales and service operations rather than operating as separate divisions. A large financial investment had also been made in implementing the concept of autonomous work groups.

THE SITUATION

An investigation was undertaken with the aim of addressing the practical applicability of organisation theory at Helgaton Ltd and the extent to which it meets the needs of the manager. This involved the analysis of published material already available within the company (secondary data) and information generated firsthand from personal interviews with managers (primary data).

Secondary data

Helgaton Ltd produces an enormous amount of literature aimed at informing and aiding the employees. This literature may be seen to reflect, in part, the management and structure of the company. Some examples are as follows.

Company manuals

Company manuals were found to be very specific in terms of policy and procedure. For example, departmental manuals explain policy in infinite detail and an accompanying manual details every step required in carrying out this policy. Employee manuals are in similar detail and include an analysis of the required manual skills.

Autonomous Work Groups (AWG)

A comprehensive set of documents have been prepared by the company which set out: the AWG environment; the need for change; what is the AWG; the vision; limits of responsibilities; benefits to the individual; benefits to the company; and hopes and concerns.

Organisational processes

The recruitment and selection process is based on scientific principles. Detailed Job Profiles are built up and for interview purposes comprehensive Candidate Profiles are constructed. If suitable candidates have the right technical qualifications and pass the appropriate psychometric testing, they are matched against the job profiles. Other 'tools' include detailed processes intended to help employees in problem solving and to improve quality.

The employee survey

This survey and analysis is carried out every year and is undertaken by an independent research company. The survey involves a wide range of questions related to subjects such as management systems and styles; working conditions; training; career development; pay; benefits; job security; team spirit; and overall job satisfaction.

The same research company also provides a comparative analysis related to other companies that they survey. Results of the survey are confidential within the company but currently overall job satisfaction within Helgaton Ltd is around the 55 per cent mark.

Primary Data

Although secondary data may provide an important source of supporting information it does not by itself provide a sufficiently sound basis on which to formulate any conclusions. In order to examine further the application of organisation theory it was necessary to obtain more specific and detailed data. For this purpose use was made of the semi-structured interview with managers.

The survey population

The broad categorisation adopted was that of a manager and non-manager dichotomy. Because of their position and experience managers were considered to be the most appropriate population for the survey and the resulting data more valid and easier to generalise. The population was quota sampled. Attempts were made to balance, as far as possible, the demographics, location, and seniority and experience of the managers. A further consideration was availability of the managers' time. Details of the interviewee statistics are given below:

Number Interviewed 15
11 male; 4 female

Function – Customer Services Division 9
       – Sales and Operations 4
       – Personnel 1
       – Finance 1

Length of Service – < 5 years 2
       – 5–10 years 1
       – 10–15 years 3
       – 15–20 years 2
       – > 20 years 7

Length of Time in Management – < 5 years 4
       – 5–10 years 3
       – 10–15 years 5
       – 15–20 years 2
       – > 20 years 1

Pilot study

In order to test the reliability of the interview a pilot study was undertaken involving a representative member of the population. This pilot study highlighted two major issues.

● Many of the questions were either too open or too closed and needed to be refined.
● Initially the responses were handwritten. This was both costly in terms of time and more importantly revealed the risk of missing vital pieces of data. It was decided therefore to tape-record the interviews and to transcribe the results at a later date.

In order to try to avoid the managers gaining a feel for any particular sort of responses expected, the questions were arranged so as not to be sequential. The revised list of questions used in the interviews is given below:

1. Do you feel that there are good channels of communication within Helgaton?
2. Do you have a clearly defined job role? If so, where is it laid out?
3. What do you feel motivates Helgaton employees?
4. How do you go about achieving your goals at work?
5. To what extent do you feel a change in technology would affect the way Helgaton operates?
6. How do you plan your work?
7. Why do you believe Helgaton has chosen the empowered working group as the way forward?
8. How would a subordinate employee describe your management style?
9. To what extent do you feel teamwork is important to (a) Helgaton and (b) yourself?
10. Do you feel Helgaton's organisational structure is hierarchical?
11. To what extent do you see Helgaton Ltd as belonging to a larger environment?
12. Do you perceive there to be many technical requirements to your job?
13. What are your personal goals at work?
14. What do you feel is the purpose of training an employee?
15. What do you believe to be the basis of promotion at Helgaton?
16. How well do you see Helgaton's management respond to change?
17. To what extent do you plan the work of others?
18. Can you rate the following five factors in order of importance to (a) Helgaton (b) yourself?
    Groups and Leadership; Communications; Output; Motivation; Job Design.
19. Do you feel that an individual's behaviour can be predicted and if so, how?
20. Do you believe there to be a clear division between Helgaton management and subordinates?
21. What other roles within Helgaton have you been involved in?
22. Do you feel Helgaton is keen to understand what satisfies an employee at work?
23. Do you feel committed to a common purpose at work?

Collecting the data

Interviews lasted on average just over one hour, were arranged when managers could best spare the time and took place over a period of about one month. Managers were informed that the interview would be taped and no one objected to this. The interview involved asking the questions, elaborating and probing where necessary, and finding out more about the manager's background in case this might affect any of the responses. *For the same reason the specific purpose of the interview was not explained to the managers.* The tapes were then transcribed and tabulated.

Results of the interview questions

Note: Because some of the questions prompted more than a single response, percentages may total more than 100.

1. Channels of communication

33 per cent argued that channels of communication were good, 53 per cent that they were poor and 14 per cent argued they were both good and poor.

2. Clearly defined job role

All managers pointed to their Tasks, Goals and Objectives (TGO) as evidence of a clearly defined job role. The TGO relates the four company goals to the employee. The most senior managers clearly stated the relationship between company goals and that of the individual. Other managers argued that the TGO provided only an overview of their job role. It was also noted that the lower down the organisational structure, the more restrictive the perception of the TGO.

3. Motivation of employees

73 per cent stated money as a clear motivator. Sales and operations managers claimed that motivation was also dependent upon function: sales staff being motivated more by money and service staff by job satisfaction. Service and personnel managers claimed it was pay. Only the most senior managers directly referred to the employee survey carried out each year.

4. Achieving goals at work

Responses were of a general nature such as: 'by attention to and following my TGO'; 'by hard work'; 'whatever I do at work doesn't really matter so long as it is seen to be related to the four common goals'.

5. Effects of technology

The responses made clear that Helgaton Ltd is a technology driven company, for example the increasing use of mobile telephones. However, two managers indicated that the sole reason for the introduction of technology is to increase productivity. The problems of introducing technology without the necessary full training was also pointed out.

6. Planning of work

60 per cent specifically stated that their work is planned by their diary. Management meetings at regular times in the month and regular meetings with customers, for example, largely dictated their movements at work. One manager estimated that 50 per cent of time was dictated by the diary.

7. Empowered working group

The importance of quality (including the work of Deming) and the influence of Japanese working methods were cited as examples. It was widely believed that the benefits to the customer, employee and business results justified the large expenditure on this concept. Many managers also highlighted the autonomous work group concept as an example of the application of organisation theory.

8. Management style

When managers were asked how their subordinates would describe their management style all apart from one (93 per cent) focused on terms such as 'fair', 'democratic', 'supportive', 'honest', 'caring' and 'humanistic'.

9. Importance of teamwork

All managers bar one felt totally committed to the importance of teamworking and believed it was the only way the business could move forward. The autonomous work group concept involved all employees including managers as well. The increasing attention given to teamworking was welcomed by the sales and operations managers who expressed their commitment to the concept as being the way forward to business success.

10. Hierarchical structure

67 per cent indicated that the structure was not hierarchical in terms of specific functions. However, 47 per cent argued that a hierarchy still existed

within Helgaton Ltd or within particular functions. One manager suggested that 'the principles of Taylor still exist within Helgaton'.

11. The larger environment

Although managers appeared to recognise that Helgaton Ltd was part of a larger environment, responses tended to identify only broad elements such as the 'Green' issue. There were no responses which referred to particular environmental factors influencing behaviour in work organisations.

12. Technical requirements of the job

All claimed that a high level of skill is needed to undertake their job role. The customer service managers had all come through the ranks and started as service engineers. At that level technical requirements are high but at management level only a broad technical knowledge is required; business skills are more important than mechanical skills. Non-service managers also recognised the need for business and management skills.

13. Personal goals at work

47 per cent claimed that their only goal at work was to achieve the targets set by the company or to be the best region in terms of customer satisfaction. No conflict between business goals and personal goals was revealed. However only senior managers clearly stated the relationship between the company goals and those of the individual. Some managers had targeted future managerial positions in accordance with the company succession planning programme but no details were disclosed.

14. The purpose of training employees

87 per cent believed in the principle of training employees so that they become more efficient. 53 per cent recognised the importance of development of the individual as a person, but this was a secondary feature. One manager quoted the principle of 'self-actualising them'.

15. Basis of promotion

In the majority of cases, managers clearly stated 'merit' or 'ability' as the overt belief. However, the 'if your face fits' syndrome was also an apparent covert reason. One senior manager argued that with the removal of a layer of management promotion chances were reduced.

16. Management response to change

73 per cent claimed that they responded very well and some claimed to actually thrive on change. 27 per cent claimed that management had severe difficulty but the implication appeared to be that this applied to other managers rather than to themselves. One manager pointed to the managing change training course offered by Helgaton to help with any problem areas.

17. Planning the work of others

Of the eleven managers with line responsibilities, 73 per cent (8) indicated that they do not specifically plan the work of their subordinates. Instead they tended to agree deadlines to work to and left subordinates to achieve tasks their own way in the given time. The remaining three managers claimed that they planned the work of others in great detail.

18. Importance of factors

Managers were asked to rate five factors in order of importance to both Helgaton Ltd and to themselves (they were permitted to tie answers). Results were then tabulated, and set out below.

For each heading, the first column shows the order of importance, the second column the importance they saw Helgaton Ltd attaching to each factor, the third column is their own ranking of the factor, and the final column looks at responses which ranked the same for both Helgaton and the manager.

Order of importance attributed to five factors

Output

Imp.	Hel.	You	Same
1	9	7	4
2	1	2	–
3	–	4	–
4	4	2	–
5	1	–	–
Total	15	15	4

Groups and leadership

Imp.	Hel.	You	Same
1	5	5	3
2	3	1	1
3	4	3	1
4	3	3	–
5	–	3	–
Total	15	15	5

Communications

Imp.	Hel.	You	Same
1	1	4	1
2	3	2	1
3	9	4	3
4	1	4	–
5	1	1	–
Total	15	15	5

Motivation

Imp.	Hel.	You	Same
1	–	7	–
2	6	3	1
3	3	1	–
4	4	3	1
5	2	1	–
Total	15	15	2

Job design

Imp.	Hel.	You	Same
1	2	2	–
2	–	2	–
3	3	1	–
4	2	1	–
5	8	9	6
Total	15	15	6

For example, according to nine respondents output is a factor that Helgaton would rate as number one importance. Seven managers rated output as *their* highest priority and of these seven, four also ranked output as of greatest importance to Helgaton. Thus 57 per cent of those managers who believed output was the most important factor to Helgaton also claimed it was their highest priority.

19. Prediction of behaviour

All the managers believed that the behaviour of an individual can be predicted providing the individual is well known to them. There were, however, no indications of whether any particular behavioural assumptions, for example relating to motivation, job satisfaction or work performance, are made in Helgaton Ltd.

20. Division between management and subordinates

93 per cent perceived there to be a division to some extent although this may be from a subordinate only view and/or that these divisions were being removed. Two managers further suggested that the division was due, at least in part, to the benefits received by managers when compared with subordinates – for example bonus schemes and choice of company car. One manager stated clearly that there was no division.

21. Other roles within Helgaton Ltd

Within the customer service division all nine managers interviewed had always worked in service. The other six managers had varied backgrounds but tended to remain in the same function. All the service managers indicated that possible future moves would still be within service.

Although the company promotes the belief that cross-functional moves are possible, this appeared to be a rare occurrence on a permanent basis. 50 per cent had moved on a temporary or secondment basis but only one manager had moved between functions on a permanent basis.

22. Satisfaction of employees

Managers felt that Helgaton Ltd was keen to find out what satisfies employees although some responses suggested this might be only a 'lip-service' exercise. It was only the most senior managers who directly linked their responses to the employee survey carried out each year. 33 per cent highlighted the interest in satisfying the employee in terms of the time and money spent in undertaking the employee survey.

23. Commitment to a common purpose

There was a claimed 100 per cent commitment felt to a common purpose at work. However, the nature of this common purpose varied. Some managers expressed that they felt committed to their TGO, some to the stated goals of Helgaton Ltd, some to their region, some to business results, and some to survival of the business.

ACTIVITY BRIEF

1 *Comment critically on the nature and value of the investigation. What difficulties does such an investigation present and how might these difficulties be best overcome?*

2 *State clearly the conclusions you draw from the investigation and discuss the extent to which it reveals practical applications of organisation theory.*

3 *Explain and justify the specific recommendations you would make to the top management of Helgaton Ltd as a result of the investigation.*

RECOMMENDED READING

1. Mullins L. J. (1993). *Management and Organisational Behaviour*, Third edition, London: Pitman, Chapter 2.
2. Pugh D. S.(ed) (1990). *Organization Theory: selected readings*, Third edition, Harmondsworth: Penguin.
3. Lee R. A. (1990). 'There is nothing so useful as an appropriate theory', in Wilson D. C. and Rosenfeld R. H. *Managing Organizations: text, readings and cases*, Maidenhead: McGraw-Hill, pp.27–31.

Sentosa Engineering – Managing in an eastern culture

Dolores Thompson Yong

The increasing internationalisation of business has led to considerable interest in the extent to which the Western assumptions underlying organisational design and managerial styles can be applied in different cultures. Such issues as communication and management control are particularly significant where employee attitudes to work are different to those on which much organisational behaviour material is based.

This case examines a number of organisational issues arising from rapid industrialisation in Singapore in a company employing a multi-ethnic workforce. It provides the opportunity to examine the problems faced in formalising organisation structures in a climate of rapid expansion. These issues are considered in the context of a multicultural interplay between Western and Eastern attitudes which accentuate a number of human relations problems.

BACKGROUND

Ship-repairing is a profitable activity for Singapore due to its strategic position and the fact that there are no other major ports in the vicinity offering major repair facilities to ships taking the long journey via South Africa to countries in the Pacific Basin.

Sentosa Shipyard handles the repair of all large vessels including warships and, by local standards, is a large company with 3,000 employees on a permanent basis. It is located in an isolated part of the island and there are a number of buildings on the site used for different aspects of the company's work. A common building houses the three catering facilities and, as the shipyard is located in a remote part of the island, staff from all levels inside the organisation make use of them. Manual employees are provided with a self-service canteen offering different types of local food. Middle management and clerical staff use the second canteen which also serves local food. The directors and guests have a restaurant with a luxurious decor where both local and Western food are served. The division of halls is such that users of each canteen can view the others through glass doors.

Sentosa Engineering, the focus of this case, is a subsidiary of Sentosa Shipyard and occupies buildings within the shipyard. It was set up two years ago in response to oil being found in neighbouring Indonesia and other nearby countries. These countries lack the facilities for the construction and installation of equipment for oil-drilling and it was believed that the expertise already existing in the company could be used to exploit this new market opportunity. The company has extended its range of products to include the building of dry docks.

The company is involved in diverse work of short duration, lasting up to six months. Such construction activities, for example, the fabrication of a pressure vessel, are carried out in fabrication workshops and are supervised by a foreman. A middle manager monitors progress closely and supplies technical expertise when needed. Alongside this work there are projects of a longer duration, typically one year in length, which comprise the majority of the company's work. These can involve a diversity of skills and are normally sub-contracted to external agencies who bring in their own employees to work on the project. This work is supervised by a team from the engineering company and, by the nature of the contracts, can generate very high profits for Sentosa Engineering.

It is a common practice for companies in developing countries who lack sufficient technical and/or managerial expertise to 'buy in' such skills through the employment of staff from developed Western countries. The employment of 'expatriate' staff at Sentosa is arranged through Lloyds Shipyard (UK) Ltd, a company with considerable experience in ship-repairing in the UK. It is associated with Sentosa Shipyard as a managing agent to supply specialist personnel as and when necessary. When Sentosa Engineering was established a similar arrangement for the supply of managerial and technical staff to the subsidiary was utilised. However, where those from the indigenous population can occupy such positions it is policy to have local personnel employed in these jobs. Lloyds' personnel are recruited under 'expatriate' conditions which can mean benefits amounting to three times the equivalent salary of local personnel. Such benefits include annual paid home-leave, air-passages for family, private schooling for children etc. The proportion of 'expatriate' personnel holding middle and senior management positions amounts to about one-third of the total.

Sentosa Engineering shares a number of facilities with the shipyard, including the catering provisions. It is also still in the process of devising its own systems for dealing with paperwork, including invoicing and payments. There is, as yet, no formal control system to predict costs. While orders are increasing the company is not clear on its profit margin on work undertaken. It is estimated that this may be as low as 4 per cent of turnover. Without any formal system for costing, the company's policy is to bid for contracts on the basis of fixed materials costs and to add on a percentage to cover labour and profit. However, since it has to pay 15 per cent materials handling costs to the shipyard some of its potential profits are being diverted to the parent company rather than being retained within the subsidiary.

As the organisation chart in figure 2.1 shows, Sentosa Shipyard's senior personnel comprises the managing director, the financial director and the personnel director who are also the senior executives of the engineering company. The personnel department of the shipyard has full responsibility for all matters related to staffing within Sentosa Engineering. As it is only in matters relating to work operations that the engineering company is autonomous it effectively operates as a sub-department of the shipyard adopting its overall policies and objectives. Both the shipyard and the engineering company come under the auspices of a board on which prominent local citizens serve.

The managing director of the Sentosa Shipyard is Norman Hodgson, an engineer by training from the North of England. He has overall responsibility for Sentosa Engineering and takes an active interest in all matters within the engineering company.

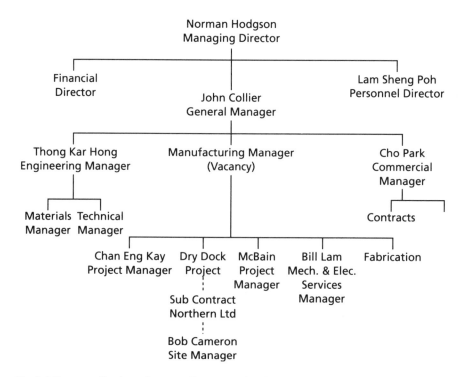

Fig 2.1 Sentosa Engineering: outline organisation structure

When the shipyard proposed the creation of Sentosa Engineering, John Collier, a middle manager at the shipyard with experience in this field, participated extensively in the plans. Subsequently the board decided to appoint him to head up the new organisation with the title of General Manager of Sentosa Engineering. Collier exercises complete autonomy in the production and project management of the company. He is responsible for the financial profitability of the company although expenditure accounts come under the auspices of the main shipyard. While the engineering company draws its expenditure funds from the shipyard's financial department, it bears responsibility for its own profits.

John Collier's management team is recruited by the personnel department of the shipyard. As the nature of most projects is such that shop-floor labour would be employed by outside contractors who bid for tenders, the only section that the general manager closely supervises is middle management. Shop-floor workers for short duration work are supplied by the shipyard as and when necessary.

As the organisational chart shows, the general manager is head of three divisions, each headed by a manager. The divisions function independently but the accomplishment of company objectives depends on successful passing of information and co-ordination of activities. At the time of writing there is no manufacturing manager as the last one returned to England and no replacement has been appointed.

The middle managers at the company are nearly all local Chinese personnel who have received their training in Singapore. Some expatriate engineers from England work alongside middle managers as part of the project team. At any point in time, there is more than one project under construction and a member of middle management may find themselves in various projects at different stages of completion.

The Singapore executive

In Singapore professional staff, particularly engineers and accountants, are highly valued in the labour market. Many professionals work for Western multinational companies in positions that usually offer substantial fringe benefits and entertainment allowances. It has been estimated that such benefits could accrue to an extra (Singapore) $200 alone per month in expense accounts. As Sentosa Engineering is a local concern these benefits do not apply and current salaries are not competitive with those offered by multinationals.

Indigenous young executives in Singapore today are exposed to both Eastern and Western influences. They aspire to rapid career advancement and have a materialistic outlook supported by fast economic growth within the Republic. Much emphasis is placed on the status derived from salary, size and make of car and official job title as well as the size of the expense account. On the other hand, the educated Singaporean is also exposed to Western management literature which stresses themes such as job satisfaction and self-fulfilment. The impact of large organisations on working life is relatively new. This is the first generation to operate in an industrial economy comparable to the First World. With rapid economic expansion and technological advance the indigenous executive is exposed to material goods and standards of living from the West. With this, goes however, the burden of the high cost of housing and the high tax imposed on motor cars. University graduates find themselves in a labour market where there is a wide choice of jobs. It is the expectation of local people that after making much sacrifice to achieve a university education that reward will come in the form of employment carrying a good remuneration package.

THE SITUATION

The board of Sentosa Shipyard is becoming increasingly anxious over a number of organisational issues and symptoms of discontent including the high turnover of staff in middle management amongst both indigenous and expatriate personnel. It is feared that if this trend persists, the very continuation of Sentosa Shipyard, and particularly Sentosa Engineering, is threatened.

While there seems to be no lack of orders to keep the engineering company in business the continuous exodus of middle-ranking university-trained managers is of major concern. The rapid expansion of the Republic's economy adds to this problem as most university-trained graduates find themselves with at least four good jobs to choose from. Indices of turnover are difficult to obtain but a major consulting firm has reported the following leaving rates for 48 leading companies in the Republic. These figures are shown below together with comparative figures for Sentosa Engineering.

Overall Executive Turnover*

	48 Orgs	*Sentosa*
At senior level	25%	40%
At middle management level	56%	75%
At junior management level	52%	70%

*Figures were calculated by dividing the numbers leaving each company during a year by those employed at the end of that year.

A number of issues have been suggested as possible contributing causes. The significant differences between indigenous and expatriate pay and conditions of employment leads to feelings of inequitable treatment. Senior management at the company are perceived to be poor communicators and variation in management style causes uncertainty amongst staff. Some employees are concerned about an overzealous application of security rules, whilst others feel that the company provides insufficient recreational facilities.

Examples of some of these issues are well demonstrated by the following incidents:

1. Ships docked at the shipyard can come from all over the world including naval warships, and some could be politically sensitive. In addition, it is estimated that in the preceding year the shipyard suffered a loss equivalent to $1,000,000 worth in tools which mysteriously disappeared. It has been deemed necessary therefore, to install security checks for all employees entering the shipyard. Every morning all personnel seeking entrance to the shipyard have to report to security and display identification including a photograph. John Collier, general manager of Singapore Engineering, occupies his office in the grounds of the shipyard. The guards have come to recognise Collier's (Mercedes) car and normally exempt him from being checked. However, when Collier was showing overseas visitors around the shipyard his car broke down and the guard on duty failed to recognise him. Collier and his visitors were subjected to the routine check. Feeling humiliated by the incident Collier made it known to the personnel department that the guard should be demoted. The guard was subsequently demoted to the job of a truck driver.

2. John Collier's team of middle management have to go through the same 'guard checking' routine every day. They claim this to be a source of frustration for them and that the apparent low morale in the company relates directly to this humiliating start to the day. The general manager feels that he is not in a position to deal with this matter as the security guards come under the responsibility of the personnel department.

3. Collier is not sympathetic to the managing director's efforts to promote good working relations by providing facilities for recreation. In his view work is business and the shipyard should not be viewed by employees as a playground. However, he reluctantly accepted the managing director's suggestion that once a month, they would sit in on a meeting with middle management to provide a forum for discussion on any topic. These meetings were set up in response to personnel department's initial alarm over the discovery that most executives stay with the company less than six months.

4. John Collier's opinion is that his hands are tied where manpower problems like labour turnover and salaries are concerned as he only sits in on

appointments; he exercises no power on staff conditions. The personnel department has a fixed scale of remuneration for engineers and middle managers which needs to be in line with that of the rest of the shipyard. He believes the experience gained working on oil out-rigger construction is invaluable and that after a year or two at Sentosa Engineering, engineers are in a position to command far better remuneration in other companies, particularly multinationals. According to him, this may have promoted the rapid mobility of managers.

Profile of key managers

The following profiles provide an introduction to the background and views held by a number of key managers within the company.

Norman Hodgson, Director, Singapore Shipyard, age 45 years

Norman Hodgson came to Singapore after holding many appointments for Lloyds Shipyard (UK) Limited throughout the world. He has been in Singapore for almost a decade and shows signs of wanting to stay semi-permanently, actively participating in local life. His appointment at Sentosa Shipyard has come only recently.

Hodgson is an engineer by profession and accepts that the skills of management is something which he has had to pick up through experience. However, his view of successful management (in the Eastern context) is very much the same as it is for the West. He wishes to provide middle management participation in decision making within the company. He is campaigning for more recreation facilities to be built within the shipyard as he realises that being in an isolated locality employees have few places to dine and meet and is aware that eating out with friends is a popular local activity. However, the personnel director, does not share these views and Norman consequently feels that his style is cramped by the personnel department.

Hodgson has introduced a series of monthly meetings involving himself, the general manager and middle management to encourage free discussion. However these meetings have not been as successful as he had hoped as although attendance is compulsory, participation is voluntary! Such meetings have resulted in the managing director and the general manager doing the talking with few contributions from other staff and no discussion of any problems. It is not customary in Eastern settings for subordinates to raise issues openly. Indeed, expatriate families who choose to leave their children in local schools find that the teacher talks most of the time and does not encourage participation. Even British personnel in middle management positions find it uncomfortable to contribute towards problem solving in such an environment. As a final effort, Norman Hodgson has resorted to summoning individuals for personal interviews with him on any topic which they choose. This he feels may give some clues to the problem of high turnover.

John Collier, General Manager of Singapore Engineering, age 42 years

John Collier worked for an engineering company in England which specialised in oil out-rigger component parts before he joined the Lloyd's Group. After three years of experience with the company in another European country, he agreed to work in the Far East as part of the management team for Sentosa Shipyard. He had already worked for the shipyard for three years as part of the Lloyds' management team in a middle management position before taking up the appointment of general manager of the engineering company.

Collier describes himself as an engineer first and a manager second. He dedicates his time to the company and takes little time off, arriving at the office at 8.00 a.m. without fail and never leaving till 7.00 or 8.00 p.m. When there are important negotiations, he will stay up until 4.00 or 5.00 a.m. but still appears promptly for work. He expects his divisional managers to do likewise. He takes upon himself all aspects of the functioning of the company and will only delegate other functions if this is absolutely necessary. He is the sales organiser, the project thinker, materials purchaser, etc. and his one aim is for the company to show immediate profits.

The general manager admits that he has difficulties in the area of communication between himself and his immediate subordinates. He is not certain whether the difficulty is one of a cultural nature or just an issue of different personality types. He claims to react best when he knows what the other person is thinking. In his experience discussions with Chan Eng Kay, a new appointee to the position of a project manager, are the most fruitful. Chan has been trained in England and is by nature outspoken. Collier finds empathy with, and co-operation from, Chan who shouts back at him. According to Collier this helps to clear the air and there are no hard feelings between them. The rest of middle management consider Chan to be Collier's protégé and favourite. They keep their opinions on the general manager to themselves.

This is Collier's first post in senior management. He has a strongly held opinion that it is impossible to combine high productivity with good human relations. This has been reinforced by suggestions made to him that Eastern workers respond better to autocratic management.

His contract with the company is due to expire in a year's time but the chairman of the board has already approached him with an offer of a renewal of his three year contract and has already raised his present salary. His know-how of out-rigger constructions is highly valued in this part of the world.

Lam Sheng Poh, Personnel Director, age 57 years

The personnel department is headed by Lam Sheng Pot, a local man from what can be described as the 'old school'. Lam was educated at the local university and views work firmly in the Eastern tradition that employees come to work to *work*, not to find other fulfilments. His view of the personnel function is that it should be restricted to that of hiring and firing. The 'softer' personnel functions, such as employee welfare and job enrichment schemes are not seen by Lam as being part of the personnel role. Lam is therefore against the introduction of recreational facilities and believes that people should come to the shipyard to do a good day's work. The staff at Sentosa Engineering feel that if they were to approach the personnel department with their problems they would be chased out, since personnel does not see its role as being responsible for employee counselling or handling grievances.

Poh is widely known to have former association with the Anti-Corruptions Board which commands some amount of awe. The Government was keen to rid the Republic of corruption and a board was set up to detect unfair business dealings.

Cho Park, Commercial Manager, age 32 years

Cho works closely with the general manager. He graduated from Singapore University and has come to Sentosa Engineering from Sheraton (one of the largest multinationals on the island). Cho is ambitious and believes that as long as he remained with a foreign company he would never move into top management because these positions would be reserved for nationals from the mother company. He joined Sentosa Engineering because he was offered a managerial promotion and also for patriotic reasons as it is directly contributing towards the growth of the Republic. In leaving Sheraton he sacrificed the considerable fringe benefits foreign firms provide such as longer holidays and expense accounts.

He describes his six months' employment period with Sentosa Engineering as being stressful and one of continual involvement in crisis management. He dreads coming to the shipyard every morning and he is tired before he begins work. Frustrations encountered on the job affect his home life and health. Often managerial personnel are expected to attend work when there are important projects in progress. His job does not have set hours, and when he puts in extra hours on Sundays he receives no acknowledgement from any member of senior management.

As commercial manager, Cho is responsible for marketing and sales transactions. He feels he does not have sufficient authority to make decisions when bidding for tenders. His frustrations at work partly stem from not being given sufficient knowledge of jobs which are in the pipeline. Cho misses the 'push button' costing system he was used to at his last job and the facilities which enabled him to make quick decisions. His chief frustration relates to the general manager's unwillingness to delegate. He thinks the general manager has no clear objectives and this affects the rest of the organisation. He perceives Collier as being particularly bright in business acumen but inconsistent in policy matters. Cho also feels unhappy about the fact that the engineering manager, Thong Kar Hong, who was his junior in college, has been in a senior position for the last five years. This is considered by Cho to be humiliating (status is an extremely sensitive point in the achievement conscious society of the overseas Chinese). He feels he is bypassed in the communication flow. New recruits who have joined Singapore Engineering refer directly to the general manager instead of coming to him for the information necessary to complete work on a project. In general Cho resents top management posts being filled by expatriates and suggests that this is the source of difficult interpersonal relations. He agrees with others in middle management who believe that these personnel should be replaced by local Singaporeans.

Cho is thinking seriously of leaving the company as he feels that he is on the verge of a nervous breakdown.

Bill Lam, Mechanical and Electrical Services Manager, age 29 years

Bill Lam has already given in his notice of resignation and is due to leave Sentosa Engineering in two months' time.

Bill Lam trained in Scotland. Since his return to Singapore five years ago he has had four jobs prior to joining Sentosa Engineering where he has been for six months. He joined the company to obtain experience in heavy engineering work but he has been responsible for estimating during most of his time with the company. He formerly worked as a regional representative of a British firm and has now decided to go back to the same company. He has been offered a better salary and as the job offers fringe benefits such as car and petrol allowance, he estimates the real gain to be as much as 1,200 Singapore dollars more per month. He is ambitious and thinks that eventually when the British company has to employ local personnel for its top management posts he would stand a good chance of a position.

He too considers that there are many frustrations within the company. Policies seem very rigid and render it impossible for staff to function at maximum potential. There is a lack of autonomy and he has not found a definite role within the organisation after six months. He is also bitter about his position in the organisational structure which he claims to be the source of much personal discontent. He is sensitive to the vertical delineations in the organisation and believes that engineers feel inferior to others when placed in a line lower than other functions. The general manager, when told about these feelings, has responded by arguing that the chart is only a means of finding out who is with what team and that people should not be so concerned with the status symbols attached.

Bill Lam finds the high turnover rate of engineers difficult for the establishment of social relations. In his words 'there are new faces so often that you don't bother' and feels that socialising is confined to top management. He thinks that the general manager lives in an ivory tower and has made no effort to mix with the staff. On the whole he feels that he is overworked at Sentosa Engineering and that there is no feedback or appreciation of work done.

Thong Kar Hong, Engineering Manager, age 32 years

Thong has been in the shipyard for many years and has worked with John Collier for five. He describes himself as very much a technical man. He is one of the few who seems unworried about company problems. He believes that if others would concentrate on the job in hand everything else would fall into place. Unlike Bill Lam he places little importance on positions in the organisation chart and like the general manager believes that other engineers should only use the chart as a guideline to trace individuals involved in various projects.

Thong obtained his engineering degree from Singapore University. There is mutual respect between himself and the general manager and he has no thoughts of leaving. He has a high regard for the quality of the work undertaken in the machine shop, and is satisfied with his salary package. He is directly responsible to John Collier and admits that at times he suffers the pressure of work at Sentosa Engineering. This he attributes to factors like 'lack of men available' and 'lack of help from the shipyard'. He does not believe in rigid job demarcation and suggests that staff in a position to know more about a project than others should be prepared to help out for the sake of the company. He has no sympathy with the prevalent discontent in the company.

Bob Cameron, Engineering Site Manager, age 50 years

Scotsman Bob Cameron is site manager for Northern Ltd, a construction company, and is currently engaged in contract work in the Republic for the major project of the year – the 40,000 dry weight tonnage dry dock which the engineering company is building. Bob is not employed by Sentosa but frequently deals with middle management at the company. In his view the engineers he encounters are first class workers. He has seen little evidence of humour on the construction site and he has been made very much aware of ethnic consciousness not only between Europeans and locals, but also between locals (Chinese and Indians mostly). He feels that he is dealing not with a team but with separate individuals and finds that most personnel never admit to errors. He gets the impression that the engineers are not trained in the management of people, but have had to pick this up the hard way, through bitter experience. Bob works closely with McBain who is from the Lloyd's Shipyard team and who is a project manager for Sentosa Engineering at the same grade as other local personnel. He thinks that McBain has found the formula for leading a team, since McBain's strategy of socialising with staff appears to pay dividends.

In Cameron's view the structure used to manage the company would cause problems in any country and understands why the one at Sentosa has been a source of contention. His general view is the British in Singapore manage in the wrong way – as though they were in nineteenth century England. In addition he believes that the managing director's recent introduction of three separate staff restaurants has been bad for human relations.

ACTIVITY BRIEF

1 *As a management consultant suggest intervention strategies which would enable you to investigate the organisational behaviour problems facing Sentosa Engineering.*

2 *Consider the following issues identified in the case study:*
   (a) organisation and control
   (b) management styles and employee relations
   (c) communications
   (d) cross-cultural management.
   Advise John Collier on the action he should take to manage each of these issues.

3 *Utilising the concept of the psychological contract explain why mismatches have occurred between John Collier and his immediate management team. What action should Collier take to improve these personal relationships?*

4 *Role play – participants may like to assume the different roles outlined and arrange a meeting to sort out the problem of high turnover for Sentosa Engineering. (From the shipyard both Norman Hodgson and Lam Sheng Poh should be included.)*

RECOMMENDED READING

Ferraro, A. (1990). *The Cultural Dimension of International Business,* New Jersey: Prentice-Hall.
Handy, C. (1988). *Understanding Organisations,* Harmondsworth: Penguin Business.

The role of intimacy at work: Interactions and relationships in the modern organisation

Joanna Brewis

This case study derives from qualitative research undertaken in two university departments, one large and well established, the other much smaller and newer. The former broadly demonstrates the bureaucratic principle of the exclusion of personalised relationships, the other is a far more intimate and close-knit environment. The aim is to illustrate different organisational cultures and offer suggestions as to the effect each might have on individuals and organisational processes, for example communications, co-ordination of different projects and measurement of organisational effectiveness. Intimacy here refers to relationships which revolve around reacting to the other person as an individual rather than an organisational position; the continuum of intimacy extends from casual acquaintanceship at one end through to close friendship and romance at the other. Typically intimacy has been characterised as problematic at work given the lack of objectivity such a relationship implies; one cannot, it is argued, make viable business decisions concerning promotions for example if one is personally involved with those who will be affected. But it is also possible to argue that a closer, friendlier atmosphere at work allows for a higher level of motivation and improved communications. Recent developments in management theory have addressed the use of culture to achieve improvements like these; the case can therefore be used to highlight such work.

BACKGROUND

British academia presently faces a number of important challenges. These include the fact that resources are being continually cut while student numbers at many institutions are rising, the removal of tenure (lifetime employment) for lecturers, and the introduction of quality initiatives in academic teaching. It is also the case that direct competition for students between institutions has intensified due to the old polytechnics achieving university status. The institution cited in the case is certainly facing all of these pressures, which must be assumed to be impacting on the two departments used in the study. Department A is a large, multi-site department which dates back to the inception of the university itself. It employs 70 academic staff. The undergraduate course numbers approximately 600 students across 3 years and there are 150 postgraduates. Department B is much smaller and operates from a single location. It has relatively recently become a research and teaching centre in its own right. Department B employs 28 academic staff, 9 researchers and has 160 postgraduate students. The subjects taught and researched in both departments are scientific.

The research conducted in these two departments consisted of semi-structured interviews, designed by the author, which focused on the respondents' thoughts concerning the way in which members of the department communicated and interacted with each other. Interviews were conducted with individuals at all organisational levels and with both men and women.

THE SITUATION

Department A

The culture in this department was reported as revolving mainly around the work ethic; respondents commented that the feeling was very much one that the staff were here to work and any extraneous contact beyond the demands of a particular project was 'just politics' and therefore dangerous, unnecessary and distracting. There is no room for what was dubbed 'sentiment'. It is also the case that external constraints have impacted on the department, as one man remarked, 'it's difficult to find five minutes to have a chat about the weather any more.' This was attributed to tighter funding and an increasing student roll. Intimacy and friendship then would 'get in the way' of the tasks at hand; the achievement of departmental research and teaching goals.

It is hardly surprising, given the above findings, that very few of the respondents claimed that they had close friends at work and even those that did said they were by no means as close as those outside of work; other people at work were more usually described as 'colleagues', 'pals', 'working friends', 'very close acquaintances' and so on. Relationships that did exist tended to be between same-status individuals. Interaction was emphasised for the most part to be very professional; 'I would say this is one of the most person-respecting set of people I've come across', 'it's very civilised', 'informal but on a professional level'. This was put down by some respondents to the fact that it was an academic institution rather than an industrial establishment.

Romance was certainly absent from the agenda. It is felt generally that any particularly 'inappropriate' behaviour, for example a staff–student liaison, would be dealt with extremely quickly and from a high level. It was also noted that any such arrangements would be highly incongruous; most respondents found it extremely hard to picture any kind of involvements (between members of staff or between staff and students) taking place in the department, it simply seemed alien to them, '. . . a foreign idea'. An academic jokingly made reference to the David Lodge novels about academia and wondered what kind of an institution he taught at to find so much romantic intrigue there. A postgraduate student further claimed that 'I can categorically say that we don't go to the extent of romance'.

The distance between colleagues is illustrated by a secretary's anecdote concerning her boss, who is a professor. When he wishes to communicate something to someone he will always give it to her to type up and send as a formal memo; this even happens when it is being sent to the academic who occupies the office next door to his. A similar procedure is enacted when he telephones someone; he always requests that his secretary telephone first and 'announce' him as it were. Indeed this professor also finds disciplinary matters hard to deal with because they involve interpersonal communication; he will engage his secretary to deal with these as they arise on his behalf. Communication on the whole tends to be work-related and formalised. Another secretary commented that 'a lot of them round here are not very good at communicating . . . you find as if you're working at having conversations . . . talking about anything that's not to do with work . . . they don't seem to be able to approach you . . .'.

Hierarchy is an important element in departmental culture. A female academic observed that, even though appointments of women to academic positions were on the increase, those in posts had made little real impact because they were not in positions of power. A secretary also made the point that

> in a company, apart from M.D.s, management and the rest of the staff are more or less equal, they all treat each other the same, but academics and non-academics are just completely (unequal) . . . the academics are very condescending and I mean I'm one of the youngest members of staff so I'm treated as a baby in some respects which I don't like at all . . . they don't have much respect . . . they think a secretary is just going to have a baby and then she gives up.

There is also little communication between the different departmental sites – there are four spread across campus – and although one could put this down to geographical distance there are ample telephone, internal mail and computer links to enable communication. Furthermore, while it is the case that contact is sought on the basis of shared work interests (members of research groups tend to be familiar with each other), one respondent commented that if two laboratories were engaged in separate work they would be unlikely to communicate at all even if the rooms were next to each other on a corridor. It was further noted that the lack of a communal common room made mingling unlikely, and that at the annual Christmas dinner everyone sat together in research groups and very little mixing took place. When asked whether they thought such an event brought the department closer together, some commented that it did, but only in so far as they were gathered in the same room! One respondent commented that this departmental function was always held on campus (which is not true of similar events in other departments) and that had it not been it would perhaps have been more relaxed; 'once you leave X (workplace) somehow things change'.

Impact of culture on staff

How does this culture of distance, of lack of intimacy, affect those who work within it? The atmosphere in the department was variously characterised by its members. A member of support staff said that

> I feel that whatever close relationships there are at work, whether it be father–son, husband–wife, girlfriend–boyfriend, it does tend to cloud people's judgments when they're having to make judgments about things both from their aspect and also from the aspect of someone who's trying to either supervise or look after or be responsible for [them]. You always have that, however liberal you like to feel . . . and that's my basic view of it, I would rather leave relationships away from work.

The feeling among some respondents then is that close involvement with colleagues detracts from one's ability to perform at the optimum level at work.

The lack of intimacy is also seen as positive for other reasons. Two of the women interviewed had been seriously sexually harassed, both in other university departments. Mary's reaction was to tell her husband, who subsequently accompanied her to work to discuss the matter with her superior. She remarked of her former department that 'that's how it had always been – the men accepted it, when you worked in that office that's just the way it was. You go into somewhere where that isn't the way . . . there's no one like that here (Department A) now and if someone came in like that it would get straightened out.'

That culture had resulted in an unpleasant and uncomfortable situation for the junior women who worked within it; the harassing behaviour was certainly 'nothing personal' in that it was directed at more than one woman. The more senior women, interestingly, had not experienced harassment from the man in question.

The other woman, Brenda, had resigned when the man in question made it physically impossible for her to do her job. Subsequently she had in fact been offered her position back, slightly redefined in order to put a distance between her and the harasser. Brenda's harasser had also been her senior and again his behaviour had not been confined to her although she did comment that she was the target of his most sustained efforts. She also mentioned that the department in which these events occurred was smaller, more gossipy and that intimate relationships were far more the norm. Both she and Mary were much more comfortable with the impersonal atmosphere of Department A.

But there were also negative evaluations. The formal nature of departmental culture was seen to hinder communication in such a way that uneasy tolerance characterised most working relationships. One respondent commented that 'back stabbing' was rife, because people were unwilling or unable to communicate. Lack of sensitivity was imputed to the department by another respondent (a relatively new member of staff) who saw the departmental working environment as 'very strange . . . very competitive . . . no tolerance whatsoever'. Indeed this respondent's dealings with the department thus far had in fact taken the form of a serious disagreement with a superior, the stress resulting from which had led to the respondent becoming ill. The lack of understanding, contact and reciprocity identified by these two respondents in particular and many respondents in general is seen to mitigate against effective departmental operation first and job satisfaction second – clearly the two are also connected.

Department B

The other department studied as part of this programme was much smaller and altogether different. It is single-site, which is seen to account for some of the closeness. Lines of communication were universally described as clearer and less cluttered than in some of the larger departments. There is far less emphasis on hierarchy; a technician claimed that in other departments the academics ' . . . tend to treat the non-academic staff like slaves basically', but that in this one 'they muck in' for the most part.

Here it was the presence (rather than the absence) of communication and closeness which was identified as the glue which maintained the effectiveness of the workplace. As one respondent put it, 'it's like a family . . . you know families. I mean, I've got three sisters and we're always falling out . . . but eventually it all gets back on an even keel'. She described a 'blazing row' she'd had with a senior academic – hierarchically very much her superior – the previous week, saying that it had all been 'forgiven and forgotten'. This department is very much one where the participant 'can say what you feel without there being repercussions'. Another respondent commented that disagreements which do occur are typically smoothed over at departmental social events which are frequent ('any opportunity for a celebration there is a party here'). There is also a great deal of out-of-work socialising, which does not necessarily observe hierarchy – a secretary said that she would invite a professor to her house should she give a dinner party and a technician described her and her husband's friendship with another professor who lives near to them.

The continuum of interaction in the department also extends to the romantic. Mutual romance is frequent and accepted, even adulterous romance. There have been several staff–student liaisons for example, including one which resulted in divorce – when husband and wife both worked in the department. However, it seems that this has actually caused very little trouble; it was only pointed out that the academic and the student in question were asked not to attend the Christmas party that year in order not to disrupt the celebrations. In fact most regulation in the department does seem to take place at this very informal level; as a senior academic put it, 'one would hope there's not a reason to mention it'. Relationships are tolerated and for the most part do not create problems. As one respondent said 'it works quite well . . . if people are professional about it and don't let it interfere with their working life'. Two other departmental members have also been married to each other and subsequently divorced during their careers in the department and still continue to work together amicably.

Romance is an everyday part of working life for this particular department, but it is generally expected that people will regulate their involvements themselves, and 'regulate' is the key word. One or two members were identified as not being able to undertake this, and were castigated for their poor handling of the situations that resulted. Those examples which follow were referred to by several respondents. One individual (who admitted flirting all year) had to fight a co-worker off at a departmental social event. Another had naïvely encouraged an academic's attentions and had experienced substantial difficulty in deterring him as a result, and a further woman had reputedly 'come on' to various members of the department (both men and women) to the extent that she was practically physically assaulting them at work. Intimacy here then is seen to co-exist with departmental operations, and even enhance them, but only if carefully controlled.

Furthermore the informality and cohesiveness within the department is not always seen to be positive. Two respondents mentioned occasions when the police arguably should have been alerted to events, but were not called due to an unwillingness to, as one put it, 'wash the dirty linen in public'. One incident in fact constituted a serious assault and yet was 'hushed up'. It is also possible to comment that the kind of incidents described above – e.g. the problem experienced at the departmental social event – are at least partially generated by the highly sexualised atmosphere of this particular working environment. One's fellow employee is certainly likely to be a friend and possibly a partner, unlike in the larger department.

It is ironic also that the intimacy within the department seems to generate 'bitchiness', just as lack of communication does in Department A. Two respondents described themselves as good friends in two separate interviews and then went on to heartily criticise each other; one saying the other one was an over-friendly tease and one saying the other was catty and jealous. Here it seems to be a case of familiarity breeding contempt. It should also be pointed out that any such remarks made in the other department (A) were a good deal more reticent and also tended to be generalisations rather than referring to specific individuals. Department B was further described by a postgraduate student as extremely 'gossipy'; colleagues continually 'fished' for personal information about each other which then spread very quickly round the grapevine. As a result this student never discussed anything personal with other members of the department. Perhaps then the closeness which the department values is also to a certain extent counter-productive, in terms of relationships and of departmental achievement.

It is also the case that the veneer of mutual respect sometimes slips; as in the anecdote related by a secretary, who had been given a report to write by an academic and upon submission received the somewhat backhanded compliment, 'I didn't know you could write – this is very good'. It was similarly pointed out that freedom of information was restricted by the senior academics discussing important departmental matters over lunch at the somewhat exclusive Staff Centre. Again the intimacy of interaction does not impact significantly on the 'real' business of the department, which is conducted for the most part as the formal structure dictates.

ACTIVITY BRIEF

1 (a) *According to bureaucracy theory, what kind of personal relationships should exist between organisational participants? Draw upon the case for illustration.*

  (b) *How might the above model impact on*
      (i) *individuals and*
      (ii) *the achievement of organisational goals?*
      Draw upon the case for illustration.

2 (a) *Contemporary management theories advocate a different mode of interaction within the workplace. How does it differ from that described above? What is the rationale behind these recommendations?*

  (b) *Would you say that Department B demonstrates the characteristics of the new workplace, as envisaged by the theories above? Support your answer.*

3 *Suggest why the two departments differ in culture. If you were given the task of managing cultural change as suggested by the theories in question 2(a), how might you go about it? Why might current pressures on academia necessitate such a change?*

PART 2

The individual groups and leadership

The five case studies in Part 2 are in a variety of work situations located in three different European countries and Australia. Different cultures are compared and contrasted and the impact of managerial decision making on individuals and groups are considered.

The first, 'The mystery of the disappearing female hotel graduate' examines career opportunities of women in the hotel industry. It considers three explanations drawn from a variety of research evidence which suggest that well qualified women graduates have greater difficulty progressing to senior managerial positions in the hotel industry than their male counterparts.

The second, 'SAS – Mergers in the air?' examines motivation and leadership style in Scandinavia Airlines and considers cross-cultural issues emerging from a possible amalgamation between SAS and other national airlines.

The third, 'My greatest failure: A case study in leadership' provides an insight into the impact of a particular leadership style in a German company operating in the media industry with a controlling interest in a French printing firm.

The fourth provides a view of the day-to-day operation of a large manufacturing and service company in Australia. It presents a typical working day at 'Aussieco' with a series of events illustrating key issues in the field of management and organisational behaviour, including organisational structure, manpower planning and management style.

The final case, 'Thameside: Leadershhip within a local authority housing department', deals with leadership style in a local authority housing department based in England against the background of financial constraints imposed by central government policy and the need to lead and motivate staff in a changing environment.

The mystery of the disappearing female hotel graduate

Linda Hicks

This case examines a sector of the service industry – the hotel world. Hotels are potentially female empowering in that the labour force is predominantly female and the organisation setting, prima facie, typifies 'women's work'. Hotels are temporary homes where the staff have to anticipate and care for the physical needs of sleep, food and comfort of their guests. Hotels mirror the stereotype of women's domestic role and offer a working situation which is dependent on personal relationships, which, again reflects the skills in which women stereotypically excel. It should be expected that women should do well in this particular industry and the industry would indeed be female empowering in that the skills commonly thought as 'women's work' could be rewarded in occupational terms.

However, women are outnumbered by men in management positions and this case poses the question – why?

This case looks at a variety of research evidence and collates this in producing explanations for the gender differences. Readers are asked to consider and evaluate the explanations and apply the arguments to other organisational settings.

BACKGROUND

Statistical Evidence

Currently, the hotel and catering industry is a major employer of women with nearly 17 per cent of the total female workforce. In hotels 65 per cent of all employees are women.

The majority of women are employed in operative jobs (88 per cent) and 64 per cent of women work as either kitchen or counter hands, bar staff, domestic staff, porters or stewards compared to 15 per cent of men.

However, the proportion of women to men reverses at managerial level, with men outnumbering women. Although women are represented more highly than in any other industry, holding 47 per cent of all management jobs, the proportion varies across the different sectors within the industry and is, in any case, much less than would be expected if women were distributed equally across occupations in the industry. If women were represented equally in management the proportion of women managers in each sector should be comparable to the proportion of women in those sectors as a whole. Thus in hotels, women managers would be around 65 per cent rather than 36 per cent.

At senior and board level the number is dramatically reduced. In 1993 of the eight leading hotel companies only four have women on their boards and of these only one woman is actively involved in the running of a business. It should be added that in two cases the woman is either related to, or is the co-founder of the business (Bartlett, 1993).

The proportion of female managers is not a reflection of differentials in skill levels, in that the number of graduates leaving hotel courses at college show that on Hotel and Catering Management courses 75 per cent of all students are women and this statistic has remained stable over a period of ten years. Similar proportions have been reported on BTEC courses except for the HNC course (generally carried out on a day release scheme) which registers more men than women.

These statistics indicate that not only are women attracted into hotel and catering, but that on every course, apart from the sponsored day release course, women are attending in greater numbers than men by a ratio of 3:1. There should, in theory, be a greater proportion of suitable women than men entering hotel and catering management, and that they do not poses the question of what happens to them.

- A first explanation could be that the females who stay in the industry have different and lowered aspirations and motivations than the males. In other words, is it something about the women themselves that prevents them from becoming managers?
- A second reason that women do not make progress within the hotel industry could be because there are a number of barriers and obstacles in their way. These may not be direct or visible, since they may consist of attitudes and beliefs which are woven into the cultural context of the industry about the way management and women are conceived.
- A third explanation could be that the career and developmental process of becoming a manager necessitates certain types of experiences and background, and these qualities may be perceived as being more important than higher educational qualifications.

This case will examine these three alternative explanations:

1. The aspirations of female employees in the hotel industry.
2. The cultural milieu of the hotel industry.
3. The processes of management development.

EXPLANATION 1: ASPIRATIONS AND MOTIVATIONS OF WOMEN GRADUATES

The extent to which women hotel and catering graduates hold differing aspirations to men was raised in a study by the HCITB (1984). This study was important if only because it was the first to focus on women in the UK industry. Their brief was to study the extent to which women were disadvantaged in achieving a management position. The report, whilst identifying a range of barriers and recommending a series of measures which industry and colleges could take, largely stressed that initiatives need to come from the women themselves. 'The most positive action must come from the women themselves. If women wish to make a career in hotel and catering management and wish to compete on an equal level with their male colleagues, the first step they must take is to carefully define their career plan' (HCITB, 1984, p.23). A prime reason for women not achieving managerial positions was their own passivity and they suggested that mapping out career decisions and future goals would make women more active and determined to reach their goals.

Statistics from an earlier study (HCITB/ETAC, 1983) showed there was little gender differences in the long-term goals of the graduates but significant differences in their first appointment. More women than men selected jobs at a sub-managerial level and at a lower level than their qualifications warranted. The females who selected these jobs evidently claimed that it was 'important that they acquired adequate knowledge before attempting to move upwards'. The researchers evidently took a negative view of these comments because, they continued 'This did not seem to be a view held by the men interviewed, and could be interpreted as reflecting a lack of confidence on the part of the women' (HCITB/ETAC, 1983, p.19).

It is perhaps interesting that the male perspective was the one adopted as good practice, even though the alternative of the more considered approach of the females, the intention to gain wide experience at a somewhat slower pace and to feel in control and effective at each stage, may in the long run lead to very successful management.

Outside of the hotel industry, explanations for gender differences vary. While women appear to become deliberate in their career development, there is evidence to suggest that there are far more similarities between managers than differences. Women managers appear to be as equally ambitious as men.

However, it would be unusual for a study not to refer to life outside the workplace when discussing women's aspirations. Women's motivations are placed in a wider context than for men, often making reference to life stage reached or responsibilities outside the workplace.

The interpretation of women's attitudes within this wider context of work and home may encourage the belief that men and women's attitudes are more different than they really are. Is it possible therefore to justify the explanation that women have lower aspirations than men in the hotel industry?

EXPLANATION 2: THE CULTURAL MILIEU OF THE HOTEL INDUSTRY

This second explanation directs attention to the cultural milieu of the hotel industry to assess the likelihood that womens' progress is hindered, limited or perhaps blocked by prevailing attitudes and beliefs. Initially a descriptive historical perspective will be taken to identify those elements of the hotel industry which appear to be critical to the experience of working in hotels. These key elements of hotel life, namely the notion of service and the nature of working relationships, will begin to draw attention to the likely character of managerial work and the type of managers required to perform the tasks of management effectively. The aim of this section is to focus on the ways in which these cultural elements may affect women. What are the possible influences that the major enduring features of the hotel industry could have in influencing the ways in which women are perceived in hotels which may prevent their progress into management?

History of hotel industry and its effect on women

Historians of the industry have outlined the growth and development of hotels and noted that it coincided with the development of transport, particularly railways and roads. Traditional luxury hotels, notably the Savoy Company, were considered as dominating the thinking of the hotel industry. Victorian hotels were closely allied to domestic service and the structure of the labour force was akin to a private house of the gentry. The Victorian hoteliers attempted to please their guests by constant attention to their needs and whims.

One of the first identifiable features of the hotel industry with clear historical roots is the notion of personal service and detail. Certainly this feature should serve to advantage women who have traditionally been responsible with work concerning care and attention. Women have always had their place in the history of hotels. Typically, however, they tended to play a dominant part of the housekeeping team, rather than in operations requiring close and face-to-face personal service. Although it could be acknowledged the role that some exceptional women played, there is evidence to show the decorative role that women were excepted to play in brightening up the surroundings and the supportive role that women played in their role of wife to the manager (Taylor and Bush, 1974).

Indeed for women in the past, hotel work has not been concerned with the personal contact but has typically been concerned with background work, cleaning rooms. Aspects of bonding between guests and staff tend to occur in the front office/hall and in the restaurant. These departments, until 25 years ago were typically held by men and even now food and beverage operations in hotels are still predominantly male.

This leads to the conclusion that although the personal touch and service is an overall goal of hotels, not all the work in hotels is of a servicing or caring kind. Work in hotels comprises some of the most anonymous and lonely jobs and some of the most dirty and unsocial activities (i.e. being a lone chambermaid cleaning rooms, a kitchen porter stacking dishes, a laundry worker or a night porter).

The term 'servicing' covers a multitude of different work and hotels comprise an assortment of occupations, many of them of a low-skilled nature.

Although emphasis is still placed on elements of service and more recently on hospitality, it is recognised that many activities and tasks have little directly to do with personal service or care and this may have implications for women.

Relationships within hotels

Mars and Mitchell (1976) recognised the importance of working relationships in hotels and identified the triadic relationship (between staff, customers and management) as a stable and enduring feature which has an important influence on the behaviour of all participants. The stability of this triad is remarkable and unique to this working world. The relationship is reinforced by payment of tips where the employee receives (often low) wages from the employer and additional payments directly from the guest.

One of the consequences of this relationship are secretive individual contracts. The way that contracts are established and the rules that govern the contract are for the three parties only. Great efforts are made by all three parties to maintain secrecy and retain assumed preferential treatment. This provides the employee with power to counteract the authority of management and prevents collective action. It also suggests that ambiguity enables a measure of management control: 'It is the ability of management to control and manipulate the less visible and accountable aspects of the total rewards system in favour of individual workers, which has given them the autonomy they need for the smooth running of hotels' (Mars, Bryant and Mitchell, 1979).

Thus the way in which control is exercised by managers would appear to be *ad hoc*, and dependant upon situational factors and the counteracting power of certain employees and customers. It would seem that the toleration of ambiguities is a part of the custom and practice of hotel working and hotel management. Secrecy and ambiguity makes possible a system of preferential treatment towards individual employees or groups of employees. If there are groups of employees who customarily expect preferential treatment and/or see themselves as having a special status, and, if these groups are predominantly male, then female staff can be seen at a disadvantage.

Rivalry is commonplace amongst hotel departments and certain departments seem able to maintain a high level of autonomy. The kitchen is one area which has virtually no guest contact, but does have a great deal of kudos and importance in establishing and maintaining a hotel's reputation. The history of hotels is replete with folk heroes from the kitchens, all of whom are male. The kitchen is notably, then, a department which has always held a special and preferential status within hotels and is also predominantly male.

The evidence suggests that certain key departments can wield more power and control than others, have a preferential status and have always been predominantly male. This emphasises the distinctiveness of different groups of workers within hotels with differing sub-cultures. Some 'core' workers may have skills which are more highly valued and may have negotiated a favourable individual contract and other 'peripheral' workers have limited opportunities in low-status positions and may form a part of the workforce which is constantly changing.

The existence of these sub-cultures may be strengthened in some hotels by the conditions of work. The fact that hotels do not close, indeed are typically open for 24 hours a day presents a direct and erratic nature of customer demand. To cope with these demands it is common for hotel workers to adopt a shift hour pattern of working and frequently staff 'live-in' the hotel. The dual conditions of shift hours and accommodation on the premises creates a definite boundary between the hotel and society outside. Hours are out of synchronisation and this can negatively foster isolation or, positively, a sense of community. In the event, living in the place of work is going to have a more critical affect on attitudes than leaving the place of work each day. It is likely that the spatial isolation and the peculiar working hours of hotels intensifies relationships between groups of workers and strengthens and perhaps hardens attitudes and beliefs.

Hotel life is full of paradoxes; although staff may live and work as a community, they share different rewards, have different negotiated contracts and enjoy different levels of status. It should also be noted that secrecy and individualism have ramifications for managing and controlling relationships and so too do sub-cultures which have particular expectations and beliefs about their status and value. What is of significance to the position of women is that they tend to be excluded from valued departments and tend to be working in peripheral activities primarily dominated by women. Thus they could be at a disadvantage in competing for management tasks and may be perceived in particular ways as a result of being identified with a low-status group.

Furthermore the HCITB report (1984, p.15) described earlier revealed different training opportunities for men and women: whereas the men received training suitable for a general management position, the women tended to receive more specialist training for ancillary posts and critically, many women did not receive training in food and beverage areas.

The researchers pointed out that women were not conscious of receiving a different type of training to men. Given the nature of the industry, with its self-contained small units, it would seem more likely that individuals are reliant on their immediate managers for career development and, as such, their awareness of training opportunities may be limited by their own experiences. The study did not make clear whether men were more conscious of their training needs, nor did it discuss the individuals' ability to perceive and diagnose their own training and development needs.

The study thus emphasised the importance of the management development process and the power that key managers hold in directing and influencing their trainees.

Although there may be barriers which are visible and which prevent women from gaining management experiences many of the barriers discussed in this section are invisible and concern the ways in which hotel work is constructed. Such barriers are more difficult to identify as they are part of the culture and understood ways of hotel life.

EXPLANATION 3: THE PROCESS OF MANAGEMENT DEVELOPMENT IN THE HOTEL INDUSTRY

This third explanation is closely related to the previous one, since it is difficult to separate the underlying beliefs and attitudes which make up the cultural context of the organisation from the ways in which management is perceived. As in any industry the dominant attitudes of the industry have led to a particular style of management and management activity.

The aim of this section is to identify the activities of management which result from the ways that hotels are conceptualised and to establish whether women are excluded from this process. It seems appropriate to first establish the nature of hotel management, building from the evidence described in previous sections, secondly to consider the profile of the 'ideal' manager and finally to consider the ways in which aspiring managers are developed to become this 'ideal'.

Nature of hotel management

The notion that hotel management is concerned with personal attention and service has already been highlighted as a major significant belief within the industry. The Victorian hoteliers' main responsibility was to provide personal attention and service and to play the role of 'mine host'. They were expected to 'be there' at all times and to be able to display both skills and knowledge on demand. Hotel management was therefore associated with continual presence, however, presence was subject to considerable interpretation, not only as to when managers would 'be there' but also with regard to how they would be spending their time. These features outlined by historians have remained as constant characteristics of modern hotel management with ambiguity and interpretation as a continuing feature. It is likely that the combination of being 'multi-skilled' and the concept of 'continual presence' have been important causal elements creating the management style labelled as *ad hoc* by Mars and Mitchell (1976). The term *ad hoc* implies that managers are ready to cope with any situation and are flexible to deal with the changing and fluctuating pattern created by customer demand. The 'multi-skilled' characteristic of managers has strong historical roots in that managers were expected to demonstrate the appropriate skills and knowledge as and when necessary. This characteristic has substantial support from recent studies across Europe.

The picture is of a manager busily preoccupied with daily problem solving at an operational level. The major features of the work require the job holder to be multi-skilled, particularly in craft skills and to 'be there' acting as 'mine host'. The activities of the manager's job necessitate immediate problem solving on an *ad hoc* basis. Away from the cultural context of hotels, it would be difficult to support the notion that the statements are gender bound in any way. There would seem to be no inherent reason why women should not perform these operational tasks unless they are interpreted within a gender context.

For instance being multi-skilled may only refer to kitchen work which excludes many women, and playing the role of mine host could have gender interpretations. The next section identifies the profiles of hotel managers and these possible gender interpretations.

Who are the hotel managers?

Biographical data, although scant, only confirms what is already known about the lack of women in positions of responsibility.

Arnaldo's research (Arnaldo, 1981) produced a profile of a hotel manager who would be a male, in his thirties, who had completed a four year college course with eleven to fifteen years experience in the industry and had worked for his present company for one to five years. Immediately this profile excludes women.

Pickworth in his survey of the managerial jobs in chain organisations in the US comments on the paucity of women in management positions and states that 'The principal bright spot for women in the hotel sector was the position of front office manager; 22 per cent personnel in this position were female and in hotels with fewer than 300 rooms that figure rose to 36 per cent' (Pickworth, 1982).

His review makes the comment that it is surprising given the importance of rooms division within hotels that Executive Housekeepers are the lowest paid of any of the hotel management positions and cites a quote from one female corporation executive who says that they 'plan to appoint an increasing number of males to the position of executive housekeeper to enhance its status' (Pickworth, 1982, p.33). The evidence not only supports the notion that housekeeping has a low value in hotels but also that women have a low status. It draws even greater attention to the interaction of the beliefs of the hotel industry and the way in which women are perceived. It is difficult to separate this issue from the cultural context of hotels.

The notion of personality is central in the profile of a hotelier, but what is understood to be 'personality' has more to do with subjective interpretations reflecting the belief system of the culture than it has to do with quantitative measures. It may well be the case that women do not fit this notion of 'personality', perhaps it is a masculine concept, linked to the image of what constitutes a 'mine host'.

Becoming a hotel manager

A different focus is to look at what managers do. This is particularly important given the description that managers in hotels prefer to work on concrete operations, solving daily problems.

The description by Guerrier (1987) confirms this point that the traditional ideal type is a person who '. . . would be strongly anchored in the occupation and the industry. He would have served a lengthy apprenticeship in all the basic hotel operations, particularly the food and beverage operations'.

She found that careers of hotel managers typically take the following route: a general apprenticeship served during the early part of the career, often the sandwich element of a college course. Following college a few years are spent as a trainee and as an assistant manager, this experience provides training for the 'ad hoc' management style. Generally the trainees and assistant managers have to be prepared to help out as and when necessary, in any department. They are expected to improve their skills and to be competent craftsmen. Experience in all departments is considered vital for promotion but emphasis is given to experience within the food and beverage operation. Although the variety can be gained by working for one company, it is more likely that rising managers will change companies (possibly without intention as mergers and takeovers are common within the industry).

Practical skills have always been valued highly and more highly than paper qualifications. It may therefore be that even though women may have their degrees/diplomas these are not valued as highly as practical skills, particularly those earned in the food and beverage departments.

Becoming a hotel manager would seem therefore to depend on a progression of jobs involving differing functional experiences, achieving competence in operational skills, particularly in departments which are highly valued and in hotels which have prestige. However, career development in organisations does not only rest with development of skills, nor with a profile of personality traits. The process seems to be accelerated when the individual can demonstrate that their personality matches the culture of the organisation and are willing to play the game of corporate politics.

Encouragement is arguably another important feature of career success. In an industry which is insular and bounded (see Explanation 2), it would seem probable that there is greater importance placed on identifying potential managerial talent. To ensure that the most effective trainees are developed there is high dependence on the management of the hotels to assess and judge future potential and to ensure that the trainees receive the most appropriate experience, at the right time, in the most applicable hotel. This individual monitoring between management (usually the general manager in small/medium hotels) and trainees places significant importance on the role played by managers and their judgements of the trainees working for them.

Attention to networks has long been considered an essential managerial activity. A network 'can be a more powerful determinant of the objectives to be pursued and how they are to be acted upon than the formal organisation' (Kakabadse, 1987). Getting on and being developed may therefore have more to do with becoming visible, becoming known and building up alliances.

A formalised method of this networking has been established by the use of mentors (or sponsors). Kanter suggest that sponsors have three major functions; first, they can fight for their protégé, second, they enable the protégé to bypass the hierarchy and, third, they provide reflected power. The relationship therefore not only provides the formal coaching and training, but also, and more significantly, signals messages to other people in the organisation that the protégé has been singled out for development, thus increasing the individual's visibility and enabling greater access to the networks within the organisation (Kanter, 1977).

It could therefore be that women are at a disadvantage in building up informal relationships and networks.

CONCLUSION

Research in the hotel world has established that women do not achieve managerial posts in the number that might be expected. Reasons for this have been explored in this case.

The first explanation concerned the women themselves – are their aspirations similar to those of men? Are they too passive or are their actions and reactions interpreted in a negative way?

The second explanation explored the possibility that the history and nature of hotel life works against the development of women. Men dominate the high status operations and women face an immediate disadvantage in developing the skills and experience perceived as necessary to succeed in management. In addition, the level of interpretation that was apparent in working relationships was hypothesised as working against women because situations were frequently interpreted within a masculine framework.

The process of developing managers was examined in the third section in order to identify any barriers that exist. Evidence shows that the hotel world has a history of tradition and conservatism which has remained resilient to changes in management and style. The extent to which practices may exclude women were explored and discussed.

These explanations should be critically evaluated. It may be more appropriate to view them all as partial and non-competitive or to consider other reasons for women's lack of managerial achievement in the hotel sector. It may be that the explanations are circular: *because* there are barriers and because managers do not expect female graduates to be serious managerial contenders the trainees begin to lower their aspirations. If these explanations are circular how can the circle be broken?

REFERENCES

Arnaldo, M. (1981). 'Hotel General Managers: A Profile', *Cornell HRA Quarterly*, November, pp.53–56.
Bartlett, N. (1993). 'Women in Slow Lane', *Caterer and Hotelkeeper*, 28 January.
Guerrier, Y. (1987). 'Hotel Managers' Career and Their Impact on Hotels in Britain', *International Journal of Hospitality Management*, Vol 6, No 3, p.129.
HCITB/ETAC (1983). *Hotel and Catering Skills – Now and in the Future*, Wembley: HCITB.
HCITB/(1984). *Women's Path to Management in the Hotel and Catering Industry*, London: HCITB.
Kakabadse, A., Ludlow, R. and Vinnicombe, S. (1987). *Working in Organisations*, Harmondsworth: Penguin, p.266.
Kanter, Rosabeth Moss (1977). *Men and Women of the Corporation*, New York: Basic Books.
Mars, G. and Mitchell, P. (1976). *Room for Reform? A Case Study of Industrial Relations in the Hotel Industry*, Open University Press.
Mars, G., Bryant, D. and Mitchell, P. (1979). *Manpower Problems in the Hotel Industry*, Saxon House, p.8.

Pickworth, J. R. (1982). 'Managerial Jobs in Chain Organisations', *Cornell Quarterly Review* February, pp.30–33.

Taylor, D. and Bush, D. (1974). *The Golden Age of British Hotels*, Northwood.

ACTIVITY BRIEF

1 *Evaluate the three given explanations and indicate the issues which you believe provide the most powerful arguments for gender differences.*
In your answer consider alternative explanations which could account for the lower number of female managers - both
internal factors – e.g. specific male attitudes/expectations
external factors – e.g. roles that men/women are expected to play outside the workplace.

2 *To what extent would you agree with the proposition that females are disadvantaged in the hotel world? In your answer draw on specific issues and make comparisons with other organisations.*

3 *The importance of networks and informal processes was discussed in the case. Explore the importance of relationships at work and consider the problems that could develop in the selection and development of young managers.*

4 *Is the hotel industry unique in its level of ambiguity and range of paradoxical situations? Identify these issues in the case and analyse an organisation with which you are familiar for levels of ambiguity, uncertainty and confusions.*

5 *It was suggested that masculine framework has been placed upon the work situation in hotels. What does this mean and what are its effects on the culture and its members?*

6 *Bearing in mind the details of the case what advice would you give to women about to embark on a career in hotel management?*

RECOMMENDED READING

Alban, Metcalfe B. and West M. (1991). 'Women Managers', in Firth-Cozens J. and West M. (ed.) *Women at Work*, Buckingham: Open University Press.

Hansard Society Commission Report (1990). *Women at the Top.*

Mills, Albert J. (1992). 'Organisation, Gender and Culture' in (ed.) Mills, A. J. and Tancred, P., *Gendering Organisational Analysis*, London: Sage.

Morgan, G. (1986). *Images of Organisations*, London: Sage.

Kanter, Rosabeth Moss (1977). *Men and Women of the Corporation*, New York: Basic Books.

Marshall, J. (1984). *Women Managers: Travellers in a Male World*, Chichester: Wiley.

SAS – Mergers in the air?

Per Darmer

During the 1980s the Scandinavian Airlines System (SAS) was regarded a major success story whose approach to management could be used by other organisations as a useful learning experience of ways in which they might obtain competitive advantage. The managing director of SAS – Jan Carlzon – was typified as the visionary leader of the future who was able to tear down the hierarchies of organisations and in his own words 'Turn the pyramids upside down'.

However, SAS is no longer riding on a wave of success. This case relates the present situation of SAS and the personal influence of Carlzon on the company and its staff to the issue of employee motivation and particularly the impact of leadership on work organisations. It also provides an opportunity to consider some cross-cultural issues emerging from a possible amalgamation between SAS and other national airlines.

BACKGROUND

SAS is the airline corporation of three nations: Denmark, Norway and Sweden. It employs around 25,000 staff in these three countries. While it operates as a commercial airline the governments of Denmark, Norway and Sweden are among the owners of the corporation. Between them the governments own some 50 per cent of the shares in the company and so there can be a significant political voice in the running of SAS. The headquarters of SAS is located in Stockholm, Sweden, while the main airport for the company's operations is in Copenhagen, Denmark.

Towards the end of the 1970s SAS found itself in financial trouble and for the first time in 17 years posted a loss of about 75m Danish kroner (approximately £7.5m) in both 1979/80 and 1980/81. Jan Carlzon was appointed managing director of SAS in 1981 and was charged with the task of heading the financial turnaround of the corporation. By 1982/83 SAS was again on the money-making track with an operating surplus of approximately 620m Danish kroner. The turnaround was achieved by taking SAS from being a technical-oriented organisation and refocusing it as a service-oriented airline and modelling itself as the businessman's airline. The second part of this strategy was later to have serious implications for the company. In 1982 its success was recognised when it received the accolade of the most punctual airline by a European flight association.

During this period Carlzon used his excellent communication skills and flair for handling the media to the benefit of SAS. Typical of Carlzon's style was a somewhat stage-managed affair when he personally assisted in the loading of an SAS flight at Copenhagen Airport. His purpose was to demonstrate to both the media and the employees the importance of such routine tasks. The event attracted substantial publicity for the principle of SAS employees working together to help the company succeed.

A key element of Carlzon's approach was to centre attention on the frontline personnel who, in 'moments of truth' (the confrontations with the customers), were seen to be the keys to success or failure for the corporation. In order to implement this philosophy it was, therefore, of the utmost importance that these frontline personnel were given authority to make decisions in these moments of truth without recourse to senior managers, if they were to be able to give the customer the excellent service that would encourage the customer to fly SAS in the future. Carlzon, therefore, delegated decision-making power to the frontline personnel and made sure that employees were kept aware of how important they were for the success of the company. This message was reinforced through both internal SAS magazines and the mass media.

The 'new SAS' was a success with its staff of hard-working, highly motivated and committed employees. Carlzon was seen as the man who saved SAS and was regarded a very successful leader – 'The best Carlzon in the world'. At that time Carlzon was seen as a hero by employees who would, if need be, go to hell and back for him.

Today, however, SAS is no longer the success story it was in the 1980s. In the early 1990s history appears to be repeating itself, and SAS has again encountered financial difficulties. The present troubles of the SAS are partly due to the worldwide depression of the airline business following the Gulf War, partly due to the company's preparation for the European Community Internal Market which will make the competition in the airline business tougher, and finally the result of strategic decisions made by the leadership of SAS.

Strategic decisions

In the 1980s SAS bought a large share (40 per cent of the stock) in Intercontinental Hotels. This decision was made on the assumption that customers would welcome the opportunity to book their hotel reservation at the same time as making their flight arrangements. SAS would then take care of both passenger and their luggage from departure at the airport to arrival at the hotel. To implement this strategy, SAS targeted their promotional campaign at the businessmen themselves. This, however, failed to recognise that most flight and hotel bookings are actually made by their secretaries. In addition, businessmen tend to be conservative people and prefer hotels with which they are familiar. SAS's campaign was unable to overcome this inertia and the failure of the strategy contributed to the loss of approximately 100 million Danish kroner in 1991. In September 1991 Curt Nicolin, chairman of SAS, commenting on the purchase of shares in Intercontinental Hotels said: 'The decision was right when it was taken, but the development we have seen since then has proved that the decision was wrong.'

Also during the 1980s SAS sought to widen its operational base and take advantage of the bouyant American airline market. Accordingly it bought shares in Continental Airlines. However, the worldwide depression in the industry and the resulting difficulties it caused led to suggestions that SAS had overstretched itself.

The losses following the share purchases in Intercontinental Hotels and Continental Airlines caused a financial crisis in SAS which was solved by cutting its operational expenses. The focus on cost reduction meant a cutback in staff. In 1991 SAS decided to reduce staffing levels by 3,500 employees. Jobs were lost at all levels and locations throughout the company. Copenhagen Airport was the hardest hit bearing 1,900 of the redundancies and there were also significant reductions at the headquarters in Stockholm. Many of those made redundant had been with SAS for all their working lives. For them it was more than a job that was lost; SAS was a major part of their lives.

The company's involvement with Intercontinental Hotels and Continental Airlines has changed the employees' view of Carlzon. He is most certainly no longer held in the same esteem as he was during the high-flying 1980s. The employees hold Carlzon personally responsible for these mistakes and have lost their confidence in him and his abilities as a leader to the extent that voices have been raised suggesting SAS would be better off by replacing him as managing director. They believe it is unfair that Carlzon's mistakes are being paid for by some of their collegues losing their jobs. John Vangen, spokesman for the Danish flight personnel (a Danish trade union for air cabin crew) put it this way in September 1991: 'None of Carlzon's strategies have succeeded since 1984. He has to take responsibility for that. If he cannot make the company run he should leave it. We need a management we can trust.'

SITUATION

Competition in the airline business is fierce and there are few signs that this will change in the immediate future. The major competitors for SAS in Europe are British Airways, Lufthansa (German) and Air France while competition from the developing East European airlines is increasingly significant.

While competition is a threat for all in the airline business those companies in most immediate danger are the smaller operations like SAS. The generally favoured solution to this problem is therefore growth through either mergers or acquisitions.

During a press conference on 23 February 1993, when the cooperation between the British Airways and TAT (the French airline corporation) was announced, the European head of British Airways put it this way: 'Those able to keep a cool head for the next ten years will win the battle of the air.' Faced with this competition SAS has adopted a strategy which aims to make it one of the major European airlines securing its future into the next century. Accordingly at the beginning of 1993 SAS began negotiations with three other national airline corporations: KLM (The Netherlands), Swissair and Austrian Airlines, as part of this strategy.

A merger between these four airlines seems a promising business idea. None of the airlines are able to make a major impact on their own, but together they could become a major player in the airline business. Together, the four airlines would become the largest European airline company and the second largest in the world measured by the number of passengers carried. In Europe alone the four airlines handle 25 per cent of the traffic between European countries.

For two months 16 project groups have examined the legal, commercial and operational possibilities and limits of a closer co-operation between the four airlines. The proposal resulting from these groups' report was the creation of a common management group and shared accounting systems for the four airlines. For the moment they still operate under their own masts but will, at the same time, have a common name. 'The European Airlines' has been mentioned as one possibility. In the long run it is proposed that the four airlines should become a single fully integrated corporation. The three largest partners – SAS, KLM, and Swissair – will each own 30 per cent of the new company while Austrian Airlines will own the remaining 10 per cent. The report further suggests that a common headquarters is located at either Copenhagen, Amsterdam, Zurich or Vienna. The major airports to be used by the new corporation would be in these four cities plus Stockholm, Oslo and Geneva.

If the owners of the four airlines agree to the idea of a common airline corporation the first step will be the signing of a 'memorandum of understanding'. Indications are that the airlines are in favour of the idea. Support has also been given to the proposal by the governments of Austria, Denmark, Holland, Norway, Sweden and Switzerland, who as part owners have an important voice in the decision.

Problems facing SAS

Although it seems that in joining the new corporation 'European Airlines' SAS is on its way to accomplishing its strategy and one of its major goals, it still has some major problems on the home front. The conflict between management and employees originating in the difficulties described earlier, has reached new heights. These problems have been nourished by SAS's international developments with the other four airlines. Employees do not appear to be quite as thrilled with the idea of a new common airline as management and shareholders seem to be. They fear that the new corporation will mean further staff reductions in SAS personnel.

Employees are concerned that some of the important intercontinental flights will move from Copenhagen, where they are currently based, to the airport where the headquarters of the new corporation will be located even though the location has not yet been decided. They do not share the optimism of management who are confident that Copenhagen Airport will benefit from the creation of the new common corporation in general and especially if the headquarters are located in Copenhagen, which they see as the only 'natural' choice. SAS employees however are not convinced. They perceive the indecisiveness surrounding the decision on the location of the headquarters as a deliberate strategic move by the management of the new corporation who, they believe, want to postpone such decisions and tough choices to a time when all other major decisions have been made. It is felt, for example, that the choice of the location of headquarters could very easily create turbulence amongst the partners and make it harder for some of them to sign the 'memorandum of understanding'. This could delay the process, or even worse, put an end to it.

As a consequence of their dissatisfaction the SAS employees have sent a letter to the members of the Danish government and some large Danish companies in their words, to, 'inform them of what is going on.' The headline of the letter sent by the four unions representing SAS personnel at Copenhagen Airport reads:

> **What is it we risk, if we leave the decisions to a few persons in the leadership of SAS?** The risks are to lose the intercontinental flights and 14,500 jobs at the airport and many more in supporting industries.

SAS management reacted strongly to the letter. They counter-attacked by pressing charges against the four unions for disloyal behaviour. Management and employees now stand trial on this case in the Danish Court of Industrial Relations. Gerhard Dall, information officer in SAS, explains why SAS has taken this very unusual step: 'The four unions cast doubt upon the will of the leadership of SAS to fight for Copenhagen as the centre for SAS's traffic and that is disloyal. The reality is quite the opposite.'

On May 7th 1993 Jan Carlzon called the employees of SAS to a meeting in Stockholm. During this meeting Carlzon revealed a little more about the future plans of the new corporation, particularly concerning the location of intercontinental flights.

The corporation will establish three major airports for the intercontinental flights. Copenhagen will become the gateway to Asia (mainly China and Japan). Amsterdam will become the centre for flights to the South and North American continent. The gateway to Africa will be Zurich which will also handle some of the flights to Asia and South America. The other major airports of the new corporation – Stockholm (Sweden), Oslo (Norway) and Vienna (Austria) will handle the flights between the three major cities. In addition, Vienna will handle most of the traffic to the Middle East. Carlzon attempted to calm the fears of employees by telling them that some of the intercontinental flights to the US would still be operating from Stockholm to ensure that American-based airlines will not take over these routes.

While location of the headquarters of the new corporation has still not been decided, it seems that this step of locating different parts of the international traffic at three major airports is a compromise that gives everybody a 'slice of the action'. A closer look at how the international flights are shared among the three major airports, however, indicates that Amsterdam, with the very important cross-Atlantic flights, has put itself into an advantageous position for becoming the headquarters of the new corporation.

ACTIVITY BRIEF

1 *How would you suggest management of the new airline should deal with cross–cultural issues posed by a workforce made up of four nationalities.*

2 *Jan Carlzon was characterised as a charaismatic leader admired by the employees of SAS. Why does his charisma no longer seem to be working?*

3 *Should SAS remove Carlzon as managing director, as suggested by some of the employees, or should he remain despite the negative view held of him by his staff?*

4 *SAS used to be 'one big happy family'; what has happened to that 'family-feeling' and what can be done in order to restore SAS as a united company and develop employee motivation?*

RECOMMENDED READING

Adler, N. (1991). *International Dimensions of Organizational Behavior*, Boston: PWS–Kent.

Hofstede, G. (1984). *Cultures Consequences*, Calif.: Sage.

Mullins, L. (1993). *Management and Organisational Behaviour*, London: Pitman.

Robbins, P. (1993). *Organizational Behavior*, New Jersey: Prentice-Hall.

My greatest failure:
A case study in leadership

Henner Hentze

There has been a noticeable increase over the past few years in the number of companies traditionally trading within their home markets seeking to expand their activities into other member states of the European Community. One way for organisations to achieve this objective is to acquire ownership of companies based in other member states. This trend has been reinforced by the establishment of the Single European Market with its resulting free flow of capital, goods, services and labour between the 12 national states. However, this strategy has important operational implications for organisations, particularly where it leads to employees from different national cultures being recruited.

The following case deals with a German company operating in the media industry which, among other activities, has taken a controlling interest in a French printing firm. The issues relating to leadership have been a significant factor in the day-to-day running of the subsidiary company and, when a replacement was needed for a senior manager, the company head office in Germany decided to fill the position with a German manager. Following the appointment, considerable problems arose which were, to a large part, attributed to a change in the style of leadership.

The case provides opportunities to consider the issues that may arise when different cultural styles of leadership (in this case French and German) clash and how such a change in leadership might be managed in order to limit the problems that can occur.

BACKGROUND

Media AG is a German company founded some 50 years ago as a small printing operation. Over the past few years the company has, through skilful management, expanded rapidly and now has interests in many other areas of the media industry. As part of this strategy the company decided in the early 1990s to take advantage of the opportunities provided by the

Single European Market to expand its interests into other countries in Europe.

A particular opportunity arose to purchase a majority share in a French company which specialises in security printing including the production of cheques and banknotes. The French company operated exclusively in its home market of which it had a significant share. It had been built up after the Second World War by a technically well qualified team and was financially sound. These factors led the German parent company to decide initially that the subsidiary should operate autonomously and to limit its involvement to long-term strategic decisions.

The French company is headed by Monsieur Warner, the *President Directeur General* (PGD). He graduated from one of the leading French '*Grand Ecoles*' and worked for ten years in the Ministry of Finance in Paris. During this time he developed a close working relationship with the French subsidiary which had many national contracts with the Ministry for the production of banknotes and other security work. When the position of PGD became vacant, M. Warner expressed an interest in the post which provided him with the opportunity to move from the civil service and into industry, a move which had been a long-term objective of his career.

French institutions are, regardless of their size, highly centralised. The PGD manages through a strict hierarchy according to functional lines and top-down communications; the matrix structures found in many enterprise cultures are very rare in France and communication and authority lines run vertically from, and to, the PGD. In taking up this position M. Warner entered at the top of this formal hierarchy with no experience of managing in the private sector or of the detailed work going in the company. He therefore relies heavily on the experience of his senior managers in the day-to-day management of the company.

The responsibility for production matters within the company rests with Monsieur Abel, the production director, who reports directly to the PGD. He has been with the company for most of his working life and has held his present position for 20 years. His background is very different to that of the PGD. He received no formal higher education and his career progression has been achieved through his dedication and effective performance within the company.

M. Abel's leadership style reflects the typical behaviour of the French 'patron'; a style still found today in many medium-sized French companies. It can be characterised as being highly task orientated with social relations between the 'patron' and employees conducted on a paternalistic basis. Abel has worked hard at improving the performance of the company, relying on his lengthy experience of the business to make his decisions. His detailed knowledge of the business, with which no one in the company can compete, has led to his authority within the company being beyond dispute. Consequently he exercises what he perceives to be his right to make decisions independently and without consultation. His colleagues and sub-ordinates are not, therefore, involved in the decision making process, there is limited delegation and subordinates are regularly required to seek M. Abel's advice over production matters. This approach has led to the staff having a high level of dependency but it has equally created a high degree of security for his employees. Abel's approach seems to complement the attitudes of the workforce, many of whom are middle-aged or older. These employees seem strongly influenced by such traditional work ethic criteria as duty, obedience and following orders without criticism.

An important element of French business culture is the 'cadre'. The term 'cadre' symbolises an independent and professional strata of employees with its own access criteria and regulations. Membership reflects a degree of competence and becomes a key recruitment criteria for companies when hiring managers. Cadre personnel benefit from a special legal status with additional periods of notice and enhanced pension rights. Access to the group of cadres is possible through three different routes:

- Without any higher education qualifications, entry is restricted to those who can demonstrate competence over a period of a number of years with one employer. This is the case with M. Abel.
- With a higher education qualification, taking up to two years study to obtain, additional relevant experience of between five and ten years is required.
- Immediate access to cadre status is given normally to graduates of the leading 'Grand Ecoles'. This is the case with M. Warner.

THE SITUATION

M. Abel has recently suffered from two heart attacks and the PGD believed that it would be wise to replace him with a younger manager. Abel is close to retirement age and with the additional pension benefit entitlement due to him through his membership of the cadre his standard of living would not be significantly affected by this decision. Abel accepted the decision and the company began the search for a replacement. However, when the idea was proposed to the German parent company the head office felt that this would be an appropriate time to become more closely involved in the affairs of the subsidiary. They decided to initiate a management exchange between the two countries and to make M. Abel's replacement the first of these appointments.

The person chosen as the new production director of the French sub-sidiary was Dr Bernard. He is 35 years old, an engineer by training, with a Masters degree in engineering and a Ph.D. in business studies obtained at the technical university of Munich. His thesis dealt with the topic of 'Profit sharing – a comparison of American and German views and ethics'. His educational career has placed a premium on the acquisition of intellectual capability and the ability to solve problems systematically. During several of his vacations from college he undertook work placements in France and on his own initiative he took an intensive French language course in Paris. Dr Bernard joined Media AG some five years ago as the personal assistant to the chairman. While in this post he has successfully completed a number of projects, some at his own initiative, in the areas of finance, sales and, particularly, production. The combination of his academic training, language skills and experience, together with his insights into the strategic issues at the parent company made him, in the view of head office, an ideal candidate for the post.

Even though the French were not particularly in favour of Bernard's appointment (they would have preferred a Frenchman), they accepted the decision, recognising that it would create stronger links between the two companies. One of Abel's colleagues, commenting on the change of leadership said, ' I knew Abel 40 years ago when the company was being built up. He started in charge of printing and worked himself up through the company. We often had arguments with him and he occasionally treated the workers as if he was a dictator, but production ran smoothly and in the case of an emergency, we all stood behind him. Dr Bernard is a sensible guy, has excellent qualifications, but is always so serious, somehow cold. As a German he will find it difficult here.'

Dr Bernard relished the challenge of his new position as Production Director in a foreign country and had developed firm ideas on how he would tackle his management role. He had closely studied the features of participative leadership styles and was determined to introduce them to the company. Delegation wherever possible, teamwork and joint decision making, if necessary all the way down to the shop-floor, regular two-way communication and the systematic enhancement of skills through training were to be foundations of his approach. In particular he planned to introduce a management by objectives scheme similar to that operating in the parent company. Before taking up his appointment he had discussed these matters with senior management at Media AG and received their support for his ideas.

Bernard had been told several times about M. Abel's leadership style and realised how different it appeared to the approach he planned to take. He was sure, however, that the employees would like his style which would develop the potential within the workforce, not least because of the greater involvement and autonomy his way would provide for them. For the first eight months Dr Bernard was satisfied with the way things were going at the subsidiary. Productivity levels had been maintained while the employees had adjusted to his style of management. Three employees had resigned from the company during this period; two fully qualified operators and one young technician. As was typical of his approach, Bernard examined their reasons for leaving very carefully and established that all three had left for reasons unconnected with their jobs. In one case, the employee's father-in-law had died and he had inherited the tobacconists shop the relative had owned. Another had built his own house outside of the town and had found a similar job nearby and the technician had been offered a job which promised much faster progression than he could expect at the company.

Bernard is very surprised, therefore, when, a couple of months later, he is called to Warner's office and handed a letter by the PGD who says 'read this and tell me what you think'. He takes the letter and recognises the author as being Andre Maillot, the head of production planning and one of Bernard's immediate subordinates. Maillot is a serious person, 61 years old, a dedicated company employee and extremely competent in his job. Bernard has a high regard for Maillot's work and has taken every opportunity to personally recognise his contribution to the company.

Maillot writes:

> Dear M. Warner,
>
> Over the past few weeks I have asked myself many times whether I should write this letter. Please do not misunderstand my intentions in the criticism I am about to make of the Production Director. I recognise that he is technically very good in his field, but at present the production operation is not working as well as it used to. Soon, I believe, there will be even greater difficulties and it is in order to prevent these that I am writing to you. I have explained all the problem areas to Dr Bernard but in vain. His way of working makes it difficult for him to understand what I and the rest of the staff are feeling. Perhaps I can best explain our worries more clearly by comparing Dr Bernard with M. Abel.
>
> When M. Abel had to deal with one of us on a production matter he would call us into his office, tell us the details of the problem, the solution he required and what we were to do and by when. When we left the office we knew clearly what was expected of us. With Dr Bernard it is very different. We frequently have meetings (I counted them in July – of 184 working hours 58 were spent in meetings called by him), where we would have long discussions at the end of which Dr Bernard did not come to a decision. What he repeatedly says is 'the success of the company depends upon us working together as a team to find a solution with which we are all satisfied'. It sounds great and we are doing our best to help but at the end of the day we are each only responsible for our own area of work.
>
> If we took a question to Abel we would either get a straight answer or, if he felt we should know the answer, we would get a telling off. I remember him saying to me on more than one occasion, 'After 24 years you should have learnt this by now'. Well, you certainly got an answer! We were all used to his way and realised that nothing personal was intended. Abel knew all there was to know about printing and the decisions he made always worked.

Dr Bernard, on the other hand, always starts by asking us what the problem is and we have to systematically explain everything. Then he asks, 'What would you suggest as the solution? – What are the advantages? – Disadvantages?' and 'Do you want to discuss this with Mr X or Mr Y and see what he thinks?' At the end of the meeting we are no wiser than we were at the start. The only thing that has been achieved is the time of another meeting a few days later to discuss solutions.

Dr Bernard encourages us to take responsibility for making our own decisions and to use our initiative in work matters. But two years ago when, on my own initiative, I gave the go-ahead to print an order for eurocheques, I nearly lost my job as no one told me that the contract had been cancelled eight weeks prior to the scheduled start of production. The stress that I felt as a result of this incident forced me to take several weeks off work.

Also significant is Jean Fleur, the print technician's reason for resigning. He pointed out a technical inadequacy on one of the machines to Dr Bernard. Bernard was very appreciative and friendly and told him to come up with a solution within the next three months. Fleur was so surprised and concerned that he took a job in another company because he was afraid he could not solve the problem and would be sacked. After this event the employees feel that it is better not to make any suggestions to Dr Bernard if they want to keep their jobs.

Abel was frequently found in the production area; he talked to all the staff and occasionally joked with them. He could spot when people were not pulling their weight and would tell them off there and then but he was always available if people needed help. Dr Bernard goes through the production area every day but because virtually everything is discussed in meetings personal contact is rare and he is like a stranger to most of the staff. They also believe that he has no sense of humour. When he first started at the company some of the employees tried to speak to him in the same way as they had to Abel but he did not seem interested in conversation so now none of them speak to him anymore except to say 'good morning'.

Abel was, at the same time, the most loved and the most hated person in the company but we all knew where we stood with him. We are much less sure of Dr Bernard's management style and his personality is alien to most of us. The training courses on management by objectives which he set up were interesting and we know that he wants to introduce this scheme into the company and so change the way it is managed. I am not alone in believing that these ideas will just not work in our company. We are all very worried about the future.

He does not take our concerns seriously. His standard reply is that we should all want the company to prosper and to make work more satisfying for everyone. At the moment, however, satisfaction has decreased.

(Following this there was another apology and a statement that he would inform Bernard of the contents of the letter if necessary but preferred it to remain confidential for the time being.)

Dr Bernard laid the letter down. The contents came as a complete shock to him. He felt that through his participative, reasoning approach to management the staff would see the benefits it offered themselves and the company. Their reaction went against everything he had learnt about leadership and he is upset that they did not understand his managerial philosophy. He accepts he is not good at social conversation but is hurt that despite his politeness and inner belief in people his attitude was viewed so negatively by the employees.

Bernard reflects upon the events that have occurred and thinks to himself 'This has been my greatest failure'.

ACTIVITY BRIEF

1 *Analyse how the leadership crisis at the French subsidiary has developed. The analysis should take into account national cultural differences and the leadership styles of the key participants.*

2 *What are the reasons for believing that a leadership style similar to M. Abel's will not be appropriate for the company in the future.*

3 *After the events detailed in the case, M. Warner has discussed the situation with head office in Germany. He is advised that Dr Bernard should remain in his position. Develop an action plan which would overcome the leadership difficulties in the French subsidiary.*

RECOMMENDED READING

Schien, E. H. (1985). *Organisational Culture and Leadership: A Dynamic View,* San Francisco: Josey–Bass.

Hofstede, G. (1980). *Culture's Consequences: International Differences in Work Related Values,* Beverley Hills: Sage.

Mullins, L. J. (1993). *Management and Organisational Behaviour,* London: Pitman, Chapters 8, 12 and 13.

Reality catches up with Aussieco

Robert Jones and Peter Gal

This case study describes an Australian company which, despite enormous potential in the form of a unique product and little serious competition, now finds itself in a precarious situation. The case commences by sketching the background to the company and its operations. Details of the behaviour of the people and the issues involved are presented in the form of a series of events dramatised within the context of a typical working day at the company. The case continues by examining a select number of policies pursued by the organisation in its business operations, and concludes with a brief description of several problems now facing the company.

The case study illustrates a number of key issues in the field of management and organisational behaviour, particularly the effect of leadership, organisational structure, manpower planning, and managerial behaviour, effectiveness, and style on such variables as motivation, employee commitment and work quality.

BACKGROUND

Aussieco is a large manufacturing and service company, fully Australian owned and operated. It has built its reputation on a single product in which it now holds about 60 per cent of the Australian market, down from 90 per cent in 1980. During the past ten years it has attempted to diversify into other products and markets, with mixed success, mainly due to management's failure to understand the special situations in the markets concerned. All its products are based on the same principle of computer-controlled, high-precision mechanical hardware.

The company operates from a single location in an industrial suburb close to the city of Melbourne. Its 600 employees are mainly housed in three large interconnected buildings, all held freehold by the company – an important fact because these properties are often used as security for business loans.

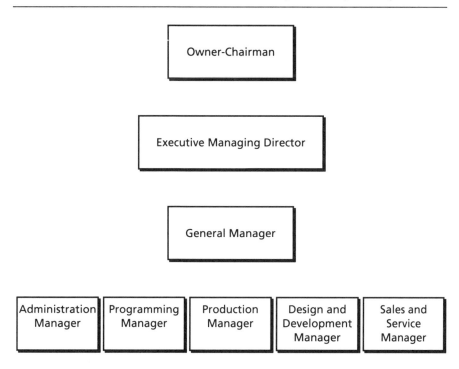

Fig 7.1 Senior management structure of Aussieco

The owner established the company in 1962 as a small manufacturing and service operation, supplying a small customer base in the Melbourne area. Throughout its expansion he has been able to retain full control and ownership, currently acting as chairman and chief executive officer. Although most final decisions are made by him, he is not involved with the daily running of the company.

The executive managing director is the owner's nephew. He came to the company in 1984 straight from university with no practical or industrial experience other than several work-experience stints during vacations. The position was created for him to learn the business and he is credited with the company's recent attempts to diversify its product range. However, the key person in the day-to-day operations of the company is the general manager. He performs his role by 'kicking around' (this phrase used to the authors during conversation) five main sector managers as shown in Fig. 7.1.

THE SITUATION

A working day at Aussieco

Employees and lower management commence work at 7.30 a.m. The company has not provided parking for employees' cars since 1989 when a series of prefabricated buildings were constructed on the previous parking area. Most staff arrive frustrated from looking for parking space in the surrounding area or after a 20 minute walk from the closest railway station. Employees rush to punch time clocks fitted in the entrance to the premises. At exactly 7.35 a.m. a personnel clerk removes the cards of missing staff and takes them to the personnel office. Employees arriving after this time must report to their supervisor and then to the personnel office to retrieve their card.

At 7.25 a.m. the first bell rings. At 7.30 a.m. a second bell rings. After the second bell everybody should start working. Staff move slowly to their positions. Female operatives in Printed Circuit Board (PCB) Assembly are waiting a second day for a supply of resistors. The stores computer shows a stock of 4,700 pieces, but none can be located. Ordering is refusing to obtain more until the programme is corrected to show the accurate stock. In the meantime one of the repair technicians is instructed by his supervisor to leave the premises and buy some resistors from a local electronics retail store. Thirty minutes later he is back, carrying a small bag with 200 resistors (retail price $AUS 8), paid for by the supervisor. He holds little hope of being reimbursed. Supply is enough to cover his team for a week.

Middle and senior management arrive between 9.00 and 10.00 a.m. Assembly-line workers hold back production with weak and vague excuses. The company has a large order to meet and if daily limits are not achieved, operatives can work overtime. Every excuse is good because the production supervisor is a qualified carpet fitter and has little knowledge of the day-to-day tasks of his subordinates. Most of the time he has no idea what his foremen are talking about. Rumour has it that he holds the job because he is the best friend of the production manager.

In the meantime, a senior programmer has received a work order with a five-day deadline to prepare several programs to meet the legal and specification requirements of a particular country. His request to do them at home has been granted. However, he intends to use this time to take his wife on holiday to Queensland. He had actually done the same job some years ago but this had been overlooked due to the appointment of a new programming manager in 1991. Programming is the smallest sector in the company and was originally the responsibility of the production manager. However, following a mass resignation of programmers in 1991, alleging incompetence on the part of the production manager, the whole group was promoted one step up.

Before lunch comes big news. The company has received an order for over $AUS 1 million. The bad news is that the order is from a customer in Perth, Western Australia, who did not pay for his first shipment about a year ago and the machines were brought back to Melbourne. Total loss $AUS 100,000. A second order was billed six months ago but not dispatched. The company asked for payment in advance, but when this was not forthcoming the machines were stripped for spare parts. Total loss $AUS 60,000. Since then nobody in the company has wanted to deal with this customer. Today the owner proudly announced that he had accepted the order personally. The complaining production manager was ordered out of his office. The production manager is the busiest and lowest paid sector manager in the company. In the history of the organisation nobody has lasted in this position for more than three years. The present incumbent looks like going the same way. In his last attempt to prevent another loss he tried to contact the administration manager, who cannot be reached as he is playing golf. The executive managing director is playing golf with him. The general manager says he has no idea what is going on. The owner never tells him anything but 'deals with my people whenever he feels like it'. Lunch break is from noon to 12.30 p.m. Everyone must leave the workplace and go to the canteen. The exceptions are senior management who have their own dining-room, and sales staff who use the showroom for lunch. Both serve unlimited quantities of alcohol, an observation not lost on operatives, who are not permitted to drink in the workplace (not only alcohol, but any kind of drink).

After lunch the general manager starts his walk around the building. The reason for this is unknown, because he does not talk to anyone, he does not answer any questions, he just wanders around. He is quite safe. He is unlikely to receive complaints or be asked questions because, with the exception of senior managers, nobody knows who he is. He either avoids visiting the company's two workshops or else moves through them as rapidly as possible. Workshops are open, with no doors, cluttered and filthy. Windows are never washed. A large number are boarded up. The tin roofs are without insulation and leak during heavy rain. Buckets must be strategically placed to catch the water. Those operatives most affected by the leaks have bought their own buckets in order to keep their immediate work area dry. The dilapidated state of the buildings contrasts starkly with the state-of-the-art (but under-utilised) machinery housed within them. Last winter a heavy night's rain forced through a new hole in the roof and blew out a computerised robot worth $AUS 500,000. After this incident, every expensive machine was fitted with its own small roof.

A significant amount of revenue has traditionally been derived from the manufacturing operations of the company's metal and wood workshops. They receive orders from outside customers to manufacture items totally unrelated to the main production. This situation appears to have evolved gradually over a long period of time through a series of *ad hoc* events, but even the longest-serving employees appear unable to explain any specific reasons for the current situation. The capacity of these two workshops is more than double that of the whole factory due to modernisation with robots and fully automated machinery in 1990. However, recession since then has kept the two workshops largely idle.

The afternoon brings a crop of personnel problems. A process worker is fired for complaining to his foreman about putting handles on machines which must later be removed in order to have access to the interior for the assembly of other parts. In the metal workshop a new foreman discovers a man with no apparent work. An investigation reveals that he is a welder forgotten by the company since the fitting of a new welding automat.

Personnel 'clangers' in the hiring of new staff abound and are readily and humorously related to outsiders ears: a secretary for the drawing office who had never seen drawings before but was now expected to finish them; a programmer with no experience of working with the program exclusively used in production; assembly workers unable to read or speak English (assembly is performed piece by piece according to specification sheets hanging on machine chassis). Those managers most affected have unsuccessfully tried to change the system. They attempt to cope by training unsatisfactory new staff, although little or no money is budgeted for such activities. The hope is that the new personnel manager will improve matters although this post has been vacant for over two months following the dismissal of the previous incumbent for sexual harassment. At 3.55 p.m. the bell rings to stop work and staff gather their belongings and queue for the time clocks. At 4.00 p.m. the second bell rings and everybody runs from the building. The word 'run' is not an exaggeration; the act of leaving the premises can be equated with a 100 metre dash. Back on the assembly line a select group of workers cosily pull out newspapers and coffee mugs prior to the commencement of their overtime; they have successfully played the 'overtime game'.

Aussieco's policies

The company has operated in the same way for many years. Its product is unique. It is more complicated to build a TV and video recorder combination (retailing for $AUS 1,500) and yet the company's machines sell for $AUS 9,500, with no middleman involved. The management of the company operates in an autocratic way. Orders are sent from the top to the bottom. Ideas and personal opinions are neither sought nor valued.

The company adheres to a number of policies when conducting its business operations.

Staffing and promotion

The company employs only migrant labour at the operative level, mostly with limited English and unqualified. Training them for certain operations is not very difficult and turnover is low because of the difficulty in finding alternative employment. Even key personnel (such as programmers, engineers, and technicians) are mainly of migrant origin, or people lacking formal qualifications, but who possess talent at their particular job. These staff members are treated well and usually receive excellent pay to keep them in the company.

The organisation appears loathe to promote its own staff. If anybody leaves, external replacements are found. During the past six years only one position has been filled through internal promotion. The system of finding jobs for family or friends (known in local parlance as 'mates') seems prevalent. The company does not supply references at the end of employment (regardless of the reason for leaving).

Manufacturing

The whole manufacturing process is broken down into simple operations and these are strictly timed. The company calls this 'efficiency measurement'. The exercise is repeated regularly, to the ridicule of staff who, when tested, work at deliberately slow speeds to avoid later harassment for not meeting daily standards. Numerical targets are set for the whole company and broken down through the main sectors to departments and individuals. These numbers are checked weekly and charted. The company refers to these charts as the 'efficiency data list'. No rewards are given for the attainment of targets. Bonuses are sometimes paid at Christmas, depending on profitability, at the whim of the owner. Workers unable to meet targets are dismissed.

Suppliers

The company continuously changes suppliers in order to source the cheapest possible materials. It doggedly adheres to this policy in spite of several expensive failures. Recently, a previous supplier of blank PCB charging $20 per unit and with a 99.5 per cent quality level was abandoned in favour of another supplier charging $12. These units proved less reliable. Faulty boards were discovered only after assembly (worth $300). A significant number were destroyed under power. The rest were rectified at an average expense of $35 per piece.

Problems

Although the company faces no immediate commercial danger, a number of problems are immediately recognisable within the company.

Profitability

Despite the enormous financial potential of the company, profitability is virtually nil. Its inability to build up any substantial cash reserve is significant. The owner takes about $AUS one million out of the company annually. For the past financial year it has been surviving from month to month, forcing management to concentrate on earning sufficient income to meet expenses and payroll.

Employee morale

Staff find little to be proud of in belonging to the company. The whole process is driven by fear. Employees are afraid to say or do anything in fear of losing their job. Long-serving unqualified managers live with similar feelings. Technocrats of the company are in a different position. They are potentially more mobile but have a comfortable and easy life with good pay. Relatively few take the challenge and leave the company.

During one promotional campaign for a trade show the company issued car bumper stickers with the company logo and appealed to employees to use them voluntarily on their private cars. Very few complied. A noticeable exception was on the owner's vehicle. Jokes are still made today that it was the only limousine in town ever to sport a bumper sticker.

Quality of Senior Management

The owner's dictatorial attitude, ignorance of modern trends, and age-related dispositions (memory loss, child-like behaviour, tantrums) are of increasing concern. So is his tendency to nepotistic appointments. If anybody tries to show him anything that is wrong with the company, they become his instant enemy.

The lack of interdepartmental communication causes serious problems. Some departments do not communicate at all, some supply only limited information, some live in an ivory tower with no appreciation of other developments. The owner sometimes compounds such problems by ordering work to be done at lower structures of the company without informing superiors.

Product quality

Quality of the final product is suffering quite badly. There has been a marked increase in customer complaints and the company is losing its good name. Warranty repairs have escalated. There are two reasons for this: the deteriorating quality of the final product, and the unqualified nature of site installation staff who damage about 20 per cent of stock, often software.

ACTIVITY BRIEF

1 *Discuss the various issues of leadership raised by this case study.*

2 *Identify how the lack of managerial effectiveness has impacted upon the organisation.*

3 *Draw up an action plan for practical remedial action for Aussieco. Particular attention should be paid to:*
   - *What must be done and by when.*
   - *How it is to be done (policies/procedures etc, resource implications).*
   - *Who should be involved.*

RECOMMENDED READING

Mullins, L. J. (1993). *Management and Organisational Behaviour*, London: Pitman.

Vechio, R. D. (1991). *Organisational Behaviour*, Orlando: Dryden Press.

Gordon, J. R., Mondy, R. W., Sharplin, A. and Premeaux, S. R. (1990). *Management and Organisational Behaviour*, Hemel Hempstead: Allyn and Bacon.

Thameside: Leadership within a local authority housing department

Sarah L. Henson and Fred Turner

'Anyone who has ever been responsible for organising or co-ordinating the work of others, who has sought to get things done through other people, has encountered some of the problems of the management of groups' (Handy 1993).

Leadership is a diverse topic and can be viewed from a number of perspectives, but essentially it is a relationship through which one person influences the behaviour of other people. It is a dynamic form of behaviour and there are many variables which affect the nature of the leadership–follower relationship. The purpose of this case is to draw attention to some of these within a local authority housing department, which in turn reflects such organisational influences as power, organisational structure, culture and individual motivation.

BACKGROUND

Local government structure

Central government policy over the last few decades has been increasingly concerned with improving the efficiency and overall management of the services provided by the public sector. Local government has been no exception [for an extensive discussion of the Goverment's changes to the structure and management of local authorities see the following reports: (i) The Maud Report 1967; (ii) The Bains Report 1972; (iii) The Widdicombe Report 1986].

In general, local authorities are providers of numerous services to the local community, from education to recreation and tourism. Their secondary purpose rests with their ability to influence government, employers, agencies and the local community and to act as an instrument of democratic self-government. Each authority has considerable freedom available to order their own organisation and internal processes in pursuit of these objectives, but it needs the skill, patience and commitment of good leadership for this freedom to be fully utilised. While the administrative style varies enormously between each local authority, all tend to conduct their work in similar ways through: meetings of the council, consisting of all elected members; and through committees and sub-committees of small groups (approximately 8–10) of elected members whose numbers differ from authority to authority.

This structure forms the basis for democratic self-government. The committee system generally ensures detailed coverage of council business. Different items can be dealt with in the committees and the informal nature of these proceedings encourages frank discussion between councillors and the full time paid council officers. This process can help build a more effective working relationship.

Two important internal processes facilitate council management and policy making. At the councillor level a policy and resources committee co-ordinates and controls the implementation of policy and prioritises resources in the local authority. At officer level there is a chief executive whose role is to advise the policy and resources committee and head a small management team (consisting mainly of chief departmental officers) which prepares plans and programmes, as well as co-ordinates policy implementation.

An outline of the organisation and committee structure at the Thameside Authority is shown in Figure 8.1.

The Role of Councillors

Briefly, councillors are representatives of their local communities, they are typically part time, unpaid and often involved in heavy workloads. They are by

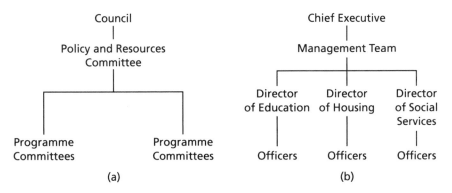

Fig 8.1 Thameside's local authority structure: (a) outline of the committee structure and (b) outline of the departmental structure

no means a homogeneous group of people; their interests, outlooks and backgrounds vary enormously. The majority are from professional, employer/manager and non-manual backgrounds. They tend to be middle-aged and a large percentage of them are elected in the name of a political party.

Most councillors are backbenchers, not policy makers, and about the only vital service they see themselves doing is casework for their constituents. The main roles which councillors tend to adopt fall into three main categories: (i) 75 per cent are mainly concerned with representing ward and constituent's interests; (ii) 5 per cent serve as general policy makers; and (iii) 20 per cent serve as policy makers in specific areas, highlighting their diversity.

In reality, most of the important policies are decided outside of formal meetings by the leader of the council and a handful of his/her confidants and then put to the full meeting of the council or its committees for 'rubber stamping'.

The role of officers

Officers in local government are those who have most contact with councillors and whose role is both to advise on policy and be responsible for the efficient running of their department.

Local government officers view themselves in a 'professional' capacity, where they have traditionally brought a high degree of skill and competence to their work. More often than not, the chief officer of a department is likely to be a specialist with the appropriate technical qualifications and experience to advise councillors and implement policy decisions while subordinate staff relieve them, through delegation, of those tasks which need less specialist expertise.

In contrast to many councillors, local government officers while often politically neutral are not anonymous; and often speak in public at committees and other meetings.

Thameside Housing Department

Michael Doyle is Director of Housing at Thameside Local Authority Housing Department. He has worked for local government for the past thirty-eight years and has always believed that all functions of housing management should be carried out within a single department. This commitment to a unified arrangement is based on the structure that his predecessor persuaded the council to put in hand.

Briefly, Michael's responsibilities include the management and maintenance of the department's housing stock; about 15,000 dwellings. He also co-ordinates the collection of rents from both current and former tenants and administers the majority of allowances for those individuals unable to pay the full amount.

The housing department is fairly labour intensive and has about 190 clerical and administrative staff. Until recently, a similar number of operatives were engaged in direct labour maintenance, but the workforce was disbanded due to contracting out the work to local private companies. The housing department is responsible for overseeing the operations of the Government's 'Right to Buy' policy, liaison with statutory and voluntary welfare bodies and the maintenance of the Housing Register (waiting list) to facilitate the allocation of tenancies, mutual exchanges and transfers for those entitled to such arrangements.

In addition to the aforementioned housing responsibilities, Michael is also a member of the council's chief officer management team, whose function is generally to act as a 'think tank' to consider top-level policy, initiate long-term strategic planning and make recommendations accordingly to the local authority.

The council currently has about 59 councillors serving the local authority covering all extremes of the political spectrum.

THE SITUATION

Councillor–officer relationships at Thameside

Michael's problem is one of relationships. During his time in local government he has experienced both the very best and worst in terms of relationships between elected members and officers. In particular he has witnessed the conflict of interest which tends to exist between these groups of people.

The problem is perpetuated by two factors. First the time pressures resulting from periodic re-elections. This can result in a lack of knowledge and expertise on the part of elected members and therefore requires a significant amount of retraining and continual induction in order to help them become familiar with, and understand, the management systems and procedures of the local authority, which are necessary for effectively carrying out the work. Second, the extent to which the organisational culture encourages newly elected members to adopt a system of rule and norm following as a means for dealing with the day-to-day workload.

The outcome of these factors has caused considerable difficulties for effective leadership and management within the local authority, despite the procedures and formalised structural arrangements which are in place to deal with the council's administration.

Unlike the entrepreneurial scene normally found in private enterprise Michael feels that the local authority is governed mainly by amateurs whose motivation for standing for election vary considerably. Inevitably this has led him to become rather cynical and completely devoid of interest in any party politics.

Michael views the motives of councillors volunteering for work in local government in a number of ways, which he believes has led to a conflict of interest between staff members within the local authority. First, he feels that there are a number of individuals with the best of motives, that is to serve others, so as to secure the running of the council to best of advantage, both in economic and social terms. Considering the council members as a whole, he feels that only about 5 per cent of those concerned fit into this category. However, he considers them to be the 'salt of the earth' and their social conscience appears to carry with it a common sense approach to management which causes very little problem.

Second, the overwhelming majority of elected members seem to have taken up the vocation of councillor for alternative reasons, some for self-aggrandisement, yet others to provide themselves with some occupational therapy in order to overcome a personal problem, for example difficulties in making public speeches or perhaps, to further develop their characters. He feels that these members tend to join the local authority full of energy and ideas, but rapidly become disenchanted and then turn to being extremely destructive and generally difficult, causing an obstacle to both management and the operation of the council's business.

Third, a very small proportion of the elected members take the job on for financial reward. Although this may seem to be trivial, bearing in mind that allowances for attendance at meetings commonly amount to two thousand pounds per annum for an individual, if a person is a chairman of a major committee this can amount to considerably more than this sum and could in fact be a significant source of income to an otherwise unemployed person or low wage earner.

The operational dilemma

The relationship between officer and elected member in the housing department has highlighted a number of difficulties which Michael has foreseen for some time, not only in terms of the problems for him in effectively managing and co-ordinating a diverse group of people, but the way in which this has on more than one occasion interfered with the smooth operation of his department.

The basis of Michael's dilemma is founded on the premise that while elected members regard their work on the affairs of the local authority as little more than a hobby, some individuals devote themselves to the task with almost fanatical zeal – and not unreasonably – expect the chief officers in all the departments to do likewise. This difference of approach often results in a clash of interests between policy makers and policy implementors.

A continual problem for Michael appears when the local authority prepares for re-election. In the event that the political balance of the local authority should change this causes the administration to be replaced with a 'new' group of councillors. Most of the 'training' in terms of knowledge and the way in which the local government machine operates which he devoted to previous elected members will be lost. In his view this is an obvious waste of resources and time.

However, the problem is compounded immediately following an election when all 'new' members of the council meet the chief officers of all the departments for an informal discussion. In an attempt to be as helpful as possible the chief executive of the local authority will introduce his chief officers and tell the elected members that if they have any particular problems on any aspect of the council's service they should contact the appropriate chief officer of a department, who will endeavour to deal with it and iron out any difficulties. A consequence of this has often meant that the chief officers are inundated with reoccurring problems on a cyclical basis.

The trainee elected member

As a result of the re-election, newly elected members will shortly be confronted with familiarising themselves with the daily operations of the council and housing department. It is at this point that many councillors face the severe personal problems of the local community. However, in Michael's view these individuals will be seriously ill-equipped through lack of knowledge and experience to deal with them. The commonly amateurish attempts to improvise often give rise to complaint.

This applies particularly in the question of the allocation of tenancies, when determining priority for accommodation to those individuals on the housing waiting list. Situations where repairs have been delayed or where failure to organise some benefit entitlement have arisen may also have caused dissatisfaction.

An elected member cannot offer their constituents very much, for example an offer of a council house or an assurance that repairs will be carried out by a given time, but at best can only secure for their constituent an interview with the director of housing. Indeed it is often the willingness of Michael to see housing applicants and tenants which is used as a standard by which his worth and credibility are gauged by the elected member. It is often remarked that 'a good chief officer is one who will see people'. As a result Michael neglects his professional work in favour of meeting the requests of councillors.

It is however, the housing department's policy, put in place by the policy and resources committee, to make sure that the allocation of tenancies adopts and uses a formal 'points' scheme with a specific number of points related to a variety of personal circumstances, for example, age and number of children. Michael will therefore be in a position of having to duplicate work at the request of elected members, which is already being done in the department by his subordinates, that is, the lettings officers and their assistants. The effect of this demand for attention to routine matters by those in the management hierarchy amounts to a reversal of delegation which is a prerequisite to effective management. Michael at the end of the day will be making good the endeavours of the elected member because of their power and influence over him and other officers, and their inexperience in dealing with the affairs of the department.

Michael is consequently forced to manage and co-ordinate his department's work by trying on the one hand to adhere to set down policy while at the same time endeavouring to assist those clearly in need whose circumstances may not necessarily be a good 'fit' with the policy.

Michael becomes increasingly frustrated with the elected members. When elected members have had difficulty in dealing with their constituents housing problems they have turned to Michael in an attempt to relinquish some of their responsibility. Consequently, having often been approached with a request that he 'gets this constituent off their back', Michael has been known to remind the elected member that they had put their back nicely into place for climbing on when they volunteered for the job and should not, therefore, reasonably complain when one of their constituents does just that.

As a consequence of the example given and many like it Michael has become discouraged. His entry into the housing profession was genuinely motivated by a wish to help those in need, despite politically motivated difficulties. But his effectiveness in handling and developing high-level policy intended to make the very best use of the housing stock and to secure the efficient running of his department is blunted by the conflicting aims and motives of the elected members and officers, those that are due to the securing of political advantage as well as those which are a consequence of the structural and operational difficulties of the organisation.

Party politics

Another problem with the elected members lies in their party political zeal. Obviously Michael recognises that members have their own political futures to nurture, but he tries to remain apolitical, and tackles his job energetically in the service of whichever political party the electorate has seen in their wisdom to put in charge. Unfortunately some elected members of the minority party who serve on the various committees of the local authority see this as some political affiliation on the part of Michael; indeed he has often been told that 'when we get into power you will be the first to go'.

Perhaps the greatest problem faced by Michael is one of insecurity of tenure. When he went into local government the situation was one of job security, whereas he now sees the prospect of early retirement just because his face might not fit politically. Yet, his 'professional' standards dictate that he serves and manages his department as effectively as possible, trying not to demonstrate any favouritism or political bias. Unfortunately, because of changing faces among the elected members, few remember how well he served the council some years ago when its political colour was different.

The problem of party political affiliation comes into even sharper focus when members of the housing department staff need to speak directly with elected members. The elected members very often form opinions – sometimes justified, but often not – as to the political affiliation of those members of staff. Categorisation into those who support the policy of the local authority and those who frustrate the proceedings commonly rise to comments like 'he's obviously a red' and Michael regularly receives little support from his chairman, who interprets the situation to the extent that such a staff member ought to be 'watched' because they may be working counter to the interests of the local authority.

The tensions and conflicts of interest within Michael's department have led him to being increasingly concerned and disillusioned with his role as director of housing. Consequently he feels he has no alternative but to take early retirement.

ACTIVITY BRIEF

Your task is to critically evaluate the issues and controversies of this particular case through understanding the link between theory and practice. In order to enhance your method of enquiry you might consider viewing this case from a number of vantage points as a way of appreciating the complexities of organisational life. In your analysis you should consider some of the following questions.

1 *What do you understand by the term leadership?*

2 *(a) What conclusions do you draw concerning the effectiveness of Michael's leadership?*
(b) To what extent is the leader–follower relationship affected by situational factors? What factors can be identified in this case?

3 *Critically discuss the conflicts of interest evident in this case. To what do you attribute them?*

4 *How might leadership and management differ, if at all, within public and private sector organisations? Give your reasons.*

5 *What recommendations or further action could be taken to overcome some of the leadership difficulties you have identified in this case.*

REFERENCES

Handy C, (1993). *Understanding Organizations*, London: Penguin, Fourth Edition.

PART 3

Context of the organisation

The five cases in this part focus on organisational goals and objectives, changing organisational structures and systems and the ability of managers to cope with pressures resulting from change in the external environment.

'*Oticon – Spaghetti for the ears*' describes the organisational structure adopted by a Danish organisation faced with the need to respond to competitive market pressures and product developments. The approach adopted by managers to encourage employees to become fully committed to the process provides a basis for discussion about the way organisations might be structured in the future.

'*Finding your way*' explores the application of action research and the use of cognitive maps for developing corporate strategy in small boat-building company. Aginst the background of economic recesion and a hostile business environment managers adopt new methods to steer their business into a profitable future.

'*Leisuredome plc*' is concerned primarily with issues of organisation design and structure, control and decentralisation in the British leisure industry. Against a background of poor objectives, ill-defined policies, procedures, and practices in a division dealing with discotheques and fun pubs, acquisition of a much larger and better organised organisation offering similar services appears to be an attractive proposition for the parent company. The case examines the result of this acquisition and the ability of the organisation to manage change.

The final two cases deal with aspects of organisational design and managements' ability to cope with uncertainty and complexity in two different public sector organisations. '*The challenge of obtaining value for money in prescribing in the National Health Service*', considers questions associated with organisational effectiveness, and the accountability and responsibility of managers and professional staff within a complex organisation. '*Middle management experiences of devolution in Barsetshire County Council Social Services Department*' outlines the key structural changes taking place in a local authority in response to Government intervention and how these affect the changing roles of middle managers.

Oticon – Spaghetti for the ears

Pernille Eskerod and Per Darmer

Oticon – a Danish firm – has caught the attention beyond its national borders because of its unique attempt to restructure the organisation in response to competitive market pressures and product developments.

This case is concerned with changing organisational structures and seeks to show how far Oticon's approach is consistent with the commonly used theories in this field. It provides a basis for discussion about the way organisations might be structured in the future and to what extent Oticon provides a model for other companies facing similar pressures.

Organisations that embark upon a significant change process are unlikely to achieve the full benefits unless their employees are fully committed to the process and the objectives sought from it. The case also provides insights into Oticon's approach to change and the steps taken to minimise employee resistance to change.

BACKGROUND

Oticon was founded in 1904 by William Demant and is a major manufacturer of hearing aids with sales throughout Europe and the rest of the world. It remains a privately owned organisation through its holding company – Oticon Holding. The majority of the shares in Oticon Holding are owned by the Oticon Trust Fund which has 75 per cent of the stock. The Trust was established a number of years ago by William Demant and his wife. The current managing director of Oticon, Lars Kolind, owns in excess of 5 per cent of the shares, and the same goes for his brother Peder Kolind. The rest of the shares are owned by minor shareholders who individually have less than 5 per cent of the shares in the holding company. The company has four Danish subsidiaries, two of which are located in Copenhagen (one of these being the head office in Hellerup which is the focus of this case), one in Snekkersten, and the main factory in Thisted. Besides these Danish operations Oticon has subsidiaries abroad. These are dispersed throughout Europe including locations in Norway, Italy, Holland, France, Spain, Germany and Switzerland. Outside of Europe Oticon has subsidiaries in the US and Japan.

In total the company has some 1,000 staff, the majority of whom are employed in the Danish subsidiaries. Work at the head office, employing 130 of the staff, covers a range of activities including new product research, product development and the marketing and promotion of both new and existing products.

By 1979 Oticon was considered by many observers to be the leading manufacturer of hearing aids in the world. During the late 1970s Danish producers of hearing aids accounted for approximately 25 per cent of the world market. Over the past 15 years, however, this market share has declined to approximately 20 per cent. In addition to Oticon, which is by far the largest, the other Danish producers of hearing aids are Wildex and Danavox. In the last few years Wildex has improved its market share at the expense of the other two manufacturers. Oticon's sales revenue in 1991 was 476 million Danish kroner while for Danavox and Wildex the figures were 347 and 287 million Danish kroner respectively.

The design of traditional hearing aids is familiar to many. The power source together with the amplification system is contained in a small unit worn behind the user's ear. This traditional style, commonly known as the 'behind the ear' model, had been the cornerstone of the success of European – not only the Danish – producers of hearing aids. However, during the 1980s an alternative, more compact design of hearing aid, with the complete system worn in the ear, came on to the market and achieved some success particularly in the American market.

European producers were slow in developing and marketing an 'in the ear' model, because of their existing superiority in producing 'behind the ear' models. The European hearing aid industry was convinced that the better quality in sound of the 'behind the ear' model would eventually prove victorious in the battle with the cosmetically more attractive, but lower quality of sound of the 'in the ear' models.

However their forecast proved to be wrong. Their cause was not helped by the significant publicity given to the 'in the ear' design when Ronald Reagan, then the President of the US appeared on nationwide TV wearing a hearing aid placed in his ear rather than behind it. The 'in the ear' hearing aid was manufactured by Starkey (a fast-growing American company) and the resulting growth in sales led to major difficulties for the Danish companies (particularly Oticon and Danavox) competing in the US market. By 1993 80 per cent of the US sales were 'in the ear' hearing aids. The Danish and the other European producers of hearing aids were, therefore, facing new and hard competition in the American market particularly from the Starkey Corporation.

THE SITUATION

This setback led Oticon into serious financial difficulties in 1987, but within two years – at the beginning of 1990 – it was back on the money-making track. During this period Oticon undertook a thorough review of its operations in order to identify what could be done to make the company more competitive and, thereby, improve its market position. It was decided to make the company more service oriented and customer focused. The overall objectiving was to make the company 30 per cent more efficient in three years. This resulted in a new company structure with the focus on making Oticon an adaptable service organisation with the individual employee at the centre.

Oticon introduced its restructured organisation during 1991 and seems well on its way to achieving the ambitious goal. In 1992 Oticon had a total revenue of 539m Danish kroner (approximately £54m). This is a 13 per cent rise in revenue, compared with a 3 per cent rise in revenue during the previous years. Gross profit in 1992 was 18m Danish kroner. Oticon has regained some of its lost territories, and today it is the third largest supplier of hearing aids in the world with a 10 per cent share of the world market.

As a reflection of its growing confidence, Oticon is trying to improve this market position by introducing a new hearing aid, which automatically (without volume control) adapts the sound level to fit the noise of the surroundings. This new type of hearing aid is produced by Oticon in both the 'behind the ear' and the 'in the ear' models.

In the three year period up to 1991 Oticon has been through an almost total reconstruction of the company. During this organisational development process there have been some changes in management and staff reductions have taken place. The new structure was implemented on 8 August 1991, and on that day everyone started in a completely different workplace (Oticon having moved into new surroundings in Hellerup).

The process through which Oticon has developed has had a significant impact on almost all aspects of organisational behaviour in the company. This transformation did not of course come about without some resistance to change amongst the employees. After all, the restructuring meant a clean break with most of the usual and well known routines and habits. In planning for the new structure, the company sought ways of involving employees in the change process.

The employees had been kept informed about what was going to happen during the three year period leading up to its implementation. Managers openly discussed the reasons for changes, how it was to be done and the possible consequences for employees. Many of the employees had participated in planning and executing the restructuring of the company. Meetings were held with employees so that up-to-date information could be passed on and any questions dealt with, firsthand, at the time. The new organisation required all employees to use a personal computer (PC) which for most was a completely new experience. In order to overcome any fears or worries this might hold, employees were encouraged to take a PC home so that they could become familiar with its use. Employee turnover at Oticon was remarkably low considering the extent of the change. No one left the company during the first three months following the introduction of the restructured organisation despite the fact that not everyone felt comfortable with the new world of Oticon.

The developments at Oticon have created a project-organisation – a so-called spaghetti-organisation, which the management writer Tom Peters argues to be the most promising structure for industry in the future. The central themes in the spaghetti-organisation are the lack of a line of command, no formal organisational hierarchy, and no specific leader to whom employees report. The employees are no longer working for a department. Oticon has abolished departments and the whole organisation is built on projects. At any one time employees and project leaders may have varying levels of participation in a number of different projects.

Oticon has literally torn down the walls to create one big open plan office. Employees move from desk to desk in accordance with the projects in which they are presently involved. In order to be able to work together and discuss the project, the team members often move their desks together in a corner of the office. To make this possible everybody has a 'Rullemarie' (a small transportable table with their few necessities) so they can move about and find themselves a place at the standardised desks containing a personal computer.

Oticon has 'banned' the use of paper. All communication is now effected through a PC-network or face to face. The latter is used more frequently now that no one including project leaders has a personal office. However, even with the use of sophisticated technology there are still a number of routine administrative tasks which have to be done in support of the project teams. Employees undertaking these jobs have less freedom and control over their activities than team members since their work is much more structured.

Organisation of project teams

The number of participants in the project groups varies according to the amount of work being done and the complexity of the task. For example a project with the objective to relaunch a product by a new marketing campaign typically has 2 to 3 members in the project group, while larger product development teams may have 10 to 20 people involved. A product development project with common technology, such as the automatic hearing aid, is often tied together through a larger project. The responsibility of the co-ordinating manager is to oversee the marketing of the product and the timing of its introduction into the market.

The selection of the project leaders takes place in several ways. Sometimes the employee who has proposed the project is chosen to lead the project. At other times senior management suggests the person they feel will be best suited for the job and a range of criteria are used to make the choice depending upon the nature of the project. Typically these include, technical skills, experience, leadership ability or corporate skills combined with the fact that the person has time available when the project is due to commence.

The project leader is free to manage the project group in the manner he or she prefers. This means that the project groups are run in various ways. Some groups meet with all the project members on a regular basis. Others only meet when they find it necessary. Some groups make all decisions jointly, while others leave the decision making to those directly involved with a particular aspect of the project. Project managers are responsible for choosing the members of each project group. The usual practice is simply to go and ask, and try to persuade people to join the project. This informal process ensures that the members really want to be involved in the project (otherwise they could have refused), but it also means that some employees are more in demand than others. Clearly it is more beneficial for an individual employee's career to be involved in a successful and high profile project since they may then be noticed by other leaders and be invited to join other important projects.

To obtain good project members, resources and attention from the top management, project leaders have to be very good in promoting their projects within the organisation. If they are successful in the promotion, project leaders will get to the top of the priority list and are more likely to be successful in obtaining scarce resources for their projects.

The larger projects often start with a team meeting with the purpose of to getting to know each other and the objectives and the scope of the project. Sometimes project members meet together for a couple of days at a location away from the company and other work pressures in order to seek new inspiration and to take a fresh look at issues and problems related to the project in hand.

The project group is required to undertake all the tasks connected with product development until the product is successfully introduced in all markets. This means that the project group may exist for several years, and that the project members cover a range of other job-functions in addition to those relating to their own specialism. There are a range of different projects in progress at the company at any one time with different timescales attached to each. The product development process for example, typically lasts for 3 to 5 years and Oticon has about 10 to 15 larger product development projects running simultaneously. Other projects are of a much shorter duration lasting a few weeks or months.

Project groups meet with top management once every three months to present their work and results. The criteria for success established by the company are that project tasks should be completed within the timescale set and within the budget allowed, otherwise the project groups are free to work as they wish. Each member of the group can even work at home, if he or she prefers, providing their absence does not interfere with the successful progress of the project.

The co-ordination and communication between the project groups are not formalised. The connections between the employees are much stronger within the individual project group than between groups. The groups are fully autonomous, which means that no one outside the project team really knows what is going on inside the group. The lack of a general overview which this process creates has sometimes caused problems for the development process.

Employees are responsible for joining project groups themselves and for completing the projects they have accepted. When a project is finished (or abandoned) the employees involved in the project move on to other projects.

All employees are encouraged to suggest new projects and ideas. Because of the lack of a line of command, the ideas can be presented to anyone in the company, even to the managing director. Employees are expected to demonstrate initiative and results. Lars Kolind, the managing director, puts it this way: 'If people don't have anything to do, they need to find something – or we don't need them' (Peters, T. J., *Liberation Management*, 1992, p. 202.)

In essence Oticon has therefore become an umbrella organisation for the projects going on in the company. The borders between the projects are, of course, not always clear-cut. Projects are often interrelated and employees are frequently working on more than one project at the same time (the average is 1.5 projects per person). Therefore the projects, the processes, and the people become intertwined, and it is this seeming mess which has given rise to the use of the spaghetti-organisation metaphor.

ACTIVITY BRIEF

1 *Critically evaluate the reasons for Oticon's success in minimising resistance to change?*

2 *From your understanding of the dimensions of organisational structure explain the nature and effectiveness of Oticon's organisational structure.*

3 *What are the advantages and disadvantages of the spaghetti-organisation as used at Oticon?*

4 *What can Oticon do in order to eliminate – or at least minimise – the disadvantages of its spaghetti-organisation?*

REFERENCES

Peters, T. J. (1992) *Liberation Management*, New York: Albert A. Knopt.

RECOMMENDED READING

Mintzberg, H. (1993). *Structures in Fives*, New Jersey: Prentice-Hall.
Mullins, L. J. (1993). *Management and Organisational Behaviour*, London: Pitman.
Robbins, S. (1993). *Organisational Behavior*, New Jersey: Prentice-Hall.
Peters, T. (1992). *Liberation Management*, New York: Alfred A. Knopf.

Finding your way:
Using action research and cognitive mapping methods in strategy formulation

K. Alan Rutter

This case explores the application of action research and the use of cognitive maps for developing corporate strategies in small firms.

In times of high uncertainty, traditional strategic management models are often inappropriate, and managers are forced to rely on intuitive skills in answering the question 'What business should we be in?' Strategic uncertainty is experienced by managers in many organisations in times of high environmental turbulence, and this case study describes what happened when action research and cognitive mapping methods were adopted by a team of managers uncertain in which direction to steer their business. Their business environment appeared to be hostile as well as uncertain, yet in an apparently hopeless situation, a new promising 'business' was teased out by the team.

Action research is a method of research in which the researcher accepts that he or she becomes part of the investigation, and the subjects of the research become co-researchers; while cognitive maps are diagrams which 'map' peoples' thoughts.

The case raises issues relating to teamwork, communication and individuals' perceptions, biases, prejudices and 'mind set'.

BACKGROUND

The setting for this firm is the UK boat-building industry, which is composed of a highly fragmented and disparate group of companies. The industry is notorious for its inadequate and unreliable data and, with the onset of the recession, it experienced major environmental turbulence, with cancelled orders, rapidly dwindling markets for both leisure and work boats at home and overseas. Against this background, the application of prescriptive models used in strategic management, such as industry, competitor and market analysis proved to be a futile and pointless exercise.

Any attempt to analyse the environment in an objective and rational way failed. Yet, despite the hostile conditions, some boat builders were not only surviving, but flourishing. It appeared that certain managers could 'see' opportunities in the environment to which they could adapt or 'fit', their firms. Others either failed to 'see' these opportunities, or they were interpreted as being 'inappropriate', i.e., the choices did not 'fit' the managers' view of their business.

Attle Marine is a long established, small boat-building company based on the East Anglian coast at the mouth of a river. The firm is wholly owned by the managing director, Toby, who acquired all the shares 18 months ago from a consortium of which he was a former member. The company builds family sailing cruising yachts from 25 feet to 38 feet in overall length. These traditional looking, heavy, long keel boats have a reputation for being safe, seaworthy craft, appropriate for North Sea conditions and ocean sailing. Shortly after Toby acquired the shareholding, the firm bought the designs of two motor work boats (30 feet and 42 feet in overall length) which were modified for leisure cruising. These motor boats were a departure from the traditional sailing boat image of the company but, because they are a development from commercial boat hulls, their seagoing properties matched that of the sailing boats.

Although not a large firm even by UK boat-building standards, Attle Marine have sold a number of boats overseas in Europe and the US either direct or through agents. However, their major market is the UK, with 90 per cent of their production being sold to owners who keep their boats on the east and south coasts of England.

In 1990, when the recession began to bite deeply into the UK boat-building industry, the managers at Attle Marine cut back their labour force from over 60 to 28 people. Of these survivors, five hold managerial positions (including the managing director) and of the remainder, the majority are highly skilled boatwrights and craftsmen who fit out and finish off the bought-in glass-reinforced plastic (GRP) hulls. In the past, all the firm's hulls have been moulded by another boat builder located nearby, but a recent government contract for some small patrol boats enabled the firm to develop its own moulding technology. However, they still buy in the hulls for their standard product range, because the managers believe that the amount of difficulties that would arise in attempting to extricate themselves from their supplier could not be justified by their current low level of sales.

Being a small firm, the managers of Attle Marine were able to respond quickly to the impact of the recession, and with a number of unusual and creative short-term actions (including the winning of a government contract for the first time ever), they found themselves to be in a reasonably strong position, *vis-à-vis* their competitors. However, given the poor state of the industry, relative position against competitors was no comfort, and they realised that some new, more long-lasting initiative needed to be taken for them to secure a more stable future.

The question was in which direction should the company go? The managing director had used consultants in the past to assist him in solving specific problems, but at the strategic level, he believed that consultants do not provide the service the practising manager needs. Furthermore, the consultants were expensive and their solutions rarely 'fitted' in with how he saw his business. He believed the unsatisfactory results were due to the consultant's objectives often being in conflict with those of the managers.

It was at this stage that Toby asked a business school lecturer, who was a friend of his, to assist the management team in identifying a new direction and in formulating appropriate strategies and action plans. Toby was aware that his friend was researching the new approaches to strategy formulation and, although having some misgivings, he was prepared to try these new ideas with his management team. Between them they agreed that after an initial introductory meeting, there would be monthly strategic management meetings or sessions, and that the managers themselves would chose whether they wanted to work with the researcher individually or as a team.

The management team

As well as the managing director, Toby, the management team comprised a commercial manager, Howard; a works manager, David; a sales manager, Jason; and the receptionist, Sylvia. Although not an official manager, Sylvia possessed considerable knowledge of the marine industry and 'knew everyone' in it. Apart from the works manager, her time in the industry and with the firm far exceeded that of the other managers.

David, in his early thirties, was promoted to manager recently after having worked his way up from the shop-floor. A skilled and talented boatwright, who could turn his hand to anything practical and make a success of it, he had the ability to see strategic issues in terms of 'How can it be made?'. At first he was very resistant to the strategy sessions, but although his contributions appeared negative, he soon became enthusiastic when he realised he was able to state his views and that he was being heard.

Jason typified the young sailing set who lived for boating. In his late twenties and a nephew of Toby, he had drifted into a mundane job after leaving school, gaining fulfilment only at the weekends when out sailing. He joined Attle Marine four years ago, and is an efficient and hard-working salesman with considerable boat handling expertise. Although he had considerable sailing experience in all types of craft, his favourite form of sailing was in the traditional family cruisers that Attle Marine produced.

Howard came into the firm and the industry as an existing owner of one Attle's boats. In his mid-40s and tired of his civil service job in London, he joined the firm six years ago to 'get out of the rat race'. University educated, and highly articulate, he is an efficient administrator and communicator. He spends most of his time dealing with complex government contracts and EC regulations and directives. Sensitive to the outside world and social trends, he was able to extend the horizons of the others present.

Toby, now in his late forties, graduated from Sandhurst and served his short-service army commission mostly overseas, where he was able to indulge in his lifelong pastime, sailing. After leaving the army, he worked for a while as a representative of an insurance company, before moving on to come a partner in a chandlery business in Kent. It was while he was at the chandler that the opportunity arose to join a consortium to buy Attle Marine. Outward-going, confident and a shrewd businessman, Toby had built up the boat-building firm steadily over years until the current recession abruptly halted the trend.

THE SITUATION

Action research and cognitive mapping

Like many people uncertain of what to do, the managers of Attle Marine felt that they needed to have reasonable confidence in their chosen direction. They were conscious of the possible dangers of 'sticking to what they know best' and of following the trends of 'industry wisdom', and now felt they needed to embark on an entirely new venture, outside their core business. The managers possessed considerable knowledge and experience of the immediate business environment and some knowledge of related ones. This information however was 'in their heads'. It constituted their subjective view of the world, in other words, their enacted environment. But, as is often the case, these views were jumbled, barely conscious notions that needed to be expressed, classified and related to each other.

The researcher set out believing that people have the answer to their own problems within themselves, and what was needed was a method which enabled the managers to draw on their own resources and, through self-awareness of their own biases and blind spots, to liberate themselves from the 'old' way of seeing and responding to the environment. Through action research methods, the managers and the researcher are able to continually reflect on his or her interrelationships with the environment and each other and to respond in a way that allowed them to 'own' their own solution.

Each session with the management team was tape-recorded and transcribed so that the managers' perceptions and ideas could be monitored and evaluated. From these transcriptions, detailed cognitive maps were produced by the researcher. Cognitive maps are visual representations of an individual's or group's enacted environment. These maps were drawn up in rough form during the sessions to allow a manager to focus his or her attention on critical features, make assumptions about their organisation's environment by defining frameworks, and link events to make judgements about actions and outcomes.

The sessions

The sessions took place over a period of three months. At the introductory meeting, which lasted about an hour, the format that the strategy formulation process would follow was explained. The researcher then asked the managers whether they wanted to participate as individuals being interviewed on their own or as a team. The managers elected to carry out the exercise working as a team rather than to have individual sessions.

At the following meeting, the managers were asked to express their views of what they saw happening in the environment and their concerns about it. This first-phase exploratory session was to allow the managers to 'tell their story', until they were repeating themselves, or until they were at a loss as to what else to say. When this stage was reached, they were asked to focus on some of the issues raised and, as the terms 'environmental threats' and 'environmental opportunities' were often mentioned in conjunction with specific environmental factors but in a confused and contradictory way, the team agreed to focus on these two issues in the next session. At the third meeting, the managers were asked individually to list three threats and three opportunities. This was done by giving each manager a blank index card on which he or she had write down their three opportunities and threats. They then had to read out in turn their first opportunity. These were listed on a flip chart. Then each in turn had to read out their second opportunity. Again these were written up. This process continued until each manager had read out their last 'threat'. The complete lists, with who proposed each item, is shown below:

Threats

1. Low priced competitor products (all managers).
2. Low priced products from Eastern Europe (Jason).
3. Overseas competitors' products matching Attle's quality (David, Sylvia, Howard).
4. Major competitors are highly capitalised (Toby).
5. Some of Attle's customers perceive the company as having no direction (Jason).
6. Continuing global uncertainty (Howard).
7. Large competitors can match Attle's handcrafted product finish with modern technology (David, Sylvia, Toby).

Opportunities

1. Attle's flexibility to respond to market demands (Jason).
2. Market growth in European markets (Toby, Jason).
3. There is a chance that Attle could move up market (David).
4. The commercial boat market is more stable (i.e. not declining) (Toby, Howard, David, Sylvia).
5. Try and acquire a larger share of the current market (Jason).
6. Enter the smaller leisure boat market with lower priced products (Howard).
7. Lower interest rates must give an advantage to leisure boat builders (Sylvia, Toby).
8. Provide full service support for existing owners (Howard, David).
9. Sell direct overseas, i.e. cut out the agent/distributor (Sylvia).

Considerable discussion took place while these lists were being drawn up, and since the researcher had the tape recorder running, the dialogue was used as part of the cognitive map. After the lists were completed, the managers were asked to choose whether they wanted to focus on opportunities or 'threats'. They elected to concentrate first on threats, and to leave 'opportunities' for the next session. To start the process off, the researcher asked the team to select just one 'threat' as the focus of the discussion. They chose to fix their attention on 'low priced competitor products', since they had all included it in their list of three. The researcher then wrote the chosen 'threat' in the centre of the flip chart and asked the team to consider what events led up to this state of affairs arising. As the concepts emerged from the team, they were sketched on the flip chart to form the sketch cognitive map.

The maps

The researcher used the sketch maps to guide the conversation, to probe and to question, to show linkages and to position events. This helped to show the team how seemingly remote factors were interconnected. As the researcher was actively involved in the conversation with the team of people, his mind was on eliciting the ideas from the managers rather than on completing a detailed map. The fully detailed maps were prepared from transcripts back at the office of the researcher. These were presented to the team at the start of the next session, and they were asked to comment on them. Any misconceptions were rectified at the beginning of the new session. This ensured that the maps were 'owned' by the management team and reinforced the idea that the maps were not the artefacts of the researcher.

The researcher felt that both the 'threats' map (Figure 10.1) and the 'opportunities' map (Figure 10.2) illustrated the complexity of the problems faced by the managers. (N.B. Both maps are simplified versions of the originals.) From the maps, it can be said that there was less confusion as far as 'threats' were concerned, but considerably more when it came to the 'opportunities' and in looking for the 'right' direction to go. Both maps start in the centre with what the managers saw as the most important concept either as a threat or an opportunity. As the map developed, an attempt was made by the researcher to have the elements that the managers considered caused the key concept to flow in from above, while the perceived consequences of the concept flowed out below. There was also an attempt to categorise the elements given by the managers into the three strategic categories 'environment', 'resources' and 'values', across the page. The linkages between the concepts were agreed at the meeting. As the maps progressed, earlier stated 'threats' and 'opportunities' listed originally on the flip chart were often included, so making up a more holistic picture of the interrelated factors in the environment.

The 'Threat' map

The 'Threat map' highlights the greatest perceived threat being that of 'low competitor prices', with again perceived causes of the situation shown above the central label, and the perceived consequences for the firm coming out from below. The map shows the problem as the managers saw it at the time. Throughout the session, blind spots emerged and were frequently challenged. For example, it was stated early on that the company priced its products a fixed percentage above a competitor. At first this price ratio was accepted without question, it was only later in the session that this assumption was challenged. It then became clear that what was taken for granted by each manager (i.e. the firm's price position in relation to its competitors), was not the same for the whole team. Each member had a different idea of what the firm's price position was and it became apparent that they were making decisions based on their individual assumptions. The map helped to expose this and other misconceptions.

At the close of the session on environmental threats, the managers agreed that something needed to be done about their strategic decision making, and they became committed to proceeding with the next session.

The 'Opportunity' map

The 'Opportunity map' starts with the managers' view that there is a potential for market growth in work boats. The map shows how perceived environmental factors such as the world economy, competitor positions, market forces and the firm's own resources come into the picture and how they can be related. The map refers to the firm's overheads and the possible cost of being a waterside site. Some team members questioned the need to

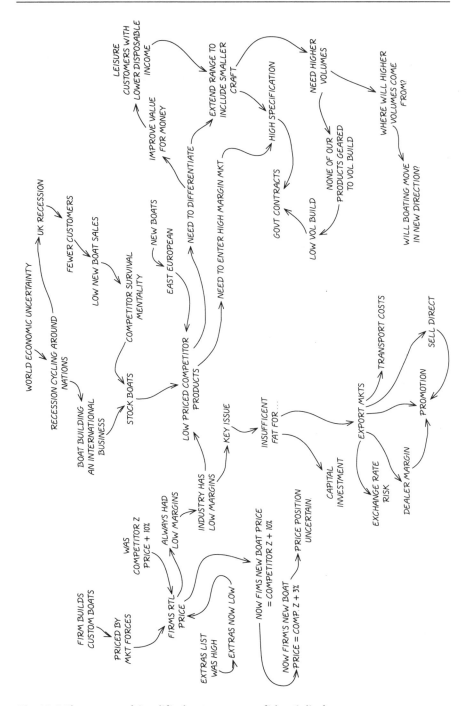

Fig 10.1 Threat map (simplified to ensure confidentiality)

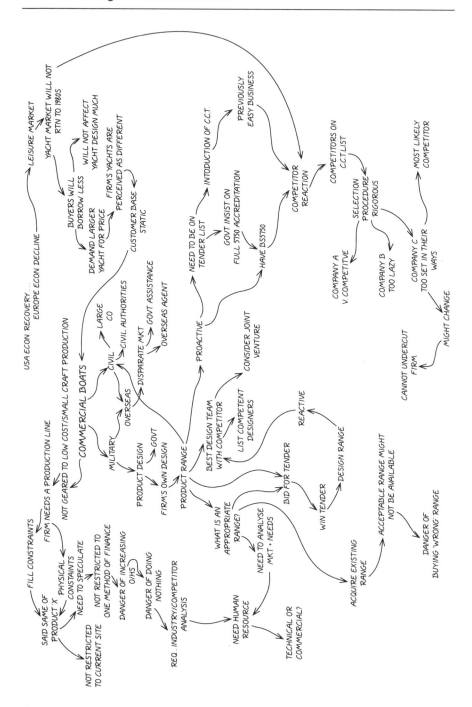

Fig 10.2 Opportunity map (simplified to ensure confidentiality)

be located where they were.

The managers see their product as being superior to that of many of their competitors. It is only later that they begin to consider what 'superior' might mean. Towards the bottom of the map, possible solutions and strategies begin to emerge, such as the employment of a specialist to concentrate on their new business. It proved to be far more difficult finding a new opportunity than identifying the threats.

The outcome of the sessions

The effect of the recession around the world led to industry prices being reduced to clear industry stocks and to penetrate overseas markets where apparent opportunities still existed. The main opportunity seemed to lie in obtaining government contracts and, although the firm has some experience of government work, they lacked what were seen as crucial resources such as possessing their own designs and product range. They also believed that they lacked sufficient managerial skill in tackling the new venture without diluting their core business. However, because the managers came up with their 'own' solution, they became confident in it and were committed to seeing it through.

During these sessions, the managers used the maps to:

1. Expose and clarify each others' perceptions of the environment in which the company operated.
2. The 'mind sets' of individual members were confronted and challenged by the others.
3. A list of alternative opportunities were drawn up and reviewed.
4. A strong commitment was made to one particular opportunity and appropriate strategies were discussed.
5. Action plans were drawn up.

The managers felt that they have learnt how to listen to one another's points of view and to have their own assumptions challenged. Consequently, they were far more aware of their own values and how these impinge on their perception of the environment and how these perceptions interrelate with their colleagues' views. Having learnt how to gain insight of their own world view and that this self-awareness had resolved their immediate problems, they felt more able to cope with subsequent ones that will arise in the future.

Issues raised by the process

During the period of these sessions, the researcher frequently reflected on what was taking place and how effective the methods really were. His thoughts revolved around four major issues.

1. Group dynamics

The first issue concerned the individuals of the team. Although David made valuable contributions, he was often 'ribbed' for being a wet blanket. Sullen and impatient, he gave the impression of someone who considered himself not a key team member and therefore he preferred to snipe from the side-lines. He frequently made comments about his being the last to be told anything in the organisation, and that he was there to sort out the mess that others left for him. It took considerable encouragement by the researcher before he was prepared to say anything at all. The response by his colleagues was dismissive in a friendly manner, and it was only through intervention by the researcher that some of David's contributions were examined in greater detail.

Sylvia made hardly any contributions at the meeting other than to nod or shake her head at what was being said. When asked for her views, she expressed these only as concurring with what one or other of those present had said, or by saying she did not know. Yet, the researcher concluded from her body language during the sessions and from what she said to him after the sessions were over, that her interest level and concentration must have been very high. The researcher suspected that she kept her opinions to herself, or that she only discussed them with Toby or Howard.

2. Concealment

It is unlikely that each participant was being entirely honest and frank (either deliberately or otherwise) and, in the few sessions that took place, it was difficult to expose any such concealment. Although there appeared to be a genuine exchange of ideas, there was the possibility that some strategic options were not disclosed for fear of revealing a strategy that could threaten individual members of the team.

3. Motives for agreeing to do the sessions

It is highly possible that Toby intended to use the sessions to 'indoctrinate' his employees, although, in practice, the team did argue quite strongly against him when they disagreed with what he said. The others might have felt obliged to join the sessions at first, but they seemed to rise to the occasion when they saw there was an opportunity to express their opinions.

4. Effectiveness of the method

Given the above issues, how effective has the method been in formulating strategies? Toby claimed at an earlier meeting with the researcher that he was the strategist for the firm. Had the process led to a more collegiate method of strategy formulation, or were the sessions merely used by Toby as an information gathering exercise?

ACTIVITY BRIEF

1 *Examine the two maps and decide what information you can extract from them. Using this information decide on an appropriate direction for Attle Marine. (This activity is best conducted in small groups, each presenting its findings at the end of the session. Time needed 1.5–2 hours)*

2 *Consider the method employed by the researcher. How valid is the action research approach, and how representative of the sessions can the maps be?*

3 *How can knowledge of organisational behaviour issues help the researcher to make the strategy formulation process more effective?*

RECOMMENDED READING

For Activity 1.

Eden, C. (1983). *Messing about in Problems,* Oxford: Pergamon Press.
Morgan, G. (1993). *Imaginization: the art of creative management,* London: Sage.
Mullins, L. J. (1993). *Management and Organisational Behaviour,* London: Pitman, Chapter 9.

For Activity 2.

Gill, J. and Johnson, P. (1991) *Research Methods for Managers,* London: Paul Chapman, Chapter 5.
McNiff, J. (1988). *Action Research: Principles and Practice,* Basingstoke: MacMillan Education.
Mullins, L. J. (1993). *Management and Organisational Behaviour,* London: Pitman, Chapters 20–21.

For Activity 3.

Mullins, L. J. (1993). *Management and Organisational Behaviour,* London: Pitman, Chapters 5–8.

Leisuredome plc – acquisition of assets or liabilities?

Karen Meudell

Leisuredome plc is an old established organisation with diverse interests in various leisure operations: casinos, amusement centres, holiday companies, restaurants and hotels. The case focuses on one particular division, Leisuredome Entertainments Ltd, which initially owned and operated 15 discotheques and 'fun pubs', mainly along the south coast of England.

The major problems facing the division were that it had poor objectives, ill-defined policies and procedures, control systems based largely on manual accounting procedures and a poor market share. It was against this background that the company decided to enlarge by the acquisition of a leisure organisation twice its size, greater geographical reach and a ready-made infrastructure of organisational support.

The case is concerned primarily with issues of organisation design in terms of structure, control and decentralisation both pre- and post-acquisition. Additional issues which can be considered are those of the identification of organisational culture, organisation development and the management of change.

BACKGROUND

Leisuredome Entertainments Ltd is a wholly owned subsidiary division of Leisuredome plc, a company capitalised to some £350 million with interests in various aspects of the leisure industry. The company has been in existence since 1920, originally operating casinos and amusement centres; a leisure division has always existed but its objectives and structure appear to have been somewhat difficult to define. However, in January 1991 the name of Leisuredome Entertainments Ltd (LEL) was taken for this division to enable investors and the general public more easily to identify with its move into the field of discotheques and fun pubs and its disposal of existing amusement centres. Figure 11.1 shows LEL in the context of Leisuredome plc.

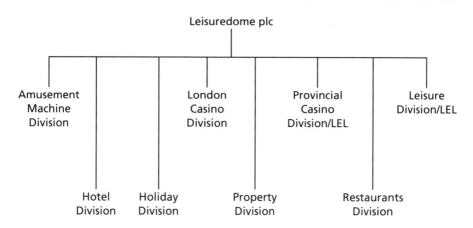

Fig 11.1 Leisuredome plc and its operating divisions

Figure 11.2 shows the organisation of LEL as at July 1991. At this time the company owned and operated fifteen discotheques and fun pubs sited mainly along the south coast but with two units further afield in Evesham and Swansea.

The market at which the company was aiming was in the 18–25 year age group but demographically this depended on the type of unit operated and seasonality. For example, Mirages discotheque had a long established and profitable reputation for catering to naval ratings whilst Norma Jean's, a fun pub, opened at lunch times during the summer months (proving very profitable because of its position on the seafront) and in the evenings provided a 'feeder market' for its sister discotheque next door, Burlingtons.

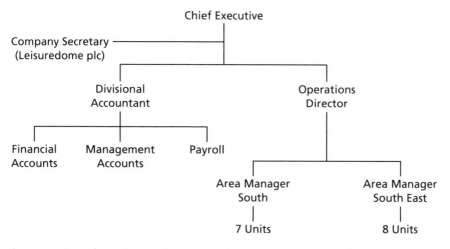

Fig 11.2 Leisuredome Entertainments Ltd: organisation chart prior to the Sundance acquisition

This particular facet of the leisure market is constantly changing as it is affected by user tastes and preferences. Technology, in the form of increasingly sophisticated lighting, and the promotional flair and ingenuity of each unit manager are important in maintaining market position. Lighting rigs alone can cost of the order of £350,000 and a complete refurbishment and redecoration as much as £750,000. The public in general, and the target market in particular, are notoriously fickle and business levels can be halved in just a few days if tastes and preferences change. Since redecoration is costly, it is common to close a unit for several weeks, render cosmetic repairs and reopen it with another name.

Also fundamental in maintaining business levels and market share is the emphasis placed on door control. Universally known as 'bouncers' but preferring the title 'steward', these are a highly paid, rare breed of employee. If door staff are not loyal to the organisation and admit undesirable clients then not only can this deter regular guests but it can also lead to disruption with police intervention and subsequent objection to the renewal of Liquor and Music and Dancing Licences. It is obvious, therefore, that the social skills of door control staff are of prime importance, particularly in those areas where units are surrounded by residential dwellings. LEL, atypically, employed its own doormen, many of whom had been employed by the company for two or more years thus aiding loyalty and commitment in an industry where labour turnover can average in excess of 400 per cent annually.

Until July 1991 the divisional head office was based in Bognor Regis in a building housing three operating units and staff accommodation. The chief executive had been appointed in January from outside the organisation but both the operations director and divisional accountant had been with the company for fifteen and ten years respectively.

The divisional accountant was, as can be seen from Figure 11.2, responsible for all aspects of financial, management and payroll control. In addition to some company secretarial matters he was also responsible for all personnel matters, pension scheme and company car purchase and disposal. Most accounts were processed manually although a microcomputer had recently been purchased to process payroll.

The operations director had been recently appointed to that position having previously been a unit and latterly an area manager. His main functions were to ensure the profitability of the units; to arrange purchasing and to negotiate contracts with breweries, glass suppliers etc. He was also responsible for liaising with solicitors for the transfer and granting of liquor licences; recruitment, transfer and dismissal of operational staff; arranging promotional events and advising on acquisitions and disposals. A self-confessed 'operator', often intervening at grass roots level, rather than administrator, he had two area managers reporting to him: one based in Southend for the South East and one based in Swansea for the South West.

As can be seen from Figure 11. 2 there existed no functional support staff in personnel, marketing, catering or security and this situation was, to a large extent, mirrored both in other divisions and the corporate offices with the exception of catering and security who both had fairly prominent positions in the two casino divisions.

Communication channels were generally informal and unstructured; administration, particularly at unit level was haphazard and undisciplined. This frequently led to frustration, conflict and inefficiency as the wrong people were informed of the wrong decisions and the two functional heads of department who, by mutual agreement following several clashes, did not speak to each other, began to build up political power bases centred upon the deliberate non-sharing of information.

It is probable that this unstructured method of communication has its roots in the culture of the company and the nature of the operation in which it was engaged. The fifteen units comprising the LEL estate had been added gradually over the previous years; positions were 'hung' from the organisation chart in an *ad hoc* fashion as the need arose and since no job descriptions had been written nor objectives set, specific job functions had never been defined and tasks had been undertaken by whoever could be persuaded or coerced with little attention being given to their ability or suitability. This was exemplified by the promotion, noted earlier, of the operations director from area manager: very much a hands-on, interactive manager, he was promoted by virtue of his experience and the fact that he was the only available in-house person, to a position which required, however, hands-off administration,

Equally discotheque managers tended to be recruited for their entrepreneurial abilities rather than their administrative skills for the reasons previously mentioned. Since the functions of the role of divisional accountant had never been formally defined, it had come to be accepted that he would 'clear up the mess' frequently made by managers when dealing with administration.

Decision making within the division tended to be reactive with no concern being given to long-term implications. Strategic planning, for example, appeared to concentrate on the principle of what one manager described as 'what shall we do this week'? This resulted in a lack of defined policies and procedures and inconsistency both in operational and behavioural terms.

As would be assumed, given the lack of communication and type of reactive decision making described above, very little control was exercised by the organisation itself and when a situation reached a point where it was necessary to establish control, this too, tended to be reactive and often draconian.

Financial control was exercised by a weekly monitoring of revenue against budget; if a unit fell short of budget for more than six weeks, consideration was given either to closing it or transferring or dismissing the manager. It is worth noting that budgets were imposed on unit managers by the operations director and divisional accountant; there was very little personal input into the mutual agreement of financial targets although they often had more local knowledge of markets and business trends.

Operational control was exercised by the monitoring of Unusual Incident Reports which were completed as necessary by the unit manager or assistant and then submitted to head office on a daily basis. Multifunctional in nature, this form was used for any incident from the loss of outdoor clothing from the cloakroom to a major disruption when police were called. As a result control was usually only exercised when the local police force intimated that they would object to Liquor Licence renewal at the next Licensing Justices Sessions. Once again the control exercised was reactive in that the unit was temporarily closed and/or the manager transferred.

THE SITUATION

LEL entered the summer of 1991 with ill-defined organisational objectives, ill-defined policies and procedures and a poor market share as the smallest company in this part of the leisure industry. The new chief executive decided to improve the latter and he realised that this could not be done without first defining objectives, policies and procedures and providing functional support staff.

It was considered preferable to enlarge the division by several small acquisitions but the opportunity arose to purchase the leisure division of a national brewer and the chief executive (now retitled managing director) began negotiations for the take-over of some 36 discotheques and 'fun pubs' comprising Sundance Entertainments. A successful outcome would not only increase the geographical reach of the division since most of the Sundance units were located in the Home Counties, Midlands and North but would also, overnight, give the division market leadership by increasing its estate from 15 to 51 units.

The acquisition plan

The decision to acquire Sundance had two major implications for the division. First it would be necessary to enlarge the organisation by the introduction, quickly, of functional support staff in personnel, security and catering and to increase the establishment in the already existing functions of financial and operations management. Second, because of the size of the new organisation, its geographical areas and the fact that the purchase price included two regional administrative offices in Bedford and Chesterfield, the decision was taken to decentralise the existing operation and relocate the divisional head office to London. London was chosen because it was more central to motorway links and office space was available in the building leased to Leisuredome plc. Figure 11.3 shows the organisation chart of LEL post-acquisition.

A further implication of the acquisition which did not come to light immediately but which was to have a major effect during the following months was the culture of, and personalities involved in, the company being acquired. It transpired that the operational management at senior level of Sundance had become accustomed to managing on the principle of 'trading favours' which had resulted in alleged irregularities and a high labour turnover of those managers who chose not to comply with this unwritten policy. Further it was discovered that the outgoing managing director and operations director had attempted a 'management buyout' but had been outbid by LEL. The two unsuccessful Sundance employees

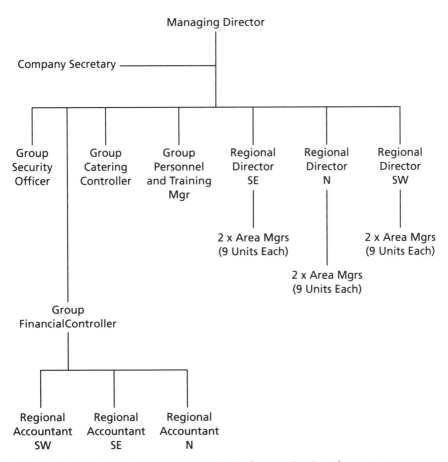

Fig 11.3 Leisuredome Entertainments Limited: organisation chart post-Sundance acquisition

subsequently raised capital to start their own business and various senior and influential positions had been offered to the two regional directors and area managers of Sundance who were instructed to join LEL until such time as the new company was operational. A further complication arose when it was discovered that the majority of the northern units operated with sub-contracted door control staff. This factor, together with the Sundance culture meant that the newly enlarged division was not only denied any real opportunity to integrate the new acquisition but it was also immediately faced with various covert and mischievous acts designed to bring about its downfall: sudden, inexplicable fights and riots in the units and threatening telephone calls to senior LEL management became the order of the day. Thus, by the end of December 1991 the division was divided into 'them' (in the majority) and 'us' (the minority) with disloyalty, suspicion and fear reigning supreme and reactive management very much to the fore.

No tangible arrangements were made to monitor the changes which occurred as a result of the acquisition. Some emphasis was placed on the 'engineering' of the take-over but most attention was given to the marketing of the operation with a series of articles and interviews in the financial and trade press. Whilst this focused public attention on the division, it did little to ensure that a smooth integration occurred.

Although the managing director has expressed concern over decentralising the division at a time when it was trebling in size, he was overruled by the main board. This decision was subsequently called into question and resulted in serious consideration being given to re-centralising some three months later.

Considerable emphasis was placed on the need for the existing Sundance staff to become easily and comfortably integrated into the Leisuredome culture. This was felt to be important not only because some senior managers were experiencing their third occasion of being 'acquired' by other companies but also because of the history of the attempted buy-out, the potential disasters arising from sub-contracted door control and the need to establish loyalties as quickly as possible. This programme of integration was planned by presentations on the company, a weekend conference and visits to all units by functional support staff. In addition, existing Leisuredome operations staff were relocated to ensure that each region had one LEL and one Sundance area manager; this strategy ensured that each region contained at least one senior manager who was 'known to be loyal'.

Whilst great concern was expressed over integrating Sundance into Leisuredome, very little emphasis was given to those existing Leisuredome employees who were also undergoing considerable feelings of stress and need to be counselled through the change. Almost overnight the roles occupied, and their perception of them, by the Bognor staff was expected to alter, unaided, from being a divisional head office to being merely a regional office. No real concerted attempt was made to explain the role of the newly created head office support staff to the Bognor staff and this resulted in confusion and feelings of inadequacy and frustration by both parties. Not only had their ability to influence major decisions and policies become diluted but the two senior executives, the divisional accountant and the operations director changed job titles. The decision had been taken to appoint a qualified financial director and company secretary above the unqualified divisional accountant and the latter was persuaded to become one of three regional accountants. In addition, the job title of the operations director was changed to regional director and he became one of three, although the bitterness of the pill was sweetened by the fact that he was also given a board appointment.

As a result, the fears of the managing director that existing Sundance management would prove disloyal and disruptive took precedence over any other concern. Whilst it could be argued that this was a foregone conclusion the attitude of existing Leisuredome management based in Bognor gave even greater cause for concern. This resulted in, in the managing director's words, 'the Bognor office declaring independence'. Control, always tenuous, was lost and was never established in the other two regions.

The leisure division, therefore, entered February 1992 with effectively three regions operating as separate companies, no integrated administration systems, no form of operational or financial control; disloyalty, confusion and discontent were evident.

In an attempt to regain control, the decision was taken to centralise the operation in Bedford with resulting redundancies and closures of the other two regional offices. Once again attention was paid to the 'engineering' of the exercise in terms of the legal and financial implications and the announcement of the decision was delayed until after the publication of the report and accounts of Leisuredome plc.

The most significant of the proposed redundancies were to be the two ex-Sundance regional directors. It was considered that it was easier and more expedient, given that the organisation had reached crisis point, to remove them rather than to attempt to gain their loyalty. The other regional director will once again revert to his former job title of operations director.

ACTIVITY BRIEF

1 *Using the concepts of organisation structure, evalute LEL's approach to its restructuring of the organisation following the acquisition of Sundance. What alternative approaches could have been taken?*

2 *Considering the expansion from 15 to 51 units at LEL, how would you manage the issues of control arising from the acquisition?*

The challenge of obtaining value for money in prescribing in the National Health Service

Jeff Watling

This case is based in a small English National Health Service (NHS) region. It describes the challenge of working in the NHS with complex structures, the vested interests of the professions and a high political profile. In particular the case is concerned with the cost of medicines prescribed on the NHS. This is a major contributor to the growth in expenditure on the NHS and it is a very sensitive issue, in that doctors have been allowed freedom to prescribe without regard to cost, as long as it was in the best interest of their patients. This case is complex and will appeal particularly to managers working in the NHS or the public sector.

The activities associated with this case point up questions associated with organisational effectiveness, value for money against clinical freedom, budgetary control, accountability and other human resources issues including the future requirements for training.

BACKGROUND

The National Health Service (NHS) is a massive and complex organisation. It is said to be the largest employer in Europe. In England, it is divided into 14 Regional Health Authorities (RHAs) of which *King Arthur's* (King Arthur's RHA) is one of the smallest, serving a population of just over three million. The NHS is always in the news, one can rarely pick up a newspaper without seeing a headline that the NHS is in crisis over something. This is nothing new to observers of the scene. Laurance (1984) began an article as follows:

> Consider this paradox. Over the first five years of the present Government, spending on the health service rose 17 per cent in real terms. The number of doc-

tors and nurses has risen, and so has the number of patients treated. Yet according to those who work in it, the health service is in crisis. Just about everyone – doctors, nurses, administrators, trade unionists – points to falling standards, inadequate services and poor conditions, and warns that the service is heading for disaster.

Former Minister of Health, Enoch Powell, described one of the reasons for this constant state of crisis as reflecting that 'those working in the NHS have a vested interest in denigration in that the only way that those working in the service can get more funds is by publicizing its inadequacies and thereby mobilizing public opinion to shame the Government into providing more money.' Hence in Powell's words, we see 'the unique spectacle of an undertaking that is run down by everyone that is engaged in it'.

Scanning the popular press, one is given the impression that nothing has changed in the NHS since the Laurance article was written, or, for that matter since Enoch Powell was Minister of Health. The internal culture of the NHS appears to have changed little and nor have attitudes of the press and public. Every time a major change is proposed there is an immediate public and political debate about the consequences. So much so that in recent years the changes in the NHS were claimed to be the main cause of the Government's defeat in the 1991 Monmouth by-election. At the time Margaret Thatcher was quoted in the *Independent on Sunday* (1991) as saying that Labour's 'disgraceful and unprincipled assault is sapping the morale of NHS staff, insulting their work and cynically exploiting and alarming the sick'.

The NHS has gone through a number of reorganisations in the last twenty years. In fact the NHS is currently undergoing a fundamental reorganisation which began with the publishing of the Government White Paper *Working for Patients* (1989).

The Government is attempting to avoid the mistakes of previous reorganisations, where there was considerable emphasis on structural change, by implementing a series of reforms which attempt to change the NHS from bureaucratic control to a system where the emphasis is on controlling outputs. This reorganisation sets out to sweep aside two tiers of management. The RHAs and the District Health Authorities (DHAs) have been allocated different roles which are quite distinct from those which they previously held. The RHAs are responsible for implementing Government policy, whilst the DHAs have become purchasers rather than providers of health care. As purchasers they are responsible for establishing the health status of the population, identifying their population's resulting health care needs and purchasing health care from an internal market of hospitals, now called Provider Units or Directly Managed Units (DMUs) and Self Governing Trusts (Trusts). The latter are no longer accountable to the DHAs or the RHAs but directly to the NHS Management Executive (NHSME or ME).

The management structure of family doctor or primary care services is similarly confusing and changing as a result of the reforms. The family doctors (GPs) are independent contractors within the NHS and are accountable to the Family Health Services Authorities (FHSAs) for the provision of primary care services against a nationally negotiated contract. This contract has recently been extended to include achievement of targets for vaccination of children and health screening such as identification of high blood pressure. In many RHAs the FHSA boundaries are coterminous with county or metropolitan council boundaries whereas DHAs are not. In King Arthur's RHA there has been a unique combination of FHSAs and DHAs into new style Health Commissions or Commissioning Agencies. There have also been some boundary changes to reduce the number of DHAs and Health Commissions.

THE SITUATION

The challenge of obtaining value for money is enormous, the total UK spend in 1992/3 being £3.1bn. In King Arthur's RHA the spend for 1992/3 being £153.8m. on primary care (family doctor or GP prescribing) and £30m. on hospital prescribing.

National growth in primary care prescribing costs have been more than 25 per cent over the last two years. The RHA is slightly down on the national average at 14.5 per cent in 1991/2 and 12.9 per cent in 1992/3. This is against a background of low inflation of 3–4 per cent. In fact inflation on the cost of medicines is also very low, below the general level. The crunch will come this year as primary care budgets have been set 6.35 per cent above current levels. There are few controls on GP prescribing. The funds are allocated directly by the Treasury and they are not cash limited, unlike most other NHS spending. Currently it is difficult to identify any form of accountability for prescribing other than some limits on the range of products available, the so-called selected list.

The growth in hospital prescribing in King Arthur's RHA is variable. Expenditure for 1992/3 against the previous year has increased by between 6 and 30 per cent.

The pharmaceutical industry, although claiming that they are hamstrung by government regulations are, in fact, very successful. They are the third highest earners of export earnings for the UK and their stock market ratings have, until recently been, the envy of most other industries. This very success makes the current Government reluctant to address the issues head on. In Germany there has been a government imposed price cut, in France there are controls on the introduction of new medicines and the prices paid for them. The Clinton administration in the United States has threatened to wage war on the industry's profits and an agreement to limit price rises to the general level of inflation is rumoured. In the UK the government limits the drug companies profitability through the Pharmaceutical Price Regulation Scheme (PPRS) and also the amount spent on promotional activities. Promotion is limited to 11 per cent of UK turnover in pharmaceuticals. In the King Arthur's RHA, the industry currently spend £16,500,000 on promotion to GPs, with an additional sum for hospitals. This is equivalent to £10,000 p.a. per GP.

The Secretary of State is threatening to increase the range of medicines which are not prescribable on the NHS. This is causing considerable concern in the pharmaceutical industry and they are threatening to move production to countries who have a more supportive attitude to the pharmaceutical industry. As a result of these problems the Government might backtrack and insist instead that the RHAs manage GP prescribing within a cash limited budget. If current growth in expenditure in GP prescribing is allowed to continue unchecked this will wipe out all potential for growth in other areas for the foreseeable future.

Pressures for change

In the past, governments have tended to change one variable at a time rather than tackle a range of variables other than structural change. 'Working for Patients' and the subsequent reforms have gone a long way to creating an environment where change can take place, even within the NHS.

Figure 12.1 illustrates the pre-purchaser/provider split organisational structure of the NHS, highlighting the accountability or lack of accountability of doctors.

Dept of Health

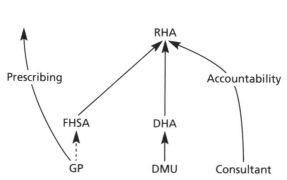

Fig 12.1 NHS structure prior to the purchaser/provider split

The problem here, is not so much the structure, as the accountability of the doctors, particularly for their prescribing practice. This point was well illustrated by Laurance (1984)

> The doctors spend the money, but they have no responsibility for and often no awareness of, their budgets. On the other hand, the administrators who control the budgets have no authority over their medical and nursing colleagues. The policy has been to provide the medical staff with resources and let them get on with it. Guaranteeing them their clinical freedom is said to ensure that every patient gets the treatment he or she needs.

Ten years ago budgets for medicines were held centrally in hospitals and they were normally 'managed' by the chief pharmacist or the Drug and Therapeutics Committee (D&Th Com). Subsequently the hospital pharmaceutical service has been computerised and is able to attribute and report expenditure to the prescriber or, in the case of inpatients, the ward to which the medicines have been issued. Some attempts have been made to devolve responsibility for prescribing budgets to consultants. However, the continuation of clinical freedom and lack of direct accountability locally have reduced the effectiveness of these changes.

In hospitals the budget-setting system is, at best, based on historical data. Budgets are set on the basis of what was in the budget last year. In most cases current budgets will take little account of developments in systems of care, for example, drug treatment replacing surgical treatment, development of new drugs, or new products which provide better control or fewer side effects or changes in workload, or GPs health screening clinics which highlight more people with high blood pressure.

GP expenditure on medicines is monitored by the Prescription Pricing Authority, (the organisation who pay high street chemists for the medicines they dispense). A sophisticated computer system (PACT) provides RHAs and FHSAs with detailed information on expenditure by each practice or individual doctor. This information is available to GPs and the medical and pharmaceutical advisors employed by the FHSAs.

Some good practice is emerging in the primary care sector. Whilst the major factor determining budgets is currently historical, systems for calculating a weighted capitation rate are emerging. The current system takes account of **A**ge, **S**ex and **T**emporary **R**esidence to calculate expected **P**rescribing **U**nits per patient, hence their name ASTRO PUs.

The medical advisory structure

While the consultants as individuals enjoy considerable freedom they have had an entrée into the management system through their own advisory structure. Each DHA and now Trust has its own Medical Advisory Committee (MAC) to advise on medical policy and these have a number of specialist sub-committees, for example, for medicine, paediatrics or surgery. The medical advisory structure is replicated at regional level where there is an RMAC and specialist sub-committees all with wide representation. GPs are similarly involved in advisory structures. There are district and regional GP advisory committees. GPs have representation on medical advisory committees and some of the multidisciplinary sub-committees listed above. GPs also have their own committee, the Local Medical Committee (LMC), which concerns itself largely with terms and conditions of service under the NHS contract.

In addition, each Trust has a number of multidisciplinary sub-committees on which consultants have a very strong voice in terms of professional power and numbers of representatives:

- The Research Ethics Committee is concerned with the design and conduct of clinical trials. This committee is almost exclusively comprised of hospital consultants, with token administrative and pharmaceutical support. This committee is often linked with the local medical school and is concerned with developing locally based research and protecting patients from poorly designed experiments which may not be in their best interest. The committee is not generally concerned with the cost benefit of potential new medicines, nor the long-term funding of them.

- The Drug and Therapeutics Committee concerns itself with the prescribing and administration of medicines. Membership will include pharmacists, a nurse, a treasurer, a manager probably as committee support and a number of consultants of whom one will be the chairman. More recently a GP has been included to ensure that primary care interests are considered, and within the last year or so, FHSA advisors are being included also. The D&Th Com will normally be responsible for producing and updating the local list of medicines approved for use in the hospital (hospital prescribing formulary or formulary) and approving the inclusion of new medicines into the formulary and hence into general use in the hospital. The D&Th Com usually has no budget, and hence approval for use does not mean that funds will be made available for a new medicine.

- The Clinical Audit Committee/Group is responsible for the promotion of quality audit, primarily of clinical practice within the hospital. In general audit is carried out against standards which are laid down by the Royal Colleges. These bodies, such as the Royal Colleges of Physicians or Surgeons, are responsible for postgraduate qualifications of doctors, which they obtain before they become consultants, and they also take responsibility for publishing standards of practice for their members. Quality Audits have in the past often been conducted by peer review between medical personnel only. The Government have, however, made it very clear that audit should be multidisciplinary and that other groups/professions should be involved. This is now happening in most organisations but spending on audit is still dominated by consultants

The main problem with all these committees has been their lack of accountability. They report to the MAC and the MAC reports to management, but they set their own professional agenda and are dominated by medical interests.

The change of structure (see Figure 12.2) has defined the accountability of the consultant in the hospital service. The NHS Trusts, in turn, are clearly accountable to their customers for delivering, through the contracts process, agreed volumes of service, for an agreed cost and to an agreed quality. Within the Trusts accountability is being more clearly defined. A small Trust board will normally have a medical director who will be a consultant and a number of operational directors who will have overall responsibility for a range of clinical services. The Trust's income will be based on delivery of contracts for treatment of a range of acutely ill patients (patients with heart attacks, acute infections, broken limbs or requiring emergency surgery) together with a number of 'elective procedures' (coronary artery bypass operations, hernias and hip replacements). In addition these contracts will have to be delivered within the contracted financial limits or the Trust will overspend its income.

These arrangements will automatically mean that consultants will become more accountable for their actions, because if they overspend beds will close to bring expenditure under control.

In the primary care sector the drug bill is still open ended, but it is highly likely that within a year it will be cash limited. The RHA has already to deliver the indicative prescribing scheme within the firm budgets allocated.

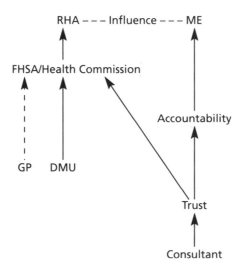

Fig 12.2 Current structure and accountability in the NHS with regard to prescribing

If the primary care drug bill is included within the cash limit, a service specification and contract for prescribing will need to be introduced. Under these circumstances the Health Commission will be uniquely placed to ensure that the interface between primary and secondary care is managed equitably.

Overspending and financial crises

As previously indicated, overspending and financial crises are not new to the NHS. Successive governments have attempted to exert control by imposing tighter limits on spending. In addition they have calculated allocations which include a requirement for annual cash releasing efficiency savings of just over 1 per cent. In the NHS budgetary control is achieved by applying downward pressure on historically based budgets and not on evaluating and making the best use of the available resources. At local level similar budgetary control methods have been adopted. There is a tendency to:

● allocate resources on previous year's budgets regardless of workload or change in practise;
● under-fund developments.

When the drug budgets overspend, managers exert pressure on the pharmacy to do something about it. The pharmacy staff produce recommendations for economies and some are taken up but while growth may be reduced, budgets rarely come in on target. The normal management reaction is to bail out the budgets on a non-recurring basis and repeat the exercise next year. In extreme emergency, managers close beds until the end of the financial year in March and open them again in April. This approach has done nothing to control expenditure on medicines in the long term and has led to demoralisation and cynicism amongst pharmacists. To date there is little evidence that the new contracting system for provision of hospital services will involve medicines. Some good practice has evolved in recent years and cases have been made before introduction of a new product, but in most instances consultants still prescribe first and ask for funding when someone says that the budget is overspending.

In the worst cases consultants have been known to say 'Oh, if the budget's overspending, we will pass prescribing off on the GPs.' As can be imagined off-loading prescribing causes fury amongst the GPs and the Secretary of State has recently reissued guidance (Department of Health (1991)) indicating that clinical responsibility for patients and prescribing responsibility should rest together, so that, GPs should not accept prescribing responsibility unless they feel competent so to do.

The NHS is poor at looking at the global resource and employing it flexibly, for example if medicines are used to replace a surgical intervention the surgical budget should be reduced to compensate for that change.

In most hospitals some control mechanisms are in place but, in general, they are soft:

- Hospital formularies limit the range of medicines prescribable by junior hospital doctors, but these do not apply to consultants. Formularies vary in content from detailed guidance on use of medicines to lists of medicines currently available for prescribing by junior medical staff.
- Pharmacy departments have combined with individual consultants to produce guidelines for treatment of common diseases but these tend to be advisory rather than more restrictive protocols or procedures which are enforceable.
- Drug and Therapeutics Committees advise on the prescribing and administration of medicines but they float somewhere in the structure without having budgets to allocate and are not tethered to any formal management structure.
- Some audits of prescribing are taking place but they are not compulsory.

Clinical trials are also a big problem. In general they measure the effectiveness of a new drug against a placebo or in some cases an alternative product. Most clinical trials are organised and funded by the pharmaceutical industry. They may establish that a product is more effective than an alternative or whether a new product has fewer side effects but rarely establish whether it is more cost effective. Little time is spent on establishing cost benefit in clinical trials and there is no widely accepted way of carrying out such studies. During clinical trials the drug company will normally supply the trial material free of charge. This causes problems at the end of the clinical trial if long-term therapy is needed for patients involved in the clinical trial. The new product is often more expensive than its predecessor and budgets rarely take account of non-availability of free clinical trial material. The end of a clinical trial may increase a single consultant's expenditure by 20 to 30 per cent with very little warning. The pharmaceutical industry will always set the price of a new product at a higher level than that of its predecessors provided that the product is thought to be more effective. Only where the product is equivalent to a competitor, a so-called *me too* drug, will a company introduce it at a lower or equivalent price. In this latter case the company concerned will often offer the product at a very low price to the hospital sector to gain market penetration and aim to recover its profits from the primary care sector where it will charge a higher price than the competition.

Hospital consultants who fall into this trap and refer patients to their GPs on such treatments will incur the wrath of the GPs as will the hospital pharmacists for allowing it to happen.

Control mechanisms in King Arthur's

Some very good control mechanisms have recently been introduced by King Arthur's RHA:

● A Regional Development and Evaluation Committee has been set up to look at the cost effectiveness of alternative forms of treatment including medicines.

This has been a significant step forward, in that it provides advice to purchasers and providers on whether new treatments offer a cost benefit. The problem is that, in most cases, the product is already being used before the case goes to the Development and Evaluation Committee. If the case for a new product is not accepted it is difficult to discontinue treatment, particularly if long-term treatment is involved. The Development and Evaluation Committee reports to the RMAC and has in general been backed by the RMAC even where decisions have not been popular with clinicians.

The Development and Evaluation Committee is the first step towards rational control of the introduction of new medicines. However the rate of development will always outstrip the availability of funds for developments. A recent paper describes a system introduced in the Royal Adelaide Hospital (RAH) (Bochner, 1992). The goal of the system was to provide a ranking of drug requests on the basis of obtaining the greatest benefit for each dollar spent. For each drug request, scores are allocated for each of a series of sub-sections under the general headings of quality and cost. Scores are obtained from information provided to the RAH Drugs Committee with the request. The final ratio of quality score over cost score is used to rank the requests. Local application of this system would assist management boards and health commissions in making decisions about developments.

● For GPs RHA has attempted to promote optimal prescribing on two fronts through introduction of the 'Regional Formulist'. The Regional Formulist is a mechanism for promoting generic prescribing, i.e. encouraging GPs to prescribe by the approved or generic name of a medicine rather than the manufacturer's trade name. This will only be valuable for medicines once their patent life of 16 years has expired, but the potential for savings is very large because the price of a generic can be as little as 10–15 per cent of the equivalent branded product. It also seeks to improve prescribing by promoting guidelines for treatment of six common diseases.

The Regional Formulist is planned to be reviewed annually and expanded at the rate of approximately six guidelines per year. It is currently envisaged that the introduction of the Formulist should be a voluntary system and incentives will be provided to encourage GPs to sign up to it. If prescribing budgets become cash limited then the Formulist will have to be expanded to restrict GPs' prescribing practise.

● In addition GPs are encouraged to go through the educational process of jointly developing a practice formulary by negotiation with their own partners. This will limit the range of products to be prescribed by GPs in the practice and promote cost-effective prescribing. This local approach is thought to be more effective than producing a formulary centrally and then imposing or promoting it around King Arthur's.

Education and training

Postgraduate medical and pharmaceutical education and training is directed towards diagnosis of disease and its treatment rather than: cost benefit analysis, health economics, pharmacoeconomics and drug use evaluation. Postgraduate education and training in public health medicine does deal with some of these issues, but there are few public health doctors and they have little influence on their consultant and GP colleagues. Similarly postgraduate training of pharmacists is biased towards clinical pharmacy and very few pharmacists receive adequate training in the areas listed above.

Research and development in the NHS is currently dominated by the medical profession and directed towards the diagnosis and treatment of disease. The government is putting significant resources into developing a research and development strategy for the NHS. There is a case for introducing a multidisciplinary approach to research and development and directing resources towards evaluating the cost benefit of alternative approaches to treatment of disease with medicines.

REFERENCES

Bochner, F. (1992). *Prioritisation of Drug Therapy Requests* – a model developed by the drug committee, Royal Adelaide Hospital.
Department of Health (1989). *Working for Patients: White Paper on the Government's Proposals following its Review of the NHS*, London: HMSO.
Department of Health (1991). *Responsibility for prescribing between hospitals and GPs* (EL(91)127), London: HMSO.
Laurance, J. (1984). 'The Doctor Dilemma', *Management Today*, page 5155.

ACTIVITY BRIEF

The activities described below are suitable for group or individual activity. It is recommended that Questions 1 and 2 are always undertaken to form a foundation for subsequent questions.

1 *You are asked, as a management consultant, to analyse the situation, past and present, using an organisational effectiveness framework such as those highlighted in Chapter 21 of Mullins.*

2 *You should prepare a paper for the General Management Team (GMT) at King Arthur's proposing ways in which they can demonstrate value for money in prescribing as a contribution towards the Government's requirement to reduce costs.*

The GMT comprises the Chief Executive and directors of Finance, Health Strategy (a doctor), Primary and Community Care, Commissioning and Performance Management and Development.

The GMT will be particularly interested in how Health Commissions are going to link this issue into contracts in a way which controls expenditure without consultants and GPs complaining of rationing to the media.

3 *You are asked to prepare a paper for the RMAC on the implementation of your proposals. You should ensure that you employ tight budgetary control systems but, at the same time, take the medical staff with you and allow decision making and monitoring to take place at local level.*

4 *You are asked by the GMT to consider the human resources and training issues associated with this case. You are asked to prepare a strategy for obtaining better value for money in prescribing and overcoming the imbalance between the medical and pharmaceutical advice and the promotional activities of the pharmaceutical industry. This must be achieved without additional expenditure on medical and pharmaceutical advisors.*

RECOMMENDED READING

Handy, C. B. (1993). *Understanding Organisations*, London: Penguin Books.

Mullins, L. J. (1993). *Management and Organisational Behaviour,* (Third Edition), London: Pitman.

Peters, T. J. and Waterman, R. (1982). *In Search of Excellence*, New York: Harper and Row.

Waterman, R. H. (1987). *The Renewal Factor*, Bantam Press.

Middle management experiences of devolution in Barsetshire County Council Social Services Department

Linda Keen

A growing volume of literature during the 1980s and 90s has focused upon the changes in the organisation structures and management systems of local authorities during this period, made in response to central government legislation and policy initiatives. These 'new' management practices can be seen as representing a general move from bureaucratic and professionally dominated *administration* to more flexible/organic and consumer-orientated *management* of service provision. However, identification of these changes in the literature are derived largely from senior management perspectives. This case study outlines briefly the key structural changes taking place in one authority and then focuses upon the views of middle managers in one department about the impact of the new devolved management system on their managerial decision-making roles. The case study questions involve using theoretical models of organisation structure and managerial roles to analyse the implications of these changes for the middle managers' work roles.

BACKGROUND

The changing organisational context

Barsetshire County Council (BCC) is one of the larger English county councils, employing over 28,000 employees (full time equivalents), and providing services for a large mixed urban/rural area with about a million inhabitants. Controlled by the Conservatives since its inception in 1889, BCC has enthusiastically adopted the organisational and managerial changes advocated by central government, frequently pioneering new initiatives in advance of legislative requirements. Following the election of a new leader in the mid-1980s, a new chief executive was appointed. He was given a specific brief to help clarify the council's strategic objectives, and to introduce the organisational and managerial changes necessary to ensure effective strategy implementation throughout the council – in both the direct service departments (Education, Social Services, Highways, etc.), and the support service departments such as Personnel, Finance, Information Systems, and Contract Services (in-house contractors providing services subject to competitive tendering, including supplies, vehicle maintenance, catering etc.).

Speaking about the requirements for change, the chief executive explained that on his arrival at Barset, although the council had always successfully maintained its spending within its budget, the various departmental budgets were simply cash sums, which the council 'spent up to' with little regard for meeting customer needs or demands: 'There was very little true management thinking. The organisation was dominated by a professional ethos – a very strong professional ethos, and a very excellent one – but I decided it was necessary to introduce a more business-like approach, bringing together that strength of *professional* ethos within the delivery of services with the *management* of resources'. The purpose and nature of the changes required were widely disseminated throughout the council by means of reports and newsletters issued regularly by the corporate management team, and a comprehensive management development programme. Nearly all of the council's middle managers attended a series of seminars at County Hall, where, for the first time for many of these managers, they met chief officers and the chief executive, and set up interdepartmental working groups to work on a project of their own choosing.

Key features of these organisational changes included:

- a coherent strategic planning system, involving business planning for each service with more emphasis on identifying customer needs and priorities, clear specification of service standards (including a 'Citizens Charter' for all major services), and rigorous monitoring review of performance against policy objectives.

- strong leadership styles through the authority, embodying core BCC beliefs and values – a clear sense of direction, closeness to the customer, being entrepreneurial, proactive, risk-taking etc.

- personnel management changes, including more flexible (fewer and wider) job grades, a formal staff development and performance review system and performance-related pay for all white collar staff (Barset withdrew from national bargaining for all white collar staff, excluding teachers).

- organisation restructuring, including a flatter structure with reduced management layers, and, under way at the time of writing, a move towards a functional regrouping, both of departments, and of activities within departments into (a) 'client' or 'purchaser' and (b) service provision or 'provider' units. For example, within the Social Services Department (SSD), in each of the six geographical areas, activities were to be divided into (a) the purchasers, who assess service needs and organise the service provision required for the two main client groups of Children and Families, and Adults (the elderly, disabled etc.), and (b) the providers who deliver the services. Under the National Health Service and Community Care Act 1990, the provider side will, and does already to an extent, include in-house SSD provider units who will compete with external providers such as voluntary organisations like Age Concern, and private sector firms running, for example, residential homes for the elderly.

● a culture change, replacing 'administration' by a culture based on devolved management, by reducing bureaucracy, and 'red tape', and by reducing the hierarchical structure with its tiers of authority, thus releasing all managers to make their own decisions within their area of activity, and to become more accountable through the development of the performance review system with its performance targets and personal action plans for all managers.

THE SITUATION

Changes in the decision-making powers of middle managers in the SSD

The position of middle managers within Barset's SSD is outlined on the simplified organisation chart of a typical area (see Figure 13.1).

The situation facing these managers is reported as a result of semi-structured interviews of 1–2 hours in length, held with a small sample of these managers located in four out of the six areas. The purpose of these interviews was to identify their perceptions about the impact of devolution on their work roles.

Devolved management in the SSD during the late 1980s and into the 1990s, involved two key aspects – devolution from the SSD Centre at County Hall to the six geographical areas, and, within each of the areas, to the line managers. The BCC chief executive envisaged devolved management in terms of devolving power and control to line managers, as far down the organisational hierarchy as possible, over resources such as finance, personnel, and information etc., within a specified organisation framework of clearly understood accountabilities and limits of authority. When asked for their own understanding of the term, some middle manager' views corresponded almost exactly with those of the chief executive.

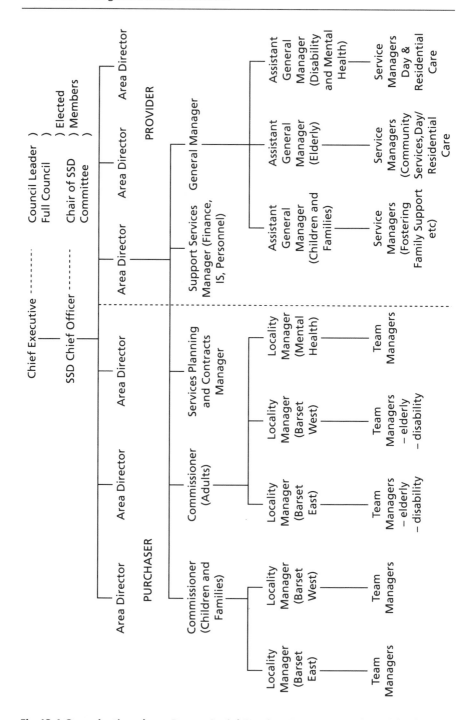

Fig 13.1 Organisation chart: Barset Social Services Department (simplified)

It has certainly meant greater responsibility and accountability for what you are doing. You do have greater freedom within the parameters of good practice, guidance, regulations and financial control – you are not continually having to ask the person above you for something, so there is a cultural shift.

(Locality Manager, Children and Families)

All of the managers attached great significance to being given greater control over their budgets:

I think devolution has meant that for the first time ever we've been able to control our budgets and our expenditure at the sharp end. And it's really forced managers to come to terms with aspects of management that previously they had no control over. I think it's primarily the budgets.

(Assistant General Manager, Elderly Services)

Many managers, whilst acknowledging the greater extent of their control and responsibilities, also queried the extent of the constraints, some to the point where they felt very little had changed:

I'm tempted to say very little in real terms – I don't think devolution in our department is genuine. Devolution for me is putting accountability down the line and saying to people 'This is yours – you get on with it with the costs and the benefits'. I don't see much evidence of that really happening. One example – devolved financial accountability. But it doesn't actually amount to: 'Here's your budget; do what you like with it'. The systems are supposed to allow people to act in an independent way but this really barely exists. I think the financial management systems are really heavily bureaucratised themselves. This is where the conflict comes in. There's this sort of, on the one hand, entrepreneurial spirit, you know -'go out and do all these things', and yet it's 'oh, you can't do that because these procedures say you must do this, that and the other.

(Assistant General Manager, Children and Families)

It gives you far more control, but – I actually think that if you are going to take responsibility for things, you've got to be accountable for them. For example, they've given us our budgets but I've got to have control of it. It's no good you saying to me 'Well, its your budget, but I'm going to take this bit off'. Or 'You don't have anything to do with the maintenance of the building, we'll do that, but you'd better put £2,000 aside on your budget'. This sort of thing. To me, that's a nonsense.

(Service Manager, Day/Residential Centre)

Devolution of service design and delivery

Barsetshire's corporate management team intended devolution to allow line managers greater discretion to run services (using their professional judgements and experience) and more scope for action, where they was no overriding reason for greater central control. All of the managers interviewed stated that they were allowed and, indeed, expected to take more responsibility for more operational decisions about service delivery. All of them provided many examples of new projects and service initiatives they had been able to develop as a consequence of their devolved responsibilities. For example, one manager had problems with delivering a meals-on-wheels service because of more stringent European Community (EC) regulations:

> We've either had to take the decision to spend fortunes updating the kitchens or contract the service out. Now, it's on the verge of collapse in Barset East, so I've just authorised the purchase of 17 hot-locks (especially designed pots to keep food hot). It's small beer – about £10,000, I suppose. But I've just been able to do it, whereas, say four or five years ago, I'd probably have had to go up through a great paraphenalia of the hierarchy to get that agreed. But it's my money, it's my budget – I can do what I like with it within reason.
>
> (*Commissioner, Adult Services*)

Several managers were very positive about the way in which the devolved management system gave them the opportunity to focus more specifically on the needs of the client – to develop needs-based rather than resource-led services. The prospect of competing with the private and voluntary sector on the service provision side, under the purchaser/provider split, had also made it necessary to define more sharply the standards and purposes of their services, and to focus more sharply on the most cost-effective way of providing them. Some managers also commented on the limits to their powers here, explaining that their discretion over service provision decisions was exercised within fairly restricted margins, circumscribed by requirements to get authorisation from their line managers, by the increasing volume of both national legislation and BCC's own procedures, and by decreasing resource allocation (both finance and staff).

> I think that devolution is down to accountability, and hence standards of accountability. I think that we are pretty well prescribed in what we do; there are a lot of rules and regulations – child protection, really, the Children's Act – child protection procedures . . . and with care management coming in (under the Community Care Act) there are going to be quite firm guidelines there.
>
> (*Locality Manager, Children and Families*)

> It feels peculiar that they have given you all this authority and then suddenly they will issue instructions about what you shall do in the event of child abuse with every t crossed, and every i dotted twice. Yet I know why – they're worried about headlines in the Sun or whatever.
>
> (*Service Manager, Children and Families*)

Limits were also reported through the purchaser/provider split for those on the provider side. Ideas to amend service delivery systems had to be referred not only to their provider side line managers but also to the purchasers who now had primary responsibility for identifying and prioritising which service needs were to be met, and which services were to be provided to meet those needs:

> In a sense the situation is less free now, because we are responding to a purchaser customer as well as to the end-user. So, particularly when working with people with learning disability, there were no care plans, or anything else, at one stage, from care managers. So we decided what we thought was best for the services we had available, and whether it was worth changing what were running, or whatever it was – that was the way we did it. Whereas now, we have to look at what they want to purchase, and mould our service accordingly.
>
> (*Assistant General Manager, Adult Services*)

One manager felt that there was almost too much freedom devolved down to line managers:

> Some would argue that there's not been *enough* centre or area interference; this has left us free to develop local patterns of service delivery, local service conditions. I do think it's the chief executive's sort of famous 'simultaneous loose-tight qualities' thing. It does seem to me that certain things they should have defined tightly have been defined loosely, and so you've got different patterns of service delivery across the county, according to what they (the areas) want, and that, I think, is wrong. I think there ought to be a county core of social work practices; this for a long time has been locally led rather than centrally led.
>
> (*Service Manager, Mental Health Services*)

Performance targets

All of the managers emphasised the increased level of accountability for performance which they were experiencing under the staff performance review scheme, which included performance targets to be achieved each year for both them and their staff:

> The pressures on people to meet their targets and come in on budget can be really good in that it focuses people on the task they have to do. I feel that they're very useful. If somebody says 'Develop a fostering service for mentally ill people', that's quite daunting. But if you say 'Provide five fostering services', that is achievable, and people can actually get hold of that.
>
> (*Commissioner, Children and Families*)

> What I'm assessed on is the managers coming in on budget. That's what I'm assessed on. I think they have missed an opportunity; staff performance is judged by how many cases have been processed, by how many care packages have been delivered rather than what I've been like as a manager . . . the business plan targets are all very much about bed occupancies, and numbers of kids in care, that sort of thing'.
>
> (*Assistant General Manager, Disability Services*).

Devolution of resource management – finance and personnel

Increased control by line managers over resources such as property, information, finance and personnel, within a clearly specified corporate framework, was a key feature of the authority's devolved management system. Most of the managers felt that they had acquired increased decision-making responsibilities for their financial resources through devolved budgeting, which was enhanced by the introduction of a computerised financial management information system:

> What I found was that I did not have to continually get permission to spend money. So I suppose that was the real thing – being allowed to make decisions without resource to higher authority. But on your head if you get it wrong!
>
> *(Locality Manager, Children and Families)*

> Before devolution, we didn't really know what money we had. The money was controlled by the old divisional managers – you didn't have any concerns about money, the money was just there. If you needed staff you got it or you didn't according to what the managers said. Now I know what money I get every year. I have a community support budget for mental health services which goes across the whole of the area. Each team manager has had that divided up between them – say £10,000 each. One of my team managers has consistently never spent his, so one of the others said 'can I have his because I can do this with it?'. So I was able to say to the non-spender 'You can't have a blank cheque. I can't sit in your account, it's got to go to a service that's being developed.' And that's what happened – I could just do it.
>
> *(Locality Manager, Mental Health Services)*

However, many managers felt that their budgetary discretion was limited in practice to small marginal sums, because the vast majority of their funds was already allocated for providing statutory (compulsory) services over which there was little discretion, and for staff costs, which left little room for manoeuvre overall. Moreover, money could be removed from their budgets, at the behest of the centre, to cover overspending in another SSD area. The scope for practices such as vieing between budget heads, carrying money forward etc. was also extremely limited – by regulations, by requirements to obtain authorisation, and, ultimately, by political/legal constraints:

> At the end of the day the bottom line's got to balance. Now, the major part of that is staffing. Then, we can't make a profit, and so that kind of restricts services. It is a fact that most of our buildings are going to need a certain amount of work on them during the year. People do need to eat. All those bits eat up most of it, and the amount that's really left over for development of any sort is pretty limited.
>
> *(Assistant General Manager, Adult Services)*

> 'I seem to be constantly writing memos to either my line manager, or the commissioner (the purchaser), or the area director, telling him we want to do something, and how much it's going to cost, and asking him if it is okay to do it.
>
> *(Service Manager, Foster Care Unit)*

Politically, you have to be quite careful about borrowing between the client groups. Traditionally, adult services have been used to bolster up children and family services, but you can't take that decision locally; that has to go up through the system and so you are a bit restricted. There's probably a limit to real devolution in local government because of the political accountability and democracy thing.

(Commissioner, Adult Services)

A similar picture emerged with the managers' personnel responsibilities. All except one of the managers felt that they had acquired new responsibilities for personnel management, particularly in the areas of staff recruitment and selection, work design and allocation, staff appraisal and development/training, again, within the framework of BCC regulations governing conditions of service:

As a line manager, I think your responsibilities are greater – there's the staff development system, and I now do my own selection (of staff) – to see that good personnel practices are carried out, and they have become part of the job now, whereas perhaps before they weren't. In pre-devolution days it would all very much be driven by personnel.

(Assistant General Manager, Children and Families)

The roles of specialist support staff – finance, personnel etc.

As part of the devolution process, many central personnel, finance and information systems specialist staff were moved out from the centre to be line managed by the service departments; they had a diagonal or 'dotted line' relationship, as BCC put it, with their head of profession at the centre in County Hall. This move was designed to encourage the staff to provide a service more directly geared towards these departments' business or service provision needs, rather than acting as centralised, remote and controlling 'millstones around the necks' of these service departments. Managers were asked about their relationships with these specialist staff devolved to the SSD, in particular, about the extent to which these staff members had moved from the traditional controlling role to a more enabling role. Several of the managers felt that the relationship had become more of a partnership:

I think they may be trying to think that way. They are providing you with something that they are more specific about, they are increasingly asking what you want from them . . . there is much more thought given to what we require and what they can offer, and making something out of it between us, and them, being responsive to our needs as well. I mean there is a long way to go on it certainly, but it's starting.

(Locality Manager, Children and Families)

Others were more critical about the specialist staff's abilities or willingness to become more integrated with the service provision needs of the SSD:

They don't really understand the issues that the service is all about. We're having to learn what *they* do, but they're not having to learn what *we* do, and I think that we sometimes feel a bit resentful about that. It's a lot of extra work, and that's why I have to stay on into the evenings if I really want to get to grips with the budget . . . There's a bit of a macho culture around about how many hours you put in, and it's all right if you don't have a family. . .

(Service Manager, Foster Care Unit)

Positive/negative responses to devolution

The managers were asked whether they were generally positive or generally negative about the impact of devolution on their work overall. The majority expressed extremely positive views, commenting on the increased job satisfaction and more challenging work arising from the additional responsibilities. Also highlighted were the increased accountabilities and greater responsiveness to client and community needs, and greater awareness of the costs of services, which, combined with clearer planning systems, enabled scarce resources to be targeted more effectively to areas of greatest need:

It's meant a great deal. It's actually owning and understanding and being responsible for budgets, and I think that's incredibly important. It doesn't actually limit one's activity; it actually improves it. And I've never found it to be meaning that I've had to cut services, but rather that they are better focused, because one has more control over them.

(Commissioner, Children and Families)

It means more work on the same day – but I love it.

(Service Manager, Day/Residential Centre)

Whilst agreeing with some of the benefits noted above, some managers remained essentially sceptical about the process, feeling that they had been given additional responsibilities, but insufficient real authority or decision-making powers:

I always feel a little bit like Gulliver, you know, sort of pinned down. I don't think they've delivered what they promised in terms of authority and responsibility. They are still making us feel so dependent on our line management and the hierarchy, to answer to them for everything. They don't actually trust us – it's an insult to our intelligence.

(Team Manager, Children and Families)

Those manuals – for years we had nothing. I remember when I joined Barset, the divisional manual was that big (half inch thick), and that was for all services. Then back in the 80s, they produced a half-baked children's manual which was that big (one inch), and now we've got *this* (two–three inch). It's interesting; there's a counter-thrust. You've got nominal devolution and yet you've got tighter control at the centre. Nearly all this stuff has come from the centre. My overall view on this is that the organisational changes have been under the *guise* of devolution, but it's actually been around, yes, tighter organisational control.

(Assistant General Manager, Children and Families)

ACTIVITY BRIEF

1 *What are the main changes which have taken place in Barset's organisational structure and management systems? Locate these changes within Mintzberg's parameters of organisational design, and consider how BCC could be placed within Mintzberg's framework of organisational configurations.*

2 *What do you understand by the term 'devolved management'? How does devolved management operate within BCC? How have BCC's integrative mechanisms changed with the introduction of devolved management?*

3 *How has the work of the middle managers changed as a consequence of the introduction of devolved management? What tensions and ambiguities can the introduction of devolved management bring about for the work roles of (a) the 'line' middle managers considered in the study (b) specialist support staff and managers, in the areas of personnel and finance, who have been devolved to the SSD.*

4 *The design parameters and management systems adopted by organisations are influenced by a number of situational or 'contingency' factors. How do the situational characteristics of BCC differ from a private sector organisation, and what impact might these characteristics have upon BCC's structure and management systems?*

RECOMMENDED READING

Mintzberg, H. (1989). *Mintzberg on Management*, New York: The Free Press.

Hales, C. (1993). *Managing Through Organisations*, London: Routledge.

Scase, R. (1989). *Reluctant Managers*, London: Unwin Hyman Ltd.

Farnham, D. and Horton, S. (1993). *Managing the New Public Services*, London: MacMillan.

Mullins, L. J. (1993). *Management of Organisation Behaviour*, London: Pitman.

PART 4

Organisational processes

The four cases in this part provide insight into the nature of work motivation morale of the workforce, job satisfaction and work performance and managerial control. *'Job satisfaction at Omega Technical Services Ltd'* provides opportunities to examine and assess the strategies available for improving job satisfaction and the design and interpretation of attitude surveys. The case presents empirical results of a survey in a service sector company providing a range of technical support services to the engineering industry in Britain.

'Quality improvement in Pall Europe' provides a context to consider the ability of managers to match individual and organisational needs through the process of Total Quality Management. It considers the link between motivation, job satisfaction and the nature of management control within a particular organisational culture. *'Neighbourhood Textiles Ltd* – Motivation and performance in a 'top-down' co-operative development project' provides a contrasting view of issues relating to motivation and morale of a workforce within a radically different organisation. A London local authority wishing to create secure jobs and training opportunities for local people, supports a co–operative model of social ownership. This case examines the link between the aims and objectives of the business, management systems and business structure and relates these to potential performance, motivation and morale of the workforce.

Finally, *'Brownloaf MacTaggart* – Control and power in a management consultancy' is concerned with issues of managerial control and power among a group of highly qualified professional consultants. Merger with a large organisation and the resultant change from a small, close-knit company to a small insignificant division in an international organisation creates tensions within the work group that result in a climate of intimidation, mistrust and unfair reward and punishment systems.

Job satisfaction at Omega Technical Services Ltd

Derek Adam-Smith and Alex Littlewood

Organisations, particularly those in the service sector, are becoming increasingly dependent upon high quality performance from their employees; a trend reflected in the growing interest in the attitude of employees towards work. Two factors have been argued to be influential. First, there exists a popular view that making work more satisfying will lead to increased motivation and performance, and to reduced absenteeism and labour turnover amongst employees. Second, it possible to identify a desire to provide satisfying work for ethical and altruistic reasons, regardless of the tangible benefits for the organisation. For these reasons the attention of managers has been drawn to strategies which attempt to increase employee satisfaction at work.

In order to develop an effective plan for improved job satisfaction it is necessary to identify existing employee attitudes to work. A commonly used method to establish the actions an organisation needs to take is an attitude or opinion survey of the workforce. The purpose of the survey is to improve the quality of decision making based on better information. This case study presents the empirical results of one such survey in a service sector company. The case provides opportunities to assess both appropriate strategies for improving the job satisfaction of staff, and the design and interpretation of attitude surveys.

BACKGROUND

Omega Technical Services Ltd is a medium-sized company established in the mid-1950s to provide a range of technical support services to the engineering industry. The majority of the company's work consists of providing a documentation service producing operational and maintenance manuals for clients involved with the design and installation of engineering projects in government departments and private sector organisations. The commercial basis of the company's work is a mixture of fixed price contracts, won through competitive tenders and a smaller number of projects run on a 'cost plus' basis. In the latter the company is paid an hourly rate for the work done but the number of hours is not specified, in advance, by the client.

In 1984 the company experienced trading difficulties as a result of increased competition in the market place and in response to falling profits a period of rationalisation began under the direction of a new financial director. This included a major redundancy programme and the relocation of the head office. Over a period of a few months there were many changes in the management of the company particularly at line manager level and in the directors of the company.

The company is currently facing external pressures as a result of the recessionary climate and some significant changes in the market within which it operates. Clients undertaking military projects have been faced with the implications of the end of the cold war and the move by others away from cost plus contracts towards fixed priced tendering has led to a degree of uncertainty for the company. As part of its strategy to maintain its competitiveness Omega is currently seeking BS 5750 accreditation.

Company organisation and staffing

Omega is structured geographically with eight regional offices located close to its main clients in the South East (SE), South West (SW), North West (NW), and North East (NE) of England, the East Midlands (EM) and West Midlands (WM), the Home Counties (HC) and Scotland. A small head office of 12 staff, together with the six company directors and the personnel manager, is based at the South West regional office.

The work in the regions is the responsibility of a regional manager who is encouraged to operate autonomously within his own market. Consequently control over personnel matters has traditionally been decentralised. The regional offices are all organised in a similar way with project leaders, reporting to the regional manager, responsible for the work of a group of staff. Each office has a small administrative support unit. The two largest branches, South West and North East, have approximately 30 employees including three project leaders and five clerical staff. The remaining six branches employ, on average, 13 direct staff. Their work is supervised by one of two project leaders and typically only two administrative support staff are employed in each of these smaller offices. In total the company employs 180 full time staff, excluding the directors and personnel manager. The average age of all employees is 44 years and 38 per cent of the workforce is female.

The outline company structure is shown in Figure 14.1.

Company Structure

Head Office
6 Directors
Personnel Manager
12 Admin. Staff

SE *Region*	*SW* *Region*	*NW* *Region*	*NE* *Region*
Regional Manager	Regional Manager	Regional Manager	Regional Manager
2 Project Leaders	3 Project Leaders	2 Project Leaders	3 Project Leaders
13 direct employees	21 direct employees	14 direct employees	20 direct employees
2 admin. support	5 admin. support	2 admin. support	5 admin. support
EM *Region*	*WM* *Region*	*HC* *Region*	*Scot.* *Region*
Regional Manager	Regional Manager	Regional Manager	Regional Manager
2 Project Leaders	2 Project Leaders	2 Project Leaders	2 Project Leaders
14 direct employees	12 direct employees	13 direct employees	13 direct employees
2 admin. support	2 admin. support	2 admin. support	2 admin. support

Fig 14.1

The company has a formal recognition agreement with the Manufacturing, Science and Finance Union (MSF) and membership is in the order of 50 per cent of the workforce. Annual negotiations are held in September of each year to agree substantive matters including pay, allowances, holidays and hours of work. Lay officials also represent union members at formal grievance and disciplinary interviews. There is no formal consultative machinery between the company and the union to deal with any matters outside of the substantive ones noted above.

Allocation of projects to individual employees is made by the regional manager in consultation with the project leaders. Liaison with clients on a day-to-day basis is the responsibility of the allocated employee and this may involve visits to the client's premises. The nature of the work requires employees with specialist knowledge of engineering work and well developed writing skills. Staff are recruited from employment backgrounds where such knowledge and skills have been developed.

By its nature the business is labour intensive; wages accounting for 80 per cent of total costs. In all areas indirect labour is kept at a minimum and other overheads are tightly controlled. In order to hold down costs following the period of rationalisation limited funds have been available to develop the overall employee benefits package. For example, membership of the private health care plan has been frozen and the quality of company cars has fallen. The training and development budget is small and there is no appraisal scheme. The company has not developed a formal communications policy which has resulted in both upward and downward communications being of an *ad hoc* nature.

THE SITUATION

With the company's drive towards improved quality and the external pressures it faces in the market place the board of directors is becoming increasingly concerned over what it perceives as a problem of low morale amongst employees and its possible impact upon performance. Middle managers have reported increased incidents of poor quality work and low productivity. The personnel manager has calculated some objective measures which may reflect morale issues. Labour turnover, obtained by dividing the total number of leavers in a 12 month period by the average number of employees, was calculated for the last full year to be 33 per cent. Absenteeism rates have increased significantly to over 10 per cent of working days.

The lack of any formal communication structure has meant that assumptions about employee attitudes have been made through subjective and random processes such as feedback from project leaders and managers. In order to assist the company in developing a strategy to improve satisfaction at work the personnel manager has been asked to undertake a formal attitude survey of all employees.

Questionnaire design

The personnel manager considered the options available to him and chose a survey technique of a tailor-made, self-administered questionnaire which he felt would ease analysis, be economical and produce results in a relatively short timescale. The use of a preplanned survey instrument was rejected since it was felt unlikely that it would tap the issues peculiar to this organisation, for example, the nature of the work and the specific skills and knowledge possessed by the type of staff employed. An initial set of discussions was held with a range of employees to identify suggestions on the content of the questionnaire.

The final questionnaire comprised 83 items of which 68 were closed statements, 12 were open-ended questions and three were of a demographic nature.

Of the closed questions 67 sought to explore issues in five areas comprising: (i) general satisfaction, (ii) communications, (iii) fairness/supervision, (iv) involvement/identification and (v) matters relating to other jobs and companies which included some pay issues. The questions were, however, randomly presented throughout the questionnaire. Respondents were asked to respond to each of these questions by ticking either the true or false box which followed the question. The remaining closed question was placed at the end of the questionnaire and sought to establish whether employee attitudes had changed significantly over the past year. It requested a yes or no response to the statement. 'If you had sent me this questionnaire a year ago, my answers would have been largely the same.'

The emphasis was placed on quantitative questions in order to aid objectivity in analysis. However, the open-ended questions, which required qualitative answers, were included in order to provide information on whether or not the closed question coverage was full enough, to seek out unanticipated problem areas, to improve the accuracy of the total analysis (by tapping salient issues) and as a means of checking the reliability of the quantitative answers.

The demographic questions asked for information on length of service, age range and gender. Respondents were asked to indicate how long they had worked for the company by ticking one of the following categories:

Less than 2 years
Over 2 but less than 5 years
Over 5 but less than 10 years
Over 10 years

Respondents were asked to indicate their age by ticking the appropriate box of the following ranges: under 20, 20–29, 30–45 and over 45.

While further analysis, for example, by grade or location might have been useful the personnel manager was keen to ensure confidentiality and with some small offices this could have been jeopardised. Further steps to ensure confidentiality included posting the questionnaire to the employees' home addresses and including a stamped addressed envelope for their return rather than the company's internal mail system.

A pilot survey of five non-employees was carried out to rectify ambiguity, readability problems, response clarity and grammatical correctness. Following a number of minor corrections to the survey instrument the questionnaire was despatched to the 180 employees of the company.

The survey results

The response rate to the opinion survey was 42 per cent; of which 72 per cent of respondents were male and 28 per cent female. This compares with the proportions of total staff employed which are 62 per cent male and 38 per cent female.

For the series of closed questions a score of one was given for an expression of satisfaction, i.e. a true answer to a positive statement or a false answer to a negative question. These were totalled to give a composite job satisfaction measure for each respondent, up to a maximum possible score of 67. The mean composite score, calculated by dividing the total number of expressions of satisfaction by the total number of respondents, was 35.

Statistical analyses were conducted to establish relationships between the demographic data and composite job satisfaction scores. A T-Test showed no significance in the difference between males and females at the 5 per cent probability level and the difference could have occurred by chance. The Pearson Product Moment Correlation was used to assess the relationship between job satisfaction and length of service and between job satisfaction and age. Both results were non-significant.

Results of closed questions

The results of this part of the questionnaire are shown in Figure 14.2–14.6 under the five headings previously identified. The figure to the right of the statement is the percentage of the survey responding 'true' and the number in parentheses is the number of the question in the questionnaire.

Results of open questions

Some employees put considerable effort into their responses to these questions; verbally fluent respondents produced long lists of responses, often written or typed on extra sheets of paper and attached to the questionnaire. Open-ended questions were coded by the personnel manager into response categories in order to bring out patterns in the data. Categories were decided by first listing all responses given and then organising them into groups. Responses were subsequently allocated to these categories. Each time an issue was mentioned it was entered into the relevant category. The questions and their grouped responses are shown below.

(i) General Satisfaction Issues

(1)	I am content with my employment at the present time	50%
(66)	I am not satisfied with my employment at the present time	46%
(36)	I feel that my job is fairly secure	30%
(18)	I have a low stress job	47%
(45)	My work carries too much responsibility	11%
(4)	My work bores me	13%
(27)	I consider myself to be quite competitive	88%
(48)	I am willing to put myself out to help the company	81%
(52)	My job is worth doing	93%
(34)	My work gives me a sense of achievement	78%
(53)	I enjoy doing work which is challenging	99%
(60)	My work offers no challenge	16%
(44)	Omega demands high standards of workmanship	64%
(5)	I take pride in producing a quality piece of work	99%
(54)	I wish I had more time to produce better quality work	70%
(55)	My work has sufficient variety	80%
(64)	I often learn new things in the course of my work	75%
(56)	I wish my job gave me more scope for learning new things	75%
(51)	Working for this company is depressing	40%

Fig 14.2

(ii) Communication Issues

(21)	The existence of a mission statement would help me in my work	60%
(57)	This company would benefit from having a greater number of formal policies	57%
(29)	I have little control over things that effect me at work	68%
(22)	I feel frustrated by things over which I have no control at work	80%
(3)	I am often asked my opinion about job-related issues	41%
(61)	Being asked my opinion about matters at work is important to me	92%
(43)	I would like to be more involved in decision making	63%
(63)	I receive regular feedback on my work from my superiors	38%
(67)	My immediate superior understands the complexities of my job well	67%
(50)	My immediate superior keeps me well informed about company issues	24%
(9)	I never know what's going on in other regions	84%
(65)	I would be able to work more effectively if I knew more about activities in the rest of the company	45%
(15)	The company newsletter is of little interest to me	48%
(11)	I read the financial results of the company with interest	51%

Fig 14.3

(iii) Fairness/Supervision Issues

(30)	I prefer to work without close supervision	95%
(16)	I am left to my own devices at work	76%
(2)	I am paid fairly for the work I do	34%
(49)	My work is undervalued	60%
(47)	My abilities are well used at work	52%
(17)	I am fairly treated by my immediate superior	89%
(20)	Omega does not treat its employees well	61%
(46)	Favouritism plays a part in promotions in this company	52%
(6)	My personal workspace is adequate	72%
(59)	The management of the company care about the conditions in which we work	22%
(10)	Lack of management support limits my productivity	54%

Fig 14.4

(iv) Involvement/Identification Issues

(40)	I stay with the company because I like my colleagues	42%
(7)	Working for Omega gives me a strong sense of belonging to a group	23%
(42)	I do not hold shares in the company	91%
(28)	I participate in the share options scheme	22%
(33)	I often discuss work-related matters with people outside the company e.g. family and friends	42%
(58)	I would recommend a friend to work for Omega	43%

Fig 14.5

The first question sought further information from those respondents who believed that the company would benefit from having a greater number of formal policies (question 57 under the heading of (ii) communication issues) and these employees were asked to 'Please give an indication of the sort of policies you feel would be useful'. The responses mainly fell into the personnel category (mentioned 14 times). Others identified included sales and marketing (7) and production issues such as job control and contracts management (6).

When asked 'What is the most rewarding aspect of your job?' replies typically included comments such as, 'producing a useful product', 'obtaining a new client' and 'doing a good days work'. This category of responses was given the title 'esteem needs' and 54 items fell into this category.

(v) Issues Relating to Other Jobs/Companies

(8)	I study the situations vacant column regularly	44%
(35)	Our competitors treat their staff better than this company does	64%
(26)	If I want to leave this company I could find a comparable job quite easily	47%
(32)	I have not applied for a job with a different company this year	32%
(13)	I anticipate still being with this company in two years time	62%
(14)	I anticipate still being with this company in five years time	23%
(23)	If the company offered to do one thing to improve my job I would ask for an increase to my wage/salary	34%
(24)	If the company offered to do one thing to improve my job I would ask for better fringe benefits	2%
(25)	If the company offered to do one thing to improve my job I would ask for improvement to an aspect of my work which does not directly relate to pay or benefits	58%
(37)	If another company offered me a 5% increase in salary to join them, I would leave	27%
(38)	If another company offered me a 10% increase in salary to join them, I would leave	52%
(39)	If another company offered me a 15% increase in salary to join them, I would leave	75%
(31)	I would like to start my own business one day	30%
(62)	If I didn't need the money, I would choose not to work at all	39%
(19)	If I won a large amount of money I would continue to work in full time employment	31%
(41)	Money is important but it is not the most important aspect of my job	89%
(12)	My salary from Omega is the only source of income in my household	27%

Fig 14.6

Responses which involved growth, e.g. 'challenge' or 'encountering new processes' were allocated to a different category of self-development since they appeared to imply a need for training and promotion. Eight items were allocated to this category.

The next question explored the employees' frustrations at work and asked for a response to the following statement: 'The most frustrating aspect of my work is:'. The largest number (26 in total) fell into the category of extrinsic job issues such as administration, lack of support, monotony and lack of materials. Other categories were: working conditions (4 items), the future (5), reward issues (10), people problems (11) and communications (6 items).

When asked 'Thinking about your job at the present time, what things do you particularly like about it?' the responses fell into categories similar to those concerning the rewarding aspects of the job. Esteem needs were the highest represented with 26 items and 12 were allocated to development needs.

The next question was similarly phrased but asked respondents to state those things that, at the present time, they particularly *disliked* about their jobs. Twenty of these were allocated to the category of production issues, e.g. lack of support, time pressures, price squeeze, being non-productive and lack of technology. Other issues mentioned were pay and benefits (10 items), working conditions (9), concern for the future (7) and people issues such as 'irritating people', 7 items.

Respondents were then asked 'For what reason do you think the company is in business?' The majority of responses (53) fell into the profit/power category. Other responses were allocated to the service provision category (9) and 2 to the provision of employment while 1 simply answered 'ask a silly question'. The personnel manager noted that many responses were written in capital letters or marked with exclamation marks, underlining or some other emphasis. Some of the answers had what the personnel manager saw as a barbed note, e.g. 'to make a big bonus for management'.

The next two open questions explored employees' perceptions of the strengths and weaknesses of the company. When asked 'Thinking about Omega as a whole, what would you say are its strong points?', the categories and the number of responses allocated to each were as follows; workforce qualities (26 items), historical strengths, e.g. client base, reputation, customer confidence (16), organisational strengths, e.g. versatility, persistence (13), financial strength (6) and technical strengths (2). In response to the question 'Thinking about Omega as a whole what would you say are its weak points?' the most common responses (29 in total) fell into the management and investment coded group e.g., 'poorly negotiated contracts', 'lack of investment in technology'. The other categories that scored highly were: future planning (17), treatment of employees (14) and communication issues (12).

By asking the next question, 'If I could realistically change one part of my job, it would be:' the personnel manager hoped to glean information on the specific issues which respondents dislike about their jobs. The highest number of responses (17) fell into the category of organisation, e.g. 'reduce administration'. Thirteen were allocated to the immediate environment category, e.g., better equipment, while 11 responses mentioned a wish for increased responsibility or greater involvement in decision making.

The next question 'Of all the things that concern me about this company the most important is:' produced the following responses. Concern with the future was expressed by 29 respondents, management and policy, and treatment of employees had 10 responses each. A small number mentioned communications.

When asked 'Omega is a successful company because:' 22 respondents simply wrote 'is it?'. Twenty of the responses referred to the workforce. Other responses included market share (10), operational standards (10) while a smaller number (7) mentioned exploitation, e.g., redundancies and low wages bill.

The last open question asked employees to respond to the following statement 'The times when I have seriously considered leaving the company have been triggered by:' Of the responses to this question, 27 fell into the reward/security category; 13 into communications; 4 were to do with job content and 3 into the people category, e.g., 'dislike for another employee'. However, 23 items were allocated by the personnel manager to a category of frustration, e.g. 'lack of respect', 'being treated like a machine', 'unfair promotions', and 'lack of support'.

The final question was closed and asked respondents to answer yes or no to the following statement: 'If you had been sent this questionnaire to me a year ago, my answers would have been largely the same.' Eighty three per cent answered 'yes'.

ACTIVITY BRIEF

1 *Critically assess the form and content of the attitude survey used by the personnel manager identifying both strengths and weaknesses.*

2 *What further action could be taken to overcome the weaknesses you have identified?*

3 *What other approaches could the personnel manager have used to assess employee attitudes and what advantage would these provide?*

Assume you are the Personnel Manager of Omega Technical Services Ltd.

4 *What conclusions do you draw form the survey concerning the current state of employee attitudes at the company?*

5 *Prepare a set of recommendations based upon the results of the questionnaire that you feel will lead to improved job satisfaction amongst the employees of the company. Your recommendations should be supported with reasons and indicate the benefits that should result from their implementation.*

6 *Draft an action plan for the implementation of your recommendations identifying implications for broader organisational issues such as culture and management style.*

RECOMMENDED READING

Mullins, L. J. (1993). *Management and Organisational Behaviour,* Third edition, London: Pitman, Chapters 14 & 15.

Robbins, S. P. (1993). *Organizational Behaviour: Concepts, Controversies, and Applications,* Sixth edition, New Jersey: Prentice Hall, Chapter 6.

McCormick, E. J. and Ilgen D. (1987). *Industrial and Organisational Psychology,* Eighth edition, London: Routledge.

Quality improvement in Pall Europe

Roger Page and Alan Peacock

This case describes the implementation of a quality improvement process in an international organisation and in particular considers the links between the organisations's product base, culture and management style at the British-based organisation Pall Europe and relates these to the philosophy of total quality improvement. It reinforces the need to consider quality improvement as the responsibility of everyone in the organisation and how this needs to be related closely to the needs of people both inside and outside the organisation.

A central feature of the application of quality improvement within Pall Europe is the perception of senior managers that systems and procedures introduced must fit the culture of the organisation and match the needs of the organisation with the needs of employees. Four leading principles have been identified which senior managers believe are central to the successful implementation of the process, all of which focus on aspects of organisational behaviour and reinforce the theme that quality improvement depends on the quality and commitment of people.

BACKGROUND

The Pall Corporation is an international organisation with approximately 6,250 employees worldwide, operating from three centres located in the US, UK and Japan. The US base trades with America, Canada and Brazil. The Japanese base trades with countries around the Pacific rim and the UK base deals with Europe, Africa, Australia and New Zealand.

The company was formed in 1946 in the US by Dr Pall who was an entrepreneurial scientist and inventor. The original product was a porous stainless steel product which filtered out impurities in fluids. In the 1950s Dr Pall developed a new generation of disposable filters that facilitate the process of fluid clarification. Fluid clarification can be a complex process but simply described means that impurities, particulates and debris can be filtered out of liquids and gases. Complete removal of bacteria from pharmaceutical products and air is an example of this.

As the business in the US expanded in the 1960s, Abe Krasnoff, an accountant, by that time was chief executive officer. Abe proved to have expert business knowledge and a charismatic style of leadership that made an impact on the growth potential of the organisation. Abe's personality and business acumen coupled with Dr Pall's products and ideas proved to be a powerful formula that successfully developed the organisation as a world leader in the specialised field of fluid clarification. Abe's charismatic leadership resulted in the development of positive staff attitudes towards the goals of the organisation and promoted an organisational culture of mutual trust and understanding between all staff. Care was also taken to ensure that Pall products were provided with a large customer support activity that today not only includes the usual sales and market services but also a strong scientific and laboratory service that is able to provide detailed advice and guidance on specific customer problems or requirements at no additional charge.

While today the product range covers a number of filtration processes, two medical applications introduced in the 1980s illustrate the nature and quality of products produced by Pall and the confidence limits required by customers. By 1980 Dr Pall had developed nylon filters for sterilising pharmaceutical products and in 1987 filters were developed for removing white cells from blood. Both these products demonstrate the degree of quality and reliability required of Pall products. Failure to operate in accordance with specification will almost certainly result in a life threatening situation for the unfortunate patient.

Against this background three central corporate values have emerged:

● Ethical – Standards promoted by the organisation must conform to all regulatory requirements and in addition the organisation requires that all information projected about the company and its products must be correct and be proved to be correct. All dealings with customers and staff must be seen to be honest and straightforward.
● Market position – Pall continues to operate in the narrow niche market of fluid clarification and current forecasts indicate that there is still room for growth in this market.
● Technological products – The nature of products will continue to be characterised by their technological nature with the required organisational structure and large customer support activity.

Pall Europe

Pall Europe was formed in 1964 under the direction of Maurice Hardy, a British engineer. Maurice managed and integrated the UK and European organisations using the corporate values outlined above and was particularly successful in implementing organisational structures and systems that took due account of cultural differences. The centre of European activity is based in England but with organisations based in France, Germany, Italy, Spain and Switzerland. Each of these organisations is managed by a director who is a national of that country and a board member of Pall Europe. Pall Europe currently employs approximately 2,250 employees with some 1,450 based in the UK. Abe Krasnoff has recently retired from his executive position and Maurice Hardy has taken on Abe's worldwide responsibilities. Two senior directors are now responsible for managing Pall Europe. One is Derek Williams, a charismatic leader, who is a good organiser and communicator with highly developed interpersonal skills and the ability to motivate staff. The other is Don Nichols who has demonstrated exceptional skills as a market strategist and given a considerable impetus to sales. Pall Europe has now achieved a size equal to that of the US business.

All Pall employees enjoy good conditions of service and the company is moving towards single status conditions for manual workers and staff. Statistics indicate a pattern of a loyal, stable workforce, with long service, low labour turnover and a perception by staff of organisational growth matched to reward patterns and resultant career opportunity. Middle and senior managers are largely long-serving employees who have progressed with the company. This is seen to promote what has been described by a senior manager as a 'horizontal management structure' where experienced long-serving managers know the organisation well and require less direction from their line managers than new staff.

THE SITUATION

In appraising their future business strategy Maurice Hardy together with his senior executives at Pall considered possible initiatives that would reinforce the organisation's corporate values and determined that it was time to introduce a quality improvement programme that would:

- Improve existing levels of profitability in the difficult economic climate.
- Relate to customer needs more closely by ensuring that good quality products are delivered on time.
- Reduce time spent on corrective action (estimated as 25 per cent of time spent at work).
- Ensure conformity to existing product liability requirements and to promote product reliability beyond these levels.
- Relate closely to the nature of business and cost structure.

Having agreed in principle to the idea of quality improvement, senior managers were charged with looking at possible ways of introducing the concept to all Pall organisations. Consultants were required who could demonstrate :

- A proven track record of successfully introducing quality improvement programmes into multinational organisations.

- A good international reputation as consultants.
- That the suggested programme would fit the culture of Pall.

Presentations were obtained from various interested consultants and a decision reached to appoint Crosby Associates (now Proudfoot Crosby). They provided the framework and support for nominated Pall Corporation staff who received extensive training in the total quality philosophy and framework which was developed and customised to suit the culture and value system of Pall and the structure of each work location.

The second phase of training involved all employees in Pall Corporation. Management consultants provided three months intensive training to a designated manager who then trained master instructors. Together they trained senior executives who received intensive training in two or three day periods, middle managers received training one day per week for six months and shop-floor workers were trained for half an hour to an hour a week for six months. This exercise was introduced some six months later in Pall Europe.

The basic philosophy of quality improvement promoted is that all policies procedures and practices of the organisation can be improved, and every employee can contribute towards that improvement. Improvements should be considered as positive experiences and no blame should be allocated to past performance.

Four leading principles have been identified with this process of quality improvement:

- Quality means conformance to requirements.
- Prevention and removal of root cause is the true sign of quality – a quick 'fix' is not sufficient.
- The standard for quality is zero defects.
- Quality should be measured by the price of non-conformance (PONC) and quantified in financial terms even if this is estimated. (The cost of not doing it right the first time.)

In order to implement the system of quality improvement an organisational structure was designed and implemented. The structure adopted was that quality work groups would consider quality improvements relating to their role in the organisation. Figure 15.1 is a simplified illustration of the structure adopted for the Total Quality Performance Process (TQPP) at the Portsmouth site; it follows the same pattern and complements the structure of the existing management hierarchical structure. Quality work groups appoint leaders to report to designated line managers who form corrective action sub-committees reporting to a quality improvement team and then on to the quality improvement co-ordinating committee.

At each level in the structure each team and committee is encouraged to consider the four principles outlined previously.

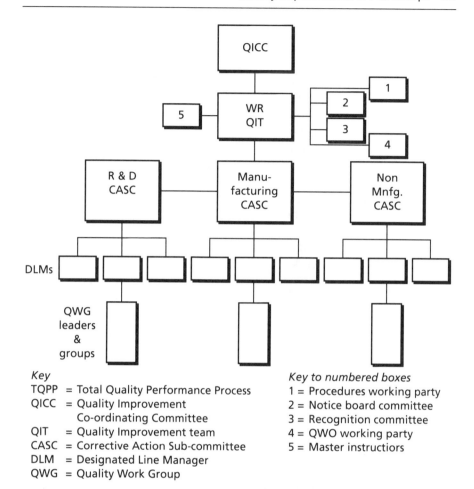

Fig 15.1 Pall Portsmouth TQPP organisation structure

Managers are expected to recognise the need to integrate the quality improvement process into everyday business activities and to demonstrate this by their own behaviour. The following guidelines issued to managers indicate this philosophy:

1. Develop a shared sense with all employees of what your respective organisations are trying to do, where each is going and how it fits into the goals and objectives of the corporation.
2. Put more emphasis on recognising individual performance that meets or exceeds expectations rather than focusing on the negatives. However, poor performance needs to be corrected and can only be successful if it is done constructively.
3. Provide employees with structure and collaborate with them to establish goals and targets critical to success and, when appropriate, be directive in assigning work.

4. Don't steal the glory from your subordinates and co-workers by hugging centre stage or giving long-winded presentations.
5. Learn to be less insistent upon always getting your own way and try to give greater credence to the opinions and solutions of co-workers.
6. Lead by example through your own dedication and work ethic and set high personal standards and work hard to meet commitments.
7. Ensure that all employees have both responsibility and accountability for their actions and objectives. Assign ownership.
8. Treat others with mutual respect. Important to maintain quality working relationships.
9. Don't take important actions without considering the down-side consequences of your decision.
10. Tie reward systems to behavioural change rather than endorsing past practices.

(Quoted from Paul Kohn 1993, Pall Corporation)

A structured approach to problem solving has been introduced with the assistance of a process model worksheet which is illustrated by Figure 15.2. This can be used as a checklist to ensure that the required inputs, outputs as well as the facilities and equipment required during the process can be identified. An example of the process working effectively and an evaluation of benefits obtained can be illustrated by considering the model applied to the process of routine meetings within the company.

Before attending a scheduled meeting attendees should determine what performance standards are required and be clear what they can contribute in terms of outputs. Everyone is expected to prepare thoroughly for the meeting so that time spent during the meeting provides maximum added value. If an individual does not contribute to the meeting and receives no measurable output (e.g. information that will be valuable to them and the organisation) they have not added value to, or received value from, the meeting and therefore should not have attended.

A further example of an issue addressed by a quality improvement team at the Portsmouth Walton Road location was to consider improvements to the internal postal delivery system operating between four sites and a main office block in the Portsmouth area. Post for internal distribution was delivered to the security gate and then sorted and taken to a central point in four sites by Pall security staff who travelled on a scheduled circuit twice per day. They also collected mail at each site at the same time for onward delivery. Administrative staff in each location were then responsible for distributing mail to different locations on their site. This system worked reasonably well but caused some frustrations when urgent mail became delayed. The quality work team have devised a system that first identifies urgent mail; arranges for this to be collected from a particular location and then promotes fast delivery of that mail by security staff on their normal circuit but to the particular postal address on each site. In this way same morning delivery is guaranteed for urgent mail. Savings have been calculated by considering the time saved less additional time spent on the quality improvement process. The *price for non-conformance* (PONC) has been quantified and estimated at a saving of some £2,000 per year.

At the other end of the PONC scale, improvement programmes in manufacturing areas have examined ways of reducing scrap during production and at a conservative estimate save £250,000 per year.

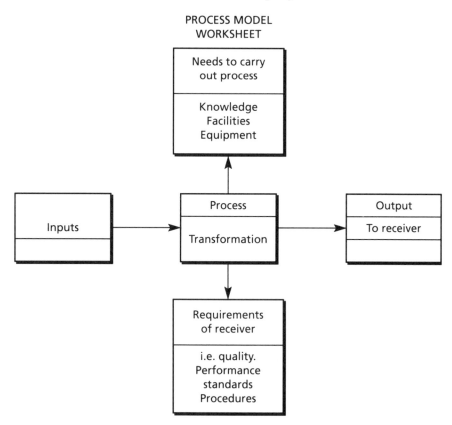

Examples of inputs and outputs

Input	*Process*	*Output*
1 Information	*Write report*	Report.
2 Test specimen	*Testing of specimen*	Report on performance of
3 Untrained student	*University course*	test specimen.
		Trained (educated, qualified) person.
4 Student with little understanding of OB	*OB module*	Student with good understanding of theories, experimental work and relationships in OB.
5 Group of people with no consensus and agreed goal	*Meeting to discuss and agree objectives and action*	Group of people co-ordinated and with a common objective.

Fig 15.2 Process model worksheet

Pall have recently extended the process to undertake improvement programmes with their customers and suppliers. These have not only resulted in financial benefits to the parties involved but also created better service, removed unnecessary paperwork and strengthened trust between customers and suppliers.

Staff are not rewarded financially for their personal contribution to quality improvement but recognition is given by senior managers who attend meetings and who are therefore aware of individual contributions and actively praise and encourage staff. Public recognition is given on quality notice boards.

In the UK there is a view that public recognition is somewhat embarrassing, but in the US an award of 'Quality Employee of the Month' provides public recognition by offering a reserved car parking space to the employee near to their workplace and also by publicising the award in internal newssheets and notice boards. For many years an employee suggestion scheme has operated successfully in Pall Europe and employees are rewarded financially for ideas adopted under this separate process. This system is still running alongside the quality improvement programme.

ACTIVITY BRIEF

1 *Identify the predominant culture and management style prevailing in Pall Europe and demonstrate by citing examples from the case how these factors have affected the implementation of the quality improvement process.*

2 *What factors will influence the motivation of staff towards continued quality improvement, and how can senior managers use this information to realise organisational goals?*

3 *Use the process model worksheet shown in Figure 15.2 to consider possible quality improvements to a process that organisations encounter regularly (e.g. a routine administrative process) and demonstrate a suitable way of quantifying the PONC.*

RECOMMENDED READING

Child, J. (1984). *Organisations: A Guide to Problems and Practice*, Second Edition, London: Paul Chapman.

Mullins, L. J. (1993). *Management of Organisational Behaviour*, Parts 6 & 7, London: Pitman.

Oakland, S. O. (1993). *Total Quality Management*, Oxford: Butterworth-Heinemann.

Woodward, J. (1980). *Industrial Organisation: Theory and Practice*, Second Edition, Oxford: Oxford University Press.

Quality of Working Life and Total Quality Management, November 1991. ACAS Work Research Unit Occasional Paper, No. 50.

Neighbourhood Textiles Ltd –
Motivation and performance in a 'top-down' co-operative development project

David Young and Tony Emerson

This case study is based upon one of the authors' experience of involvement in the development and support of a small textiles business; Neighbourhood Textiles Ltd. The project was set up by a London local authority ('Southminster') as a local economic development initiative, and developed initially by a local resource group, subsequently by the Neighbourhood Textiles Steering Committee. These groups identified the market opportunity, opted for a type of co-operative legal structure, and recruited staff for the new business. The case thus provides an illustration of the 'top-down' model (Paton and Emerson, 1988) of local co-operative economic development. The reader should be aware that significantly different models exist. Cited references provide a guide to context, critiques and alternatives.

Neighbourhood Textiles Ltd has been the subject of several studies. These include the initial feasibility studies, various internal reports, an external consultants' evaluation and a substantive case study by one of the authors – for which acknowledgement is made of the support of Rob Paton and the Co-operatives Research Unit at the Open University.

This account draws upon these reports, focusing chiefly upon issues around potential and performance, motivation and morale, within the workforce. These human resource factors are linked to management systems and business structure, and to their impact upon commercial performance, through the development, launch and trading life of the business.

Although simplified in this account, this case remains complex and controversial. Two aids to the reader have therefore been provided - a diagram of stakeholders (Figure 16.1), and a summary chronology of events (Appendix 1).

BACKGROUND

Faced by the decline of local manufacturing industry, high and rising levels of local unemployment, and shrinking employment and training opportunities for local school leavers, the London borough of Southminster decided to act. Like many other local authorities, Southminster saw an opportunity to tackle these problems through local economic development initiatives.

In intervening in the local economy, Southminster sought to create secure jobs and vocational training opportunities for local people. Politically, the council was keen on positive action to combat labour market discrimination, and was attracted to co-operative models of social ownership, as a way of promoting socially responsible, small enterprises. A 'top-down' model of local economic development was also attractive, since it apparently offered a way of using council resources to identify market opportunities, to set up firms to exploit these opportunities, and to recruit and train local people to take over the management of these firms, on a co-operative basis.

THE PRE-LAUNCH PHASE

A commercial opportunity

Accordingly, Southminster established a local resource group, made up of council officers and local councillors, one of whom was also a professional management consultant – consultant Q. The resources group drew up plans for an 'industrial community resource', a light industrial complex related to its local area, providing attractive employment with good facilities (e.g. crèche, canteen), and including a number of small 'seedbed' workspaces for new businesses. The creation of 30, rising to 50, jobs was projected.

Further feasibility research identified an opportunity for a 'cut, make and trim' (CMT) textiles firm specialising in ladies' medium to high quality fashion outerwear, sub-contracting machining work from designers and manufacturers. The feasibility study indicated that commercial viability would depend upon careful management of product quality, distribution, costing and pricing.

Key factors for commercial success would be:

- A core of skilled and efficient production workers.
- Prompt and reliable product distribution.
- Effective product quality control.
- Effective costing and pricing strategy.
- Good relations with (initially supportive) trade customers.

A meeting of Southminster Council and local voluntary organisations approved the feasibility study report, and backed the proposal to apply to the Department of Environment (DoE) for Urban Programme funding for the project.

The Steering Committee

The resource group, including consultant Q, then became absorbed into the Neighbourhood Textiles Steering Committee, which also included additional Southminster Council officers and councillors, potential future co–operative workers, and potential users of the workshop space. The Steering Committee's role was to bring the project to fruition. It thus aimed:

- To develop the feasibility study into an operable business plan.
- To raise finance, applying to the DoE for Urban Programme funding, and to the Employment Department (ED) for funding under the Enterprise Workshops Scheme (EWS).
- To identify suitable premises.
- To commence negotiations on a premises lease.
- To prepare premises for eventual occupation.
- To identify, and register under, a suitable type of co-operative limited liability legal structure.

Ultimately, the committee aimed to be in a position to transfer all management responsibility to the users of the Neighbourhood Textiles' site.

Premises, funding and the pace of development

Problems now arose in connection with premises. Southminster Council Valuers Department helped in the identification of a suitable site. Negotiations proved complex and time-consuming. The freeholders insisted upon onerous conditions, including a ten-year guarantee of rent. The Steering Committee could not provide this, nor was the council legally able to provide it. Ultimately, the council itself took on the lease, in part because it had by now invested considerably in architectural work on the site.

This delay affected both funding applications, and thus the pace of the project's development. In November of Year 2 the DoE approved the Urban Programme application for the following financial year (Year 3/4). Delays in negotiating the lease meant that the project could not be implemented at the start of this period. By the time implementation was possible, the terms of the original Urban Programme application were seriously out of date. Costings, particularly architect's estimates, had risen well beyond the rate of inflation over the period.

In the meantime, the ED EWS funding application faced problems caused by the ED's failure to clarify its support criteria. Eventually, in May of Year

3, approval was given, subject to the inspection of Neighbourhood Textiles' lease. This was not then available, and before it could be supplied, the ED was subject to public expenditure cuts which caused Neighbourhood Textiles' application to be scrapped.

To save the project, the Steering Committee negotiated revised terms with the DoE for Urban Programme funding. This came at a price, requiring a revised business plan showing a more rapid build-up of business to generate stronger cash flow, and a concomitant increase in commercial risk.

The development of the project now increased in pace. The Steering Committee rapidly appointed a production manager, on full salary, who joined in work towards the commercial launch of Neighbourhood Textiles Ltd. Under the influence of the new production manager, implementing the revised business plan, the launch timescale was shortened, the planned worker induction and training programme was reduced, and the recruitment programme for production workers was accelerated and revised. The original aim of recruiting local workers to be trained up to required production standards was replaced by a (stated) policy of recruiting workers who were 'already experienced and skilled'. Despite the adoption of this policy, there was no evidence to suggest that the local labour market could supply adequate quantities of suitably skilled workers. For precisely this reason the

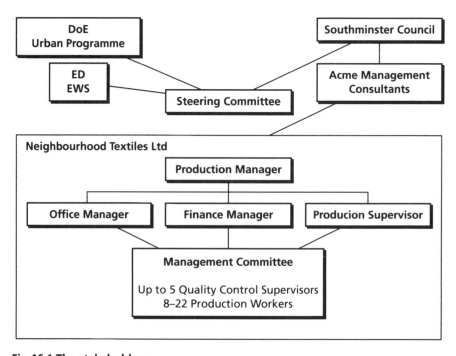

Fig 16.1 The stakeholders

original feasibility study had emphasised the need to recruit, then train, production workers in-house.

No sooner were these developments under way than, in December, the ED reversed its decision on EWS funding to Neighbourhood Textiles. After prolonged discussion, the Steering Committee agreed to decline this offer, preferring to maintain the revised business plan in order to avoid further disruption and delay.

Recruitment

From late in Year 2, the Steering Committee leafleted local housing estates, collecting the names of potential production workers and supervisors, plus crèche, canteen and ancillary workers. Contact with these people was maintained through the pre-launch period, and included invitations to attend meetings of the Steering Committee. In retrospect, the Steering Committee secretary felt that it was implied at this stage that there would be 'work for all', regardless of skills or experience.

In March, Year 3, prospective production workers were invited to take part in a machining skills test and informal interviews. Prospective supervisors and managerial staff were invited for informal interviews. Interviews were conducted by a panel consisting of the (then prospective) production manager and two members of the Steering Committee (one of whom had textile machining experience). This event was set up on the following basis:

1. Prospective supervisors and managers to observe machinists at work.
2. Prospective machinists to observe the prospective supervisors and managers observing them.
3. The Steering Committee panel to observe all parties.
4. All parties to report independently to the Steering Committee panel.

In July, a second round of interviews for prospective staff was held. The two principal criteria officially under consideration were trade skills and commitment to co-operative working.

Subsequent accounts suggest that problems arose in the recruitment process. Few of those who attended in July had attended in March. The Steering Committee secretary thought only three. No machining tests were given to those attending in July. A machinist who *did* attend in March and in July was not sure if she had been judged competent; considered the recruitment questionnaire to consist of leading questions; and knew of at least one other successful applicant who had lied about her skills and experience at interview. The production supervisor later recalled the appointment of several people with inadequate machining skills. One of these was asked informally to leave, but was subsequently appointed as a quality control supervisor, because in the opinion of her colleagues, 'she was such a positive co-op member'. The production supervisor had four years' (but not in the last eight) experience of machining. Expressing initial misgivings on taking up her post, she was advised by the production manager 'not to worry, it's like riding a bicycle'. In her later judgement the entire recruitment process was 'haphazard and confused'.

The recruitment process created a pool of prospective workers. These were drawn upon in two intakes.

THE POST-LAUNCH PHASE

Staff induction and training

Neighbourhood Textiles Co-operative Ltd was launched in December of Year 3. Year 4 began, prior to the commencement of production, with an induction and training programme for the first intake (Intake 1) of eight production workers. These workers had no prior experience of co-operative working, and so a week-long programme was provided, to introduce them to their rights and obligations, systems and procedures, effective participation in meetings including role plays, and a visit to a another working co-operative, in order to prepare them for their participation in co-operative management decision making.

Evaluation of this programme indicated that it was a success overall, generating marked increases in participants' enthusiasm and confidence. Nevertheless, further training in co-operative decision making, although planned, was not carried out. Intake 1 eventually became an 'inner core' among the production workers, with greater collective identity, cohesion and lower turnover, than among subsequent recruits.

The 14 workers of Intake 2 joined in March, Year 4. Consultant Q later recalled that the production manager had insisted upon recruiting at this time, although ahead of the recruitment plan in the revised business plan. No clear reason was given. Each Intake 2 worker had been led to expect a formal interview and a machining test, prior to starting work. These did not take place, because the production manager instructed the office manager to treat them all as immediately 'ready for work'.

Intake 2 received little or no formal training, apart from a brief talk on co-operative working, and a variety of informal machining tests. These were not consistent, and unlike real production tasks. In one case the production supervisor considered a new recruit's work to be inadequate. The production manager asked to state her case in his presence, plus that of the office manager, and the new recruit. Following this, the recruit was retained. She left some time later.

Performance and quality

Neighbourhood Textiles was now in production. However, according to several machinists, production targets were not set during the first five months of trading, and then only in the form of *averages*. The revised business plan recommended *individual* target-setting for workers, in consultation with the production supervisor.

As a result, machinists experienced feedback in exclusively negative terms – when the production supervisor returned faulty work to them. The following notes were taken during a Management Committee meeting in May:

> Worker X blamed quality of material in relation to machinery being used. Production manager blamed people for not notifying production supervisor immediately when technical problems arose. Worker Y said some machinists were not working hard enough, and argued that people should be paid according to the work they did. Production manager and production supervisor supported this. Y then queried why the second batch of machinists had been taken on. Worker Z said production manager should be seen on the shop-floor more often – he would soon pick up who was working and who was not.

The Neighbourhood Textiles Management Committee report of July, Year 4, stated that; '. . . individual machinists' targets have not been specified. Both the production supervisor and machinists felt that the production manager spent too little time on the shop-floor, and gave too little support to the production supervisor'.

Quality control

Quality control was a problem throughout the life of Neighbourhood Textiles. Intake 1 workers were inclined to judge the work of Intake 2 workers as inferior. In February, a report to the Steering Committee from the Management Committee stated that a quality control supervisor had now been appointed, that 'a quality control system is almost set up', and that 'production quality is now acceptable'. This supervisor was appointed under circumstances discussed above. Management Committee minutes in April and May referred to continuing quality problems. A June minute stated that 'a quality control system will begin next week'.

The production supervisor later stated that, 'we spent a lot on materials because work was bodged'. She felt that quality criteria were unclear to all staff, and that the production manager was always inclined to pass work of questionable quality. Consultant Q stated that in July he discovered that there had been a 50 per cent wastage rate for garments, during a period when between two and five quality control supervisors had been employed. In his estimation, the quality control problem had been 'tackled' solely through the appointment of additional supervisors.

Staff appraisal, discipline and grievance procedures

The production manager had full disciplinary powers up to the point of final written warning. He routinely denied this, on the grounds that his contract of employment did not explicitly confer these powers. No formal disciplinary measures were taken throughout the life of Neighbourhood Textiles. Several 'stand up rows' occurred between the production supervisor and individual machinists – the production supervisor was often abused when returning poor quality work to machinists. In such cases, the production manager had a 'chat' with the machinist. There were no dismissals, although several machinists left during the life of the business; some seem to have been persuaded informally to leave, most commonly because of inadequate skills. Rumours concerning such matters were in continuous circulation, as well as rumours of conflict among managers.

In May, the Management Committee (MC) set up a Staff Disciplinary Committee, consisting of all four managers, plus three machinists. This proved deeply unpopular, and in practice never operated.

Payment

Two bonus schemes were proposed at Neighbourhood Textiles. An attendance and punctuality bonus was paid, although there was constant dispute over exact times of arrival and departure. A *shared* production bonus was also mooted, but never put into practice. An *individual* bonus scheme was not possible, since individual output was never measured. Briefly, a raffle draw for those arriving early was operated, but was dropped after drawing criticism. According to one machinist, the production bonus was 'not enough to stop you taking (paid) sick leave'. Apart from the official bonus schemes, it was also the practice of the production manager to make secret bonus payments to certain workers.

The production manager was employed on a salary of £18,000 p.a. (plus car) in August, Year 3. At his six-monthly salary review in the following January he requested an increase to £25,000. The Steering Committee agreed this on the grounds that it represented 'the market rate', and recommended it for approval by the MC. At a meeting from which the production manager declined to withdraw, the decision was ratified.

The secretary to the Steering Committee occasionally queried the production manager's expenses claims, including a visit to a Paris fashion exhibition. In doing so, he met strong opposition from the finance manager, who criticised his 'penny-pinching' attitude.

Both the original feasibility study and the revised business plan assumed a flat rate for management salaries during the first year of trading. The salary of the finance manager had been set at £8,000 p.a., but in March, Year 4, an increase to £11,000 p.a. was recommended by the Steering Committee to the MC. This was approved. The minute recording acceptance referred to a revised salary of £13,000 p.a., and was duly ratified. The increase was never explained or otherwise examined.

In May, salary increase requests from the office manager and the production supervisor were refused. The June wage review for production staff was postponed by general agreement, due to the financial position, and never took place.

Marketing

Consultant Q criticised the production manager's implementation of Neighbourhood Textiles' marketing strategy on the following grounds:

- The business plan strategy was not followed.
- Excessive resources were devoted to sample work on inappropriate products (heavy coats, bullet-proof vests).
- Advertising in trade journals was inadequate.
- Too few direct approaches were made to manufacturers and designers.
- The visit to the Paris fashion exhibition was not appropriate for a small CMT firm.
- The failure to distinguish between firm and speculative orders.

In retrospect, consultant Q suggested that the bulk of Neighbourhood Textiles' orders had been obtained by other managers, or by Steering Committee members, and very few by the production manager.

A major trade customer stated that they had plenty of work for Neighbourhood Textiles, but found the co-operative unreliable after initial orders had been met satisfactorily. Apparently, this customer at one point considered buying Neighbourhood Textiles out, so confident was it of the scope of market opportunity available to the co-operative.

The office manager stated that the production manager sometimes lied to clients about progress on their orders. A machinist recalled the production manager giving exaggerated estimates of productive capacity to a visiting customer, on the shop-floor.

According to consultant Q, Neighbourhood Textiles' costing and pricing practices were inappropriate, since the production manager was working from a handbook of standard industry mass production times, rather than using local measures. The office manager also suspected underpricing. When tackled on method, the production manager stated, 'it just comes with experience'.

Meetings and decision making

Apart from Steering Committee meetings, two types of meeting took place within Neighbourhood Textiles – formal Management Committee meetings and informal production meetings. The former took place during the working day, the latter usually on Friday evenings. In the opinion of one machinist, a great deal of negative feeling was expressed at meetings. In general, she did not feel it safe to raise and discuss controversial issues at meetings. She identified child care as a notable point of conflict. Women were always in a majority in the workforce. In her opinion, older women were inclined to resent the payment of child-minding and crèche fees to younger women workers, particularly in the common case where younger workers were unlikely to attend production meetings.

Independently, and at various times, the Steering Committee secretary, the office manager and the production supervisor stated that workers had discussed with them grievances that workers were unwilling to raise at meetings. Such grievances had often been raised initially with the production manager, but without satisfactory result. The Steering Committee secretary felt that, during meetings and at other times, the production manager was inclined; to 'put down' anyone making a complaint; to make false promises about future orders and work levels; to 'rant' about problems of productivity and punctuality, criticising offenders and non-offenders alike.

Financial reporting

During the trading life of Neighbourhood Textiles Ltd the variance between projected and actual commercial performance was marked. Figure 16.2 shows sales for the period January – August (Year 4). Figure 16.3 shows the cumulative trading deficit for the period.

In this period the Steering Committee held six meetings; the Management Committee held eight. In retrospect, both the Steering Committee secretary and one of the machinists expressed unease about the general conduct of

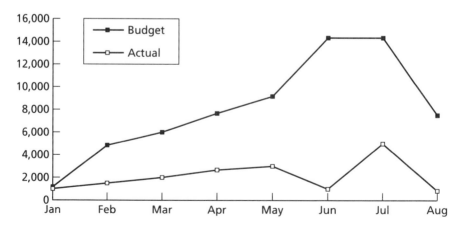

Fig 16.2 Sales

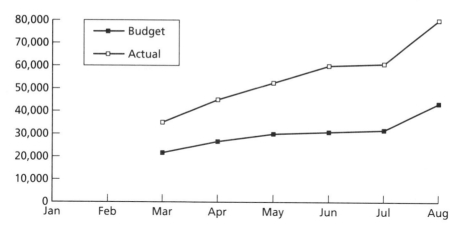

Fig 16.3 Cumulative deficit

Management Committee meetings. The office manager criticised the practice of rotating the chair at every meeting, which in her view caused poor quality chairing.

Financial reporting was principally the responsibility of the finance manager. At no more than 50 per cent of Steering Committee or Management Committee meetings in the period was a specific financial report presented. The reporting of financial information to all meetings was limited, optimistic, and usually inaccurate. There is no record of any meetings discussing financial performance indicators such as, for instance, sales revenue.

Amongst the workforce, awareness of the co-operative's true situation was slow to develop. The production supervisor first recalled 'some financial information' being posted up in July. In her opinion it was not understood, being 'just a load of figures' to everyone except the cutter, who spotted substantial inaccuracies. A machinist later stated that she 'had never understood' the figures supplied by the finance manager. Several workers referred to a rumoured incident in which the production manager had intercepted a financial report prepared by the finance manager, and altered it prior to its submission to Southminster Council.

In February, the Steering Committee was told by the production manager of several successfully acquired orders – most of which did not, in fact, materialise. The finance manager reported the installation of an accounting system which, 'is not producing information as fast as necessary but should be soon'. At the February Management Committee meeting, workers asked that financial information be presented clearly, simply and graphically. The finance manager's subsequent reports remained as tables of figures. 'More detailed figures' were promised 'as soon as possible'. These never materialised. Every worker of the several later consulted felt that the finance manager's presentations were difficult to understand.

In April, the Management Committee agenda included an item on 'Financial Report'. Discussion under this item focused almost entirely upon policy and costs concerning child-care payments, and was prolonged and heated. One line of argument was, 'Why should our bonuses be sacrificed to pay for their children?' Apart from this, as in February, the finance manager presented a further table of figures. This pattern of presentation and debate was repeated in the April Steering Committee meeting.

At the Management Committee meeting and AGM in June the production manager presented a report on forthcoming orders, pointing to:

- £40,000-worth of 'confirmed' CMT work.
- £22,000-worth 'pending'.
- £30,000 contract 'pending' from Ministry of Defence for bullet-proof vests.
- A 'highly lucrative export order' arising from the Paris visit.

He concluded by presenting the prospect of considerable overtime opportunities, and fifty extra vacancies for new machinists. None of this work came to fruition.

Financial crisis

Later in June the production manager asked Southminster Council to guarantee Neighbourhood Textiles' bank overdraft 'to cover a temporary peak deficit'. A financial report and projections accompanied the request. Southminster's corporate planning officer's reply described the information supplied as 'limited', and expressed concern over the co-operative's financial position. More detailed figures were requested, because, '. . . we cannot understand how the overheads figure is made up or how the sales forecast relates to the number of machinists and their productivity'. In July, Southminster Council made a small loan to Neighbourhood Textiles, a condition of which was full co-operation with Acme Management Consultants, appointed by the council to carry out a full investigation of the co-operative. The production manager took an immediate holiday, followed by sick leave. In September he left the country. Before leaving he attributed all Neighbourhood Textile's problems to its co-operative structure, 'which made effective management impossible'.

The report by Acme Management Consultants came, among others, to the following conclusions:

- Neighbourhood Textiles was 'one of the least efficient factories that we have ever experienced'.
- Quality control at Neighbourhood Textiles was 'non-existent'.
- Morale at Neighbourhood Textiles was 'the lowest that we have ever experienced'.

● 'The self-motivation that might be expected in a co-operative was not apparent'.

The report recommended a total reorganisation and complete retraining exercise. The consultants' report specifically noted that they did not wish to be considered for this work. Southminster accepted the report, but declined to act on its recommendations. By September, Neighbourhood Textiles Ltd was in formal liquidation.

ACTIVITY BRIEF

1 *According to the production manager, Neighbourhood Textiles' problems flowed entirely from its co–operative structure, 'which made effective management impossible'. Was Neighbourhood Textiles' commercial failure an inevitable result of its co–operative structure? Or could Neighbourhood Textiles have enjoyed commercial success as a co–operative? If so, what changes would have been necessary to achieve this, and how might its history have been different?*

2 *Neighbourhood Textiles was developed according to a classical 'top-down' model. Evaluate the impact of this development model upon communication, co–operation, motivation and morale within Neighbourhood Textiles' workforce. What other models might have been used in the development of the co–operative, and with what possible results?*

3 *In the judgement of Acme Management Consultants, 'The self–motivation that might be expected in a co–operative was not apparent'. Would you expect to find high levels of self–motivation in a co–operative? Why? What happened to this factor at Neighbourhood Textiles, and why?*

4 *Evaluate the significance of human resource factors in the performance of Neighbourhood Textiles Ltd. Overall, how would you evaluate the relative importance of human resource factors against other, 'non-human', factors in this case? To what extent do you consider that the distinction between human and other factors is valid in this case, and in general?*

5 *Give several examples of where, when and how you might have intervened in the management of Neighbourhood Textiles (a) as a production worker (b) as a member of the Steering Committee. In each case, state what you would expect to have been the consequences of your interventions.*

RECOMMENDED READING

Cornforth, C., Thomas, A., Lewis, J., and Spear, R. (1988). *Developing Successful Worker Co-operatives.* London: Sage.

Joyce, P., Woods, A., Montanheiro, L., and Zafiris, N. (1989). Workers' Co–operatives in North London: Democracy & Job Creation *Local Economy* 4, 3, November.

Mellor, M., Hannah, J. and Stirling, J. (1988). *Worker Co–operatives in Theory & Practice.* Open University Press.

Paton, R. and Emerson, T. (1988). '"Top-Down" and "Bottom-Up": Goodbye to All That?' *Local Economy*, 3, (3) November.

APPENDIX 1

Neighbourhood textiles: a chronology of events

Year 1   Southminster Borough Council establishes neighbourhood resource group.

Resource group, including management consultant Q, develops plans for a local 'Industrial Community Resource' – a textiles factory combined with independent small workshops. Feasibility report identifies an opportunity for a 'cut, make and trim' textiles business.

Southminster Council approves report and supports application to Department of Environment (DoE) for Urban Programme support.

Resource group merges into Neighbourhood Textiles Steering Committee, which takes responsibility for the further development of Neighbourhood Textiles. Application to Employment Department (ED) for Enterprise Workshop Scheme (EWS) funding submitted. Lease negotiations commence.

Year 2

November DoE agrees Urban Programme funding for financial year 3/4. Project development costs now rising sharply.

ED decision on EWS funding application delayed.

Steering Committee begins pre-recruitment process.

Year 3

March   Recruitment tests and interviews (1).

May   ED gives conditional EWS funding approval. Delay in lease negotiation delays acceptance.

July   Central government public expenditure cuts imposed on ED. All pending EWS projects scrapped – including Neighbourhood Textiles.

DoE agrees revised Urban Programme funding scheme to cover loss of ED EWS funding. This saves the project, but requires revised business plan and greater commercial risk.

Recruitment interviews (2).

August   Steering Committee appoints production manager, who implements revised business plan, affecting worker recruitment, induction and training programme.

December ED U–turn on EWS funding – funding offer restored. Steering Committee declines. production manager takes over more direct management responsibilities from Steering Committee.

Neighbourhood Textiles Co-operative Ltd registered and launched.

Year 4

January   Formal induction training for Intake 1 production workers.
          Production commences.

March   Intake 2 production workers join. No formal induction training pro-
          vided.

June   Financial crisis. Neighbourhood Textiles requests additional financial
          support from Southminster Council. Council requests further financial
          information.

July   Southminster Council provides small intermediate loan, and appoints
          independent consultants – Acme Management Consultants.

          Production manager on holiday, followed by sick leave.

          Southminster Council declines to adopt recommendations in Acme
          Management Consultants' survival plan.

September Production manager leaves the country.
          Neighbourhood Textiles goes into liquidation.

Brownloaf MacTaggart – Control and power in a management consultancy

Gary Akehurst

Watkins International is a long established firm of chartered accountants and management consultants, with international interests in accountancy and audit services, corporate finance, insolvency services, taxation and management consultancy. This case is concerned with one division of Watkins International, the Brownloaf MacTaggart Management Consultancy Division, which until merger with Watkins in 1988 had been a successful small engineering consultancy practice.

Moving from being a small, close-knit company to a small, insignificant division in an international corporate empire has created considerable tensions. Managerial control has changed rapidly from one of benevolent dictatorship to one of corporate uniformity. The end result has been a climate of intimidation, of unfair reward and punishment, uncertainty and mistrust, set against a backdrop of falling profits and plummeting morale.

This case is concerned with issues of managerial control and power among a group of highly qualified and initially, at least, highly energetic and enthusiastic professional consultants. Additional issues include changing culture within a rapidly changing organisation and how the position of senior managers can gradually change from one of respect and trust of judgement, to one of fear and loathing.

BACKGROUND

Brownloaf MacTaggart (BM) is the engineering consulting division of Watkins International, a large international firm of chartered accountants and management consultants.

Watkins was established as a chartered accountancy practice in 1893. Following decades of moderate growth it entered the management consultancy market in 1955 primarily as a 'spin-off' from audit and taxation work.

In the following years this diversification proved to be profitable. What had started as a very small sideline activity has developed into a multidivisional management consultancy business employing in the UK alone some 700 people. Worldwide Watkins employs around 70,000 people through a network of firms and associate firms. The international firm has at least one office in most countries, and in the early 1990s has established new offices, particularly in Eastern Europe.

Watkins has endeavoured to grow primarily by acquisition and internal growth, but acquisition has been by far the most successful strategy, particularly in the 1980s when a software development company and BM were acquired. The firm now has five consultancy divisions in the UK covering information technology and software engineering; public sector management; financial services and treasury; leisure and retailing; and general engineering.

Brownloaf MacTaggart and Co. had started business in 1962 as a two man partnership. Alex MacTaggart had been a successful production engineer, who had assiduously built up a long list of good contacts while working for blue chip engineering companies. Duncan Brownloaf had been a successful engineering company salesman selling diverse products such as hydraulic pit props and mining pump equipment. The two men combined their undoubted strengths by taking small premises in Walsall, in the West Midlands. The business flourished and in 1977, now employing 20 people, two additional employees were admitted into partnership – Heinrich Grubber, a German national, and William Smallpiece, a native of Shropshire.

The BM business flourished, establishing a good reputation for creative and practical solutions for engineering businesses across the world. Projects tended to be fairly small in value, averaging £10,000 to £15,000 (at current prices), with occasional larger assignments but clients were prestigious and BM gained a reputation as one of the top three in its specialised field. Success however, was to prove to be a double-edged sword.

Having admitted the two new partners, both founder partners were beginning to think of retirement. Duncan Brownloaf's health was failing and perhaps it was time for a change. In 1980 the company moved into bigger offices in the heart of Birmingham. One month after the move both Alex MacTaggart and Duncan Brownloaf were gone. It was suggested, although never proven, that both men suffered a 'palace coup' led by Heinrich Grubber.

The BM name was continued, after all the goodwill generated was considerable, and Heinrich Grubber and William Smallpiece set about planning for the future. For some time both partners worried about future strategy. Should they stay as a small stand-alone company or actively seek merger or acquisition? In 1988 the future direction was effectively settled. Watkins International had been looking to acquire an existing engineering consulting company. Merger negotiations were started with BM. These negotiations proved to be unusually protracted. Besides issues of partner capital, there were a number of issues surrounding managerial autonomy. Surprisingly, merger was nearly aborted by the insistence of the BM partners that young Eric Reliant be admitted into partnership. The partnership qualities of Eric were not immediately obvious to the senior partners of Watkins. A redemptive new age traveller, he tended to be seen as a disorganised blue sky thinker (or 'head in the clouds' visionary). Underneath however, he was an artful schemer who had carefully flattered and fawned around the BM partners. What he lacked in technical engineering skills he more than made up for in low-life cunning.

With agreement reached on the admission to partnership of Eric Reliant, the way to merger was clear. Following the merger life appeared to continue much as before. BM continued to occupy the same premises, and to all intents and purposes operated as the same company. The BM name was retained for the sound commercial reasons of client goodwill and recognition, but now operated as the Brownloaf MacTaggart Division of Watkins International.

For eighteen months it was business as usual. The head office of Watkins was two miles away – in many respects out of sight and out of mind. Surprisingly Watkins did not rein in its new division. Procedures stayed more or less the same although the house style of reports to clients now had to conform to strict and elaborate Watkins' requirements. The name of the overall firm had changed but the three partners continued to behave as if BM was an independent company. Heinrich Grubber was particularly proud of now being a partner in an international firm with all the apparent prestige and jet travel this implied.

THE SITUATION

Watkins International began to introduce firm-wide standardised practices early in 1990. First the time sheet recording system linked to client billing was changed from a manual system to a computerised system; later, standardised routines and forms were introduced for a number of administrative procedures, including holiday requests, staff appraisal, expenses and assignment control. All curricula vitae were placed into a computerised database linked to a proposal (or bidding for work) administration system. Updating of each curriculum vitae takes place after each consultancy assignment by the project manager completing the relevant form and sending it to the marketing department. Surprisingly, despite the relative sophistication of this system, matching the personnel with the requisite experience to project requirements is rather hit and miss, and depends more on an informal reward and punishment system (consultants who conform to the company culture are rewarded with interesting and prestigious assignments, which may help career advancement, while consultants who do not conform, for whatever reason, can be impeded by a succession of mediocre or difficult projects). BM employees began to recall nostalgically the 'old days' of BM before merger. Little did they know that more was yet to come.

In May 1991 Watkins secured three floors of a prestigious office block located adjacent to their head office in Birmingham. This office block consists of ten floors, four of which are occupied by a commercial bank and architectural practice. All Watkins' management consultancy divisions were located, in August and September 1991, on to one floor of the new office. Some 700 people (including all management consultancy support staff such as accounts, personnel and office management) are housed in a huge open plan office (although partners have individual, if small, offices). Individual consultants are assigned to a desk, each desk accommodates at least two consultants. If both consultants are working in the office, working space becomes a simple matter of early desk possession. All consultants are required to log on to a computerised staff locations system, which records contact telephone numbers and physical location for every hour of the working day. The same system acts as a message recording point when consultants are working outside the office.

The change from a relatively small office away from the main management consultancy to the big company environment came as quite a shock to several BM staff. For many staff there was a realisation, perhaps for the first time, that they were working in a large, rather impersonal, increasingly automated and tightly regulated environment. Above all they were expected to sink or swim in a fiercely competitive environment. There was also a realisation among staff, and indeed the BM partners, that although they may be well known in the engineering industry, within the Watkins' empire they were minute in terms of size of turnover, number of projects, number of employees and profitability.

The length and severity of recession, not just in the UK, but also in other developed countries was beginning to cause difficulties not just in the BM division but also in the information technology and software engineering division. Many engineering businesses were being taken into receivership, and while managing businesses under receivership became for a time highly profitable for BM, other more profitable work needed to be generated. The traditional feasibility study and other development type work had steadily become less easy to obtain, and in the early part of 1993 there was virtually no on-going development work. While international work had provided a cushion during the depths of the recession, UK-based work had seriously declined since the beginning of 1993. The BM divisional plan for the five years to 1997 envisages a doubling of turnover from £3.5 million to over £7 million; the number of BM consultancy staff staying the same at 30 consultancy staff (including three partners) and four support staff, and the average consultant utilisation rate (or percentage of employable time charged to a client) increasing from just under 60 per cent to 65 per cent. At a divisional meeting early in 1993 BM staff were warned that, although staff numbers were forecast to remain the same, new staff were to be recruited. Many staff saw in this statement an implied threat of dismissal or redundancy for some, while younger and less expensive consultants were to be recruited.

In order to improve its competitive advantage in a stagnant management consultancy market (by being seen to conform to the highest service quality delivery standards) Watkins introduced in 1992 a new quality management system, in an effort to secure BS 5750 Part 1 certification (the British Standards quality award). This new system required a complete rethink of the way consultancy assignments are managed, and introduced an essentially mechanistic approach to quality management based on an accountant's view of correct filing, record keeping and random assignment audits. Elaborate quality procedures became progressively refined during 1992 and became encapsulated in a beautifully printed Watkins Quality Manual. This manual was revised five times in as many months, and not surprisingly, many consultants became confused as the quality system appeared to be used by partners as part of a reward and punishment system; it is all too easy to miss completion of a form, completion of a section of a form, neglect to obtain a partner's signature on a form or miss a quality plan review. The threat of periodic quality audits hangs over every consultant and, instead of using the quality management system as a means of improving services to clients, many consultants have become increasingly antagonistic towards it. The whole quality management system has become a bureaucratic nightmare instead of the aide to successful service quality and client satisfaction it should be.

The following paragraphs briefly describe the organisational structure, recruitment policy, assignments allocations and perceived methods of advancing within the company.

At the current time the BM Division consists of three partners (Heinrich Grubber, William Smallpiece and Eric Reliant); three associates (Quintin Bottomley, Nigel Redcoat and Rupert Wormwood), four managing consultants; four senior consultants; twelve consultants; two analysts, two technical assistants, three secretaries and one researcher/librarian. Although Watkins International prides itself on ostensibly not having a rigid hierarchy, it is in fact very hierarchical, consisting (for billing and employment purposes) of four grades of technical assistant, one grade of analyst, consultant and senior consultant; two grades of managing consultant, associate and partner. Having climbed the greasy pole to partner in a division, the hierarchy continues remorselessly upwards, and includes – divisional senior partner, partner-in-charge of central departments (audit, tax, management consultancy, corporate finance and insolvency services), partner-in-charge of regional offices, managing partner of regional offices, managing partner of head office in Birmingham, chief executive and senior partner and chairman of the board. Added to this list are the partners in charge of offices in each country and of associated firms.

Recruitment policy within Watkins is generally rudimentary but calculated. There is no shortage of well-qualified applicants. In normal economic conditions the Watkins management consultancy thrives on a constant inflow and outflow of bright young staff, although in the past three years recession has generally slowed down this movement such that Watkins has made around five per cent of its management consultants redundant since the end of 1992. The typical management consultant is aged around 30, with a few years professional accounting or industrial experience. He (for the typical consultant tends to be male, although exceptionally gifted women are being recruited in greater numbers) generally has a first degree from a well-known university plus an MBA from one of the top three British business schools. Occasionally an accounting qualification has also been obtained. He or she is also highly motivated with an almost obsessional ambition to climb the career ladder. Because of this obsession with success, the typical consultant is prepared to work all hours of the day and night, and working at weekends in the office is thought to be particularly important, provided of course, a partner is made aware of this fact.

Entrants to the BM Division are somewhat different to the typical Watkins consultant. A typical BM consultant is aged around 29 to 33; has a first degree in engineering, usually from one of three universities plus membership of a professional engineering institute, such as the Institute of Mechanical Engineering. Possession of a higher degree is rare. As a consequence, the average BM consultant and partner are less well qualified than other Watkins consultants and partners. A climate of almost anti-intellectualism has therefore flourished in the BM Division, particularly since the merger with the Watkins empire, along the crude lines of 'we're only the oily engineers – ignorant but proud of it'. To reinforce this somewhat maverick ethos, and in the rare moments when everyone downs tools to relax, the BM Division has earned some notoriety in the mammoth drinking sessions in local Birmingham pubs, followed so it is alleged, by dubious parties in far flung suburbs. As with the Watkins company as a whole there is never a shortage of young hopefuls eager to join the ranks of BM and as such, the BM partners have over the years developed a callous and cavalier attitude to personnel management. Such attitude by the partnership would have been unthinkable during the time of Alex MacTaggart and Duncan Brownloaf. The Watkins management consultancy personnel function is small and subordinate to the wishes of the partners.

Motivation of staff is rarely considered and their well-being is secondary to the business of improving profitability. Heinrich Grubber in particular, takes a cool and calculating approach to staff management. He tends to select bright new consultants and then invariably burn them out with sustained hard work until the next young person comes along to take their place. It takes around eighteen months to two years of relentless hard work in the BM Division for the true nature of the situation to dawn on the more perceptive consultant – basically promotion to the next grade is rarer than a Norwegian parrot and, while one or two consultants have recently been promoted from consultant to senior consultant, only one person in the past fifteen years has been promoted from senior consultant to managing consultant.

The allocation of consultancy assignments within the BM Division is based primarily on either 'the warm body' principle (who is available) or as part of a none too subtle punishment and reward system. Generally there is a perceived hierarchy of jobs, ranging from an international assignment in some exotic location, working for Heinrich Grubber and the well-respected associate Nigel Redcoat (rated as a top job) to the managing of a small engineering business under receivership, working for Eric Reliant and the loathed and feared associate, Rupert Wormwood, famous for his unprincipled ways and ill-disguised alcoholic binges (most certainly a low-rated job). A succession of either top-rated jobs for prestigious clients or small insignificant jobs managed by poor job managers, can make or break a Watkins career in around four months.

Advancement in the steadily deteriorating atmosphere of the BM Division is always likely to be a rather haphazard process. Surprisingly, technical engineering skills *per se* are not the key to career success in this organisation. Advancement, if it comes at all, may occur by a combination of conformity to, compliance with, and dependence on the sub-culture of the BM Division, within the wider culture of the Watkins company. Conformity, compliance and dependency can be demonstrated in a number of ways – being seen to work all hours in the office; flattery of the partners resulting in appalling sycophancy; exercising personal responsibility by undertaking small marketing and selling exercises designed to bring in new assignments; completing already time pressured projects before schedule and under budget (which generally can only be achieved by under-recording time expended on a project), and the honing of good old fashioned Machiavellian techniques of back stabbing.

It is against this background of difficult trading conditions in an environment that is uncertain, together with the absorption of a relatively small firm into an international management company with all its standardised procedures, and where mistrust, intimidation and fear are common emotions, that this case is developed.

ACTIVITY BRIEF

1 *Identify the different ways in which managerial control and power are being exercised in both Watkins International as a whole and the BM Division in particular.*

2 *Having identified the different aspects of managerial control, examine how appropriate these are in managing the different types of employees in Watkins International.*

3 *Explore the nature of the apparent dichotomy and tensions created, in allowing highly qualified,creative and essentially autonomous consultants room to reach creative solutions to client problems (often under considerable time pressures within an uncertain environment) and the employing organisation's need for order, stability and reliability.*

4 *Considering the Watkins International approach to quality assurance, which appears to be primarily bureaucratic and perhaps at variance with the image management consultants would wish to present to clients, is this likely to affect the way consultants consider and make recommendations for the implementation of total quality management systems in client organisations?*

RECOMMENDED READING

Huczynski, A. and Buchanan, D. (1991). *Organizational Behaviour*, Second Edition, New York: Prentice Hall, Chapter 22 'Management Control' and Chapter 19 'Leadership and Management Style'.

Sveiby, K. E. and Lloyd, T. (1987) *Managing Knowhow. Add Value by Valuing Creativity*, London: Bloomsbury.

Mullins, L. J,. (1993). *Management and Organisational Behaviour* Third Edition, London: Pitman, Chapter 17 'The Nature of Management Control' and Chapter 20 'Organisation Development'.

Kakabadse, A. Ludlow, R. and Vinnicombe, S. (1988). *Working in Organizations*, London: Penguin, Chapter 8 'Power: A Base for Action'.

Thomas, K. W. (1976). 'Conflict and Conflict Management', in M. D. Dunnette (Ed), *Handbook of Industrial and Organizational Psychology*, Chicago: Rand McNally, pp 889–935

Morgan, G. (1986). *Images of Organization*, Newbury Park, California and London: Sage, Chapter 6 'Interests, Conflict and Power'.

PART 5

The personnel function

Personnel policies and procedures and the role of managers dealing with practices associated with them serve as the focus for five cases in Part 5. The first case,
'Dealing with HIV/AIDS in the workplace', raises issues relating to attitudes and
values, communication, equal opportunities, personnel policies and systems and
business ethics. The situation described in the case provides a framework for considering the reality of decision making in a sensitive area of personnel policy and
practice. *'Changing shiftworking arrangements in an NHS hospital trust'* examines management rationale for changing terms and conditions of service in a
unionised public sector organisation and the way in which change can be implemented. The link between procedural mechanisms and the attitudes and beliefs
of staff is explored as well as the difficulty of maintaining good individual and
collective relationships during and after the change process.

'Employee capability in a magistrates' court' provides a view of managerial
decision making from a legal perspective and relates this to other personnel
policies such as recruitment, selection and career development. The match
between the needs of the organisation and the needs of people are considered
from behavioural and legal perspectives and consideration given to the social
responsibility of managers who are required to deal with difficult human relations problems. *'Midshire Association for the Blind – The staffing implications
of restructuring'* presents a situation which unfortunately has faced many
organisations in recent years in which external forces and economic constraints
force organisations to consider the possibility of shedding labour through
redundancy. This case deals with the framework of national and European
employment legislation and, as with the previous case, provides opportunities
for considering managerial, individual and corporate responses to change in
organisational requirements.

The final case *'Competence-based recruitment and selection'* moves away
from the rule-making theme of the previous two cases and considers the concept
of competence in work roles and explores the potential application when recruiting and selecting staff. The focus on abilities necessary to do a job successfully
rather than the use of traditional predictive criteria such as age and educational qualifications could materially affect the way in which organisations
recruit and select staff and hence challenge the way some of the familiar systems and procedures adopted by personnel specialists and line managers are
used. The case provides an innovative, valuable and practical insight into the
use of competencies and considers their impact on personnel policies, procedures and practices.

Dealing with HIV/AIDS in the workplace

David Goss

This case concerns the issues which face managers and employees in dealing with HIV and AIDS in the workplace. Although the prospect of contracting the virus through normal work activity is virtually non-existent, the disease continues to be the subject of considerable uncertainty, a cause of anxiety, and sometimes a basis for prejudice and discrimination. These issues have been confronted by many organisations, especially in the areas of social and medical care, who work directly with people affected by HIV and AIDS, but they can also emerge in any organisation if an employee contracts the virus. However, relatively few organisations have addressed the latter issue and, as this case demonstrates, an ill-conceived response can pose severe problems for those affected by the virus, for managers charged with taking decisions in this regard, and for the organisation.

The case raises issues relating to attitudes and values, communication, equal opportunities, personnel policy and systems and business ethics.

BACKGROUND

Distinctive Data Processing Ltd (DDP) is an information handling company with its head office in London and 'satellite' branches in the south west, south east and north of England. For staff, the branches are kept in touch with each other and head office by a bi-monthly company newspaper. It is with events at the south east branch that the case is concerned.

As the result of winning a large new contract the south east branch has recently been expanded and restructured. It now employs 64 staff (previouly there were 30), the bulk of whom are in clerical grades engaged in computer operation and data input; 60 per cent of the workforce in the south east branch are women. The office is organised on two floors of a modern building. The ground floor, housing the computer workstations and most of the staff, is divided into sections by screens, each of which provides a base-area for the six work teams undertaking the processing work. Each team is made up of about eight staff with a team leader at supervisory grade. The upper floor is divided into offices which are used by the various managers and their support staff. These include the branch manager, the contracts manager, the technical services manager, and the personnel manager.

The expansion of the south east branch has resulted in a change in its relationship to DDP head office. It now operates as a cost/profit centre, responsible for the running of its own contracts and assessed by its performance in this respect. It is expected to achieve a level of return specified by head office but, within very broad limits, it has freedom to achieve these results as its management sees fit.

To cope with the growth in staff numbers a personnel function has been established at branch level. Previously all personnel matters had been handled either by head office (dealing with administrative systems) or by managers and supervisors on an *ad hoc* basis. There is now a personnel manager and a personnel assistant.

The personnel manager is responsible to the branch manager and has responsibility for virtually all operational aspects of personnel policy. There is no trade union presence and pay and conditions have been devolved to branch level. The branch has always prided itself on a friendly atmosphere and the fair treatment of staff. Management have been keen to preserve this after the restructuring and, in this respect, there has been no change in terms and conditions for existing staff, and current head office policies and practices are continuing for the present. For clerical grades there is an incremental pay-scale (based on annual appraisal) and an annual holiday entitlement of 28 days. There are no bonus schemes or related fringe benefits. However, although the company does not provide private health insurance (except for managers), it does have an Occupational Sick Pay scheme which provides cover from the commencement of employment and provides for three months full pay followed by three months halfpay. There is also a company pension scheme to which employees contribute 5 per cent of salary.

There is an equal opportunities policy, developed by head office, that covers discrimination on the grounds of race, sex and disability. This policy is in the form of a mission statement rather than a detailed procedural system and reads as follows: 'DDP is an equal opportunities employer. It believes that no employee should be treated less favourably because of race, colour, nationality, sex, marital status, or disability. All necessary steps will be taken to remove direct or indirect discrimination. All staff are expected to act in accordance with this policy, breaches of which may, in certain circumstances, lead to disciplinary action being taken against the offender.' This policy has been in force for five years.

Sandra Jones is the personnel manager for the south east branch. She has been in post for only ten months, having been promoted to this position from her previous job as a team supervisor. At the time of her promotion she had no experience of personnel management although she is currently undertaking a part-time Diploma in Personnel Management course. She was promoted into her present position on the recommendation of the branch manager who had been impressed by her ability to 'get on with people' during her two years service as a supervisor. Given the relatively small size of the branch and its 'stable' employment relations Sandra's lack of experience was not felt to be a problem as she was known to be capable of 'learning on the job', supplemented by her ongoing part-time training. Indeed, this expectation of competence has been fulfilled. Sandra has settled into her new position, has mastered the existing systems and is starting to feel confident in her ability to perform as an effective personnel professional. Not surprisingly she has spent most of her time since promotion working from her office, familiarising herself with the existing systems.

THE SITUATION

The situation faced by Sandra involved the case of John, a junior clerical worker in one of the data processing teams, who had taken repeated time off for sickness reasons over the last six months. John was generally considered to be a somewhat quiet but personable young man who was a diligent employee and who tended to keep himself to himself. His absences were covered by medical certificates which referred to a viral infection and, because of the company's generous sick pay scheme, had not caused Sandra any particular concern as none approached (cumulatively or individually) the three month period when the level of sick pay was reduced. Initially these absences had been for a matter of days and, as far as Sandra knew, John had returned to work without any apparent difficulty. However, on one occasion John did not return to work and, after two weeks, his mother informed Sandra that he was in hospital. Three weeks later, Sandra received a letter from John's mother saying that he had died in hospital and that the funeral had already taken place. Sandra informed John's former team of his death and said that she would visit his parents to convey condolences. When this meeting took place John's parents confided in her that he had died from an AIDS-related disease, but asked her not to reveal this to his former colleagues at work.

When she reported to the work team on her meeting with John's parents, she decided to respect their wishes and keep the cause of John's death secret. At this stage she felt comfortable with this decision: on the one hand, she did not feel it was anyone else's business and, on the other, she thought that to release the fact that John had 'died from AIDS' might start 'unpleasant' rumours about what she now assumed must have been his homosexuality. However, it soon became apparent when she met the eight people who had worked with John that this was going to be a difficult position to sustain. All appeared genuinely saddened by John's death but, when asked how he had died, she felt that her evasive answers were causing a certain amount of suspicion and she left the meeting feeling far less comfortable than she had at the outset. As a result, she decided not to publicise John's death in the obituaries section of company newspaper (as was normal practice when an employee died), fearing that this would only fuel rumour and suspicion.

A few days later, however, Sandra received a message from the supervisor of the team to which John had belonged asking for a meeting. At this meeting a number of issues were raised which made Sandra reassess the effect of John's death and the way in which she had handled it. The meeting was an emotional one in which a number of unpleasant aspects of organisational behaviour were exposed and deep feelings of distress revealed. These issues can be listed under three headings

Issues raised at the meeting

1. The rumour mill

The first issue concerned a number of rumours which were now circulating in the ground floor office, and behaviour on the part of some employees that was causing distress and anger. The team supervisor told Sandra that it was now widely believed that John had died of AIDS and that he had been a practising homosexual and a drug abuser. These rumours were proving hurtful to John's former colleagues both because they were themselves unsure of the circumstances surrounding his death and because they were convinced that the accusations of drug abuse were malicious and untrue. Indeed, these rumours were thought to be instigated by a small group of junior male employees who were making crude jokes about gays and AIDS. This had now taken on an almost ritualistic character, the perpetrators seeming to take a puerile delight in being offensive, even after the callousness of their behaviour had been pointed out to them. This was not only distressing for those who had worked closely with John, but it also raised the issue of prejudice against homosexuals which, previously, had never been considered. John's sexuality had never been the subject of discussion at work and his colleagues had no idea whether or not he was gay. The general climate was now described as one of tension and antagonism.

2. Guilt

This tension was compounding the second problem which was a sense of guilt among those who had worked with John. In the absence of any information to the contrary (and by 'putting two and two together'), it was being assumed that John had indeed died of AIDS. However, there were now concerns that his developing illness had not been treated with the sympathy it deserved. Colleagues felt that had they known of John's condition they could have made his time at work less stressful and perhaps, even extended his life. This sense of guilt was being exacerbated because the climate of rumour and secrecy now made it difficult to talk openly about the circumstances of John's death: it was seen to be somehow 'unnatural' and 'shameful', both on account of its suddenness and because of the stigma and prejudice which had emerged in the office.

3. Lack of organisational recognition

The final area of concern was a perception on the part of the team John had worked for that the company had not given sufficient recognition to his death and that it preferred secrecy and 'a quiet life' to an open defence of his reputation. Indeed, the fact that nothing had been said officially was seen to have fuelled the rumours and implicitly to have suggested that there was in fact 'something to hide'.

Sandra was somewhat shaken by these developments and told the team supervisor that she would take steps to try to rectify matters. However, when she thought over the issues a number of additional questions and concerns emerged.

Issues occurring to Sandra

- Should she have taken active steps to determine John's health state immediately he started taking time off work?
- What would/should she have done had she found out John was ill because of HIV infection?
- Had there been any risk to other employees as a result of John's HIV infection?
- What was she going to do about the prejudicial behaviour of the young male employees?
- How was she going to defuse the anxiety and tension in the office?

Reflecting on these issues, Sandra realised that she knew very little about either HIV and AIDS or how to deal with its ramifications at work. In consequence she was reluctant to take the issue to her senior managers when she had neither a full grasp of the issues involved nor any effective solutions to offer. She decided, therefore, to consult a specialist in this area before taking further action.

Action taken by Sandra

Sandra arranged an appointment with the representative of a local voluntary group offering advice and guidance on matters associated with HIV/AIDS. After discussing the issues with the specialist, named Ken, a number of possible options were suggested. These options were in three main areas: policy; training/education; and legal issues.

1. Policy

The first option was to develop a policy relating to HIV/AIDS for the branch office. This, it was suggested, might help to clarify the key issues involved in dealing with workplace HIV/AIDS issues and the organisation's stance regarding discrimination or prejudice. Ken drew Sandra's attention to an initiative developed by the National AIDS Trust (with support from several major companies and the Employment Department) called 'Companies Act!'. This suggests that 'HIV should be on every personnel manager's agenda; a non-discriminatory policy is the only practical approach. HIV and AIDS are equal opportunities issues, not exclusively health and safety ones'. The guidelines include:

- The policy must address both HIV and AIDS separately, and the company's response to each should acknowledge they are separate conditions.
- Any policy must clearly state that discrimination, in any aspect of company activity, against anyone who is HIV positive or who has AIDS will not be tolerated.
- The policy should state clearly that AIDS will be treated in the same manner as any other progressive or debilitating illness.
- The policy must contain a clear statement on confidentiality, explaining the way in which confidential information will be treated.
- The policy must make clear, by outlining or referring to discipline and grievance procedures, what action will be taken if staff breach the terms laid down.
- The best model policy will cover areas such as opportunities for redeployment, retraining, flexible working, compassionate leave etc. Where possible these should apply not only to those infected with HIV but also to carers.

2. Training

The second area of discussion centred on the issue of training and information provision. Sandra felt that both she and the staff were generally ignorant about HIV/AIDS and that some form of education would be beneficial. Her initial view was that this could be provided via booklets or fact-sheets. However, Ken's view was that some form of training or more formal education could be worth consideration. Whilst he felt that factual information had a role to play, he also thought that some type of AIDS-awareness training focusing on attitudes towards the disease would be useful, especially in dealing with the hostile and prejudicial feelings already exhibited. He added that these sorts of training sessions could be provided by a variety of bodies both locally and nationally working in the HIV/AIDS and health education field and strongly advised that this sort of provision be dealt with by experts and not undertaken by inexperienced trainers.

3. Legal Issues

Ken dealt first with the issue of testing for HIV. Unless there is an express condition in a contract of employment it will not be possible for an employer to insist that *existing* employees are subject to a test for HIV antibodies. However, an employer can insist that *potential* employees (i.e., job applicants) submit to such a test as a condition of employment. Where such testing is carried out it will be covered by rules of medical confidentiality and should take account of government guidelines which state that counselling should be given before the test is taken and when the result is disclosed. The bulk of opinion (including that of government) is that testing in relation to employment is normally neither necessary nor useful on the grounds that the test may not disclose the presence of the virus (since it has to be present in the body for around three months before its presence is detectable) and, unless carried out on a regular basis, will not detect post-test infection. In addition, it is recognised that there is no reason why someone who has HIV should not work normally for many years. In many cases people with HIV do not develop symptoms of AIDS-related disease for more than ten years following infection. At present those areas of employment law which have relevance to AIDS/HIV concern three main issues: discrimination; confidentiality; and dismissal. Ken provided the following summaries.

(a) *Discrimination*
There is no UK law relating directly to discrimination against those with HIV/AIDS; any such discrimination has to fall under the scope of the Sex Discrimination Act (SDA) or the Race Relations Act if it is to be unlawful. In terms of direct discrimination under the SDA (i.e., where on the grounds of sex a woman is treated less favourably than a man or vice versa), any discrimination associated with AIDS/HIV must be aimed at one sex alone. If an employer sacks a man on discovering that he is HIV+ there will be no actionable discrimination unless it can be shown that the employer would have treated a female employee with HIV differently. This, of course, could be the case where a man with HIV/AIDS is also known to be gay and the dismissal inspired by general prejudice towards male homosexuals. Indirect discrimination (i.e., where some condition or requirement is applied equally to men and women but a considerably smaller proportion of one sex can comply than the other) may be an issue if the requirement

for a job application, or transfer, or promotion, etc., is that a person should not be infected with HIV. Here it would be a question of medical evidence as to whether a considerably smaller proportion of one sex can comply. In Western developed nations AIDS has been most prevalent amongst men (both homosexuals and haemophiliacs) and, if this continues, it may be that indirect discrimination becomes a possibility as substantially less men could fulfil the requirement of being free of the virus than women.

(b) *Confidentiality*

The law relating to confidentiality derives from the duty of trust and confidence in the employment relationship which requires that the employer and employee keep information on the HIV status of any employee confidential unless the employee consents to disclosure. Disclosure without consent may be justified in the public interest in very exceptional cases if, for example, there is a threat to the health and safety of others' (which in most work situations is highly unlikely). Also in the absence of an express contractual term, a person with HIV/AIDS is not under an obligation to reveal this to an employer except where not to do so would lead to the risk of infection or harm to others. Again such risks are, for most people, negligible.

(c) *Dismissal*

Although it is difficult for an employee to sustain a charge of unlawful *discrimination* in relation to HIV/AIDS, it may be possible to claim unfair dismissal. However, dismissal of people with AIDS can be fair under certain circumstances although it will not normally be justified simply by the existence of HIV infection. But if a person has developed an AIDS-related disease (as opposed to being antibody positive) then the normal tests relating to long-term sickness will apply. Thus there is no legal obligation on an employer to create a special job which that person is capable of doing or to allow indefinite time off. An additional area where AIDS may have an impact is in relation to allowing employees time off to care for dependents who have the disease. Significant absence from work, for whatever reason, can amount, after warnings, to a fair reason for dismissal. The most difficult cases have been those where an employer has been faced with either the refusal of employees to work with a person with HIV/AIDS or where trade is, or expected to be, lost because a person with the disease is known to be employed. In the former case, such a dismissal may be judged unfair as tribunals are not allowed to take into account any industrial pressure by employees when deciding on the fairness of the dismissal. But where commercial considerations are involved, it could be argued that an employee can be fairly dismissed if it can be shown that the business is suffering financially from that person's continued employment. In order to show that the dismissal is fair, it would be expected that the employer had first provided education and information for those objecting, had attempted conciliation and considered the possibility of relocation or, if appropriate, disciplinary action.

Sandra took this information back to her office. She now had to decide what to do next.

ACTIVITY BRIEF

1 *Sandra has decided to advocate the development of a separate policy relating to HIV and AIDS. Using the 'Companies Act!' guidelines (shown above) draw up a suitable draft policy document. (This activity is best conducted in small groups, each group presenting its policy for discussion at the end of the session. Time needed 1.5–2 hrs).*

2 *Once a policy on HIV/AIDS has been developed, how should it be put into practice? Consider in particular, the introduction of the policy (high profile or low profile), how it will be monitored and enforced, and how it will effect other personnel policies (e.g., relating to recruitment and selection, equal opportunities, redeployment, sick leave and compassionate leave).*

3 *Identify and explore the behavioural and social processes that underlie responses to HIV and AIDS in the workplace.*

RECOMMENDED READING

For Activity 1.
Mullins, L. J. (1993). *Management and Organisational Behaviour,* London: Pitman Chapter 18, esp. p.595.
Goss, D. (1993). 'The ethics of HIV/AIDS and the workplace', *Business Ethics: A European* Review, 2, 3. pp143 – 148
or
Goss, D. (1993). *Principles of Human Resource Management,* London: Routledge, Chapter 7.

For Activity 2.
Mullins, L. J. (1993). *Management and Organisational Behaviour,* Chapters 18, 19, Chapter 20 pp 657–664.
IDS Study 528 (1993). 'AIDS returns to the Agenda', April.

For Activity 3
Mullins, L. J. (1993). *Management and Organisational Behaviour,* Chapters 5 and 6.
Banas, G. (1992). 'Nothing prepared me to manage AIDS', *Harvard Business Review,* July – August, pp 26–33.

Changing shiftworking arrangements in an NHS hospital trust

David Farnham

This case focuses on management's intentions to change the shiftwork patterns for a group of nursing staff who are employed in a newly established National Health Service hospital trust in a large conurbation. It examines management's rationale for changing shiftwork patterns and the reaction by nursing staff to management's proposals. The case also considers how and why the main staff union, the Royal College of Nursing (RCN), becomes involved in trying to resolve the issue and the roles of line management and the personnel manager in the dispute. The case illustrates not only the use of the formal procedural mechanisms used in resolving employee relations conflict. It also shows how the attitudes and beliefs of individual actors in the workplace affect their behaviour in acting out their organisational and employee relations roles.

BACKGROUND

The National Health Service (NHS)

The NHS was established in 1948 and its structure was the product of extensive negotiations and consultations amongst relevant interest groups at that time. These included government, the medical profession and some 50 staff unions, representing all grades of staff in the service. The aims of the NHS were to create a public service, funded by general taxation and free at the point of use, to all those needing it when they were ill. The three main elements in the new NHS were the hospitals, community health services and the general practitioner (GP) services.

There was a tripartite management structure in the NHS in England and Wales after 1948. Management of the hospital service was provided through the Ministry of Health, regional hospital boards and hospital management committees. Community services were administered by the local authorities, with GP services administered through family practitioner executives. Employee relations decisions in the service were highly centralised, with most staff, apart from the medical profession, having their terms and conditions of employment determined centrally, through national-level collective bargaining machinery. These comprised a general 'Whitley' council, for matters covering all NHS staff, and specialist functional Whitley councils for each major occupational group in the service.

Since 1948, there have been a number of organisational and managerial reorganisations of the service. A major one took place in 1974. This co-ordinated the health services, formerly supplied by a mixture of central and local government provision, through a four tier structure consisting of: the Department of Health and Social Security; regional hospital authorities (RHAs); area health authorities; and district health authorities (DHAs). But the family practitioner services continued to operate within a separate structure.

The most recent health service reorganisation took place in 1990, as a result of the National Health Service and Community Care Act. This created an internal market in the NHS, comprising a set of health care 'providers' and health care 'purchasers'. The NHS providers include hospitals, primary care services and community care services, while the NHS purchasers include DHAs and GPs.

Since April 1991, a further reform has taken place. This enables individual hospitals and community care units to obtain 'trust' status by making an application to the Department of Health (DoH). Where an application is approved by the Secretary of State, the hospital or community care unit is funded directly from the DoH, rather than through its RHA. The NHS trust then becomes the direct employer of health service staff. Trusts have the freedom, and responsibility, not only to manage their own budgets but also to move away from centralised personnel policies and national collective agreements.

One major group of staff now excluded from national collective bargaining on their terms of employment is nurses and midwives and the professions allied to medicine. Government removed them from the Whitley system in 1983 and they now have a pay review body which makes recommendations on their pay to the Prime Minister. Other aspects of their employment conditions, however, remain negotiable at national and local levels.

The Maintown General Hospital Trust (MGHT)

The MGHT is a large general hospital in the London area, with an annual revenue budget of some £70 million, and it employs about 6,000 staff. The trust has 12 clinical units, each headed by a clinical director who is a medical consultant, and these units are supported by six senior managers with either functional responsibilities such as the personnel manager, or hospital-wide responsibilities, such as the catering manager. Each clinical director, in turn, has a non-medical, clinical services manager.

The trust's management board consists of the general manager, the clinical directors, the other senior managers in the hospital, such as the finance director, and external, non-executive members.

The main duties of the clinical directors are to oversee the efficient and effective management of their units, and to keep themselves up-to-date with developments in their specialist field. The day-to-day managing of the clinical units is the responsibility of the clinical services managers. Their duties include: managing and directing the unit's staff; planning and monitoring services; managing the unit's budget; and ensuring that all policies and procedures, including those relating to personnel and safety, are implemented and adhered to.

THE SITUATION

The cardio-thoracic unit

The MGHT has a world-renowned cardio-thoracic unit. The patients who are treated in the unit suffer from a diversity of heart and vascular problems, undergo extensive investigations and are provided with a variety of treatments, including drugs and sophisticated surgery. Because of the complex and distressing nature of their illnesses, many patients need to have intensive care over long periods of time. This puts considerable pressures on the unit's stretched resources and makes high demands on the professional and caring skills of the medical and nursing staff.

As a self-contained unit, the cardio-thoracic unit has both in-patient facilities, including provisions for patients needing intensive care, as well as out-patient ones. There are three 20-bed wards in the unit, for various categories of patient, a theatre suite and a recovery area. Due to technological advances in investigative, operative and post-operative medical procedures, there is a continual need for well-trained, specialist medical and nursing staff in the unit.

The unit's current clinical director, Mr Archibald Smith, is a highly qualified and well respected medical consultant who leads his team enthusiastically and with flair. It is generally recognised, however, that he is less interested in the routine managerial aspects of his role and he therefore relies very heavily on his cardio-thoracic services manager, Sally Harvey, for the day-to-day running of the unit.

Sally is an ambitious and well qualified individual and is currently studying for a Diploma in Management Studies, on a part-time basis, at the local university. When under pressure, however, she can be somewhat authoritarian in her dealings with staff and she is generally regarded by the staff unions, and by the hospital's personnel manager, Peter Marks, as being anti-union.

In her three years in the hospital, she has had two or three brushes with the unions in the unit and it is only because of the intervention skills and professional expertise of Peter Marks that potential confrontations with the unions have been avoided. As an experienced and qualified personnel specialist, Peter regards Sally's frame of reference on employee relations as rather unitary and exclusively managerial. Peter's frame of reference on employment issues, in contrast, is predominantly pluralist and participative. He believes management need to gain the consent of staff when important decisions are to be made.

Sally has had particular problems in her dealings with Rob Brown, the RCN's shop steward in the unit. He is a conscientious and effective representative for the nursing staff, is well versed in the procedural aspects of employee relations and has a good working relationship with the regional officer of the RCN, Anne Bevan. He has attended training courses with the RCN and, where informal approaches have proved to be ineffective, he is always willing to take up the complaints and grievances of his members. As an assertive and confident individual, Rob Brown clearly has a reputation for not letting his members' complaints go unrecognised and unresolved by management.

Nursing management and nursing establishments in the unit

The clinical staff in the cardio-thoracic unit are led by a nurse manager, in each of the three wards. They are accountable for the day-to-day management of their areas of responsibility to Sally Harvey and they advise her on all clinical matters. Their main duties are: (1) to manage the hospital wards on a 24-hour basis, ensuring high standards of patient care; and (2) to plan shiftwork rotas, ensuring the staffing levels are met and skills mixes are adequate. They are working supervisors and therefore have to be strongly committed to both the delivery of nursing care and the managing of ward resources efficiently and effectively.

Nursing establishments in the unit are stretched, however, and, because of continual resource constraints imposed by government, additional resources are unlikely to be provided in the foreseeable future. Furthermore, there is an expanding need for specialist, trained nurses in the unit, as demand for the unit's services increases and technology and surgical techniques advance. As is the norm in nursing, staff establishments are made up of both full-time and part-time appointments, on both the day and night shifts.

However, there is no allowance in current staffing establishments for annual leave, sickness or study leave, on either the day or night shifts. Any shortfalls in nursing staff have to be remedied through bank or agency staff and this is expensive.

Existing shiftwork arrangements

In order to provide continuous and varied patient care, management has to organise an overlapping, three-shift system in the unit. This currently consists of a day shift – covering two sessions (a) the morning and early afternoon period and (b) the late afternoon and evening period – and a night shift.

The day shift is staffed by mainly full-time nurses, working 37.5 hours per week for five days a week, with part-time staff making up whole-time hours. The existing day shift was introduced by management six months ago, after very limited consultation with, and some complaints by, the nursing staff. The two-day shifts consist of:

1. the early shift from 0600 till 1415, with 15 minutes allowed for coffee and 30 minutes for lunch, giving a shift of 7.5 hours;
2. the late shift from 1215 till 2030 hours, with 15 minutes allowed for tea and 30 minutes for supper, giving a shift of 7.5 hours.

The night shift is staffed differently. It consists of only two full-time staff, with the other 13 working on a part-time basis, largely because of family commitments. The full-time night staff are also contracted for 37.5 hours per week but, in practice, work four, 10-hour shifts per week (see below). This means that they are entitled to one night off every four weeks. The night shift starts at 1945 hours and finishes at 0645 hours, with one hour deducted for a break.

The new shiftworking proposals

Last week, the cardio-thoracic services manager, Sally Harvey, announced her intention, in the unit's newsletter, of changing the night shift. This was the first time that the night staff had heard about this and they were very concerned about it. The change was announced to help ensure a three per cent cost improvement in the unit, without reducing staff levels. Sally's decision was that the night shift be changed to 1955–0617 hours, a reduction of 38 minutes per shift, but no date was set for implementation.

The staff have been told that the objectives of this management decision are: (1) to ensure that shift patterns are standardised throughout the unit; (2) to provide adequate overlap between shifts; (3) to equate the night shift to a quarter of the 37.5 hour working week, thus requiring full-time night staff to work four nights of nine hours 22.5 minutes per week; (4) to provide socially acceptable shift patterns within the unit; and (5) to ensure that shift overlaps and payments for unsocial hours are minimised, resulting in cost savings to the unit. The actual amount that is likely to be saved is estimated to be about £7,000 in a financial year.

In response to management's unilateral announcement of these changes in working practices, the night shift have turned to the RCN for help. This is because, immediately after the proposed change in shift patterns was communicated to staff, an abortive meeting between the cardio-thoracic services manager and the night shift resulted in them being told that management's decision was final. Consequently, Rob Brown has written to the cardio-thoracic services manager informing her that he has advised his members to invoke the first stage of the procedure to avoid disputes. He has also discussed the issue with the RCN's regional officer, Anne Bevan.

Due to the status quo provisions within the negotiating procedure, the RCN steward has also advised his members to continue working on the existing shifts. The status quo clause reads as follows:

> Management agrees not to implement any major alternations to conditions of service or change well-established working practices until agreement has been reached between management and the unions or the negotiating procedure has been exhausted.

In the meantime Sally has now written a letter to all the night shift which they received today. It reads:

To: All Night Staff
From: The Cardio-Thoracic Services Manager

Dear Colleague

CHANGES IN THE NIGHT SHIFT

Thank you for your comments on my proposals regarding the above. I have now decided that the benefits of the proposed arrangements far outweigh their disadvantages. I would be grateful therefore if you would let me know whether you want to opt for reducing your hours or working extra nights. If I don't hear from you by the end of the month, I shall assume that you do not wish to change your hours. The new rotas will then be introduced to incorporate the extra nights. You can be assured that my decision has been taken only after a great deal of thought and in the interests of both patients and the Unit.

Yours sincerely,

Sally Harvey
Cardio-Thoracic Services Manager

cc: Nurse Managers, Day Shifts
     Nurse Managers, Night Shifts
     Mr P Marks, Personnel Manager
     Mr R Brown, RCN Steward
     Ms A Bevan, Regional Officer, RCN

As a result of this letter, an emergency meeting has been convened involving Sally Harvey, Peter Marks, the Nurses Managers, Rob Brown, Anne Bevan and the 15 night staff who are in dispute with management.

ACTIVITY BRIEF

1 *What are meant by unitary and pluralist frames of reference in employee relations? How are these frames of reference likely to reflect – and affect – Sally Harvey's and Peter Marks' management of employee relations issues?*

2 *How could 'social action' theory be used to interpret the behaviour of the parties in this situation?*

3 *What is the significance of the **status quo** clause in the hospital's procedure to avoid disputes? How could management change it if they wished to do so?*

4 *Given the cardio-thoracic service manager's objectives in proposing to change the night shift, what were likely to have been **the night staff's immediate responses** to these objectives in terms of their impact on: standardisation of shifts; overlap of shifts; equalisation of the day and night shifts; social acceptability of shift patterns; and minimising payments for unsocial hours?*

5 *Indicate how this dispute between the cardio-thoracic services manager and the night shift might have been avoided in the first place.*

6 ***Either***
Role play the emergency meeting which has been convened between the management, night shift and the staff representatives. This will require, in the first instance, preparatory meetings of each side convening separately.

Or

What compromises might be necessary for both the management side and the staff side to make in order to reach a mutually agreed settlement between them at their emergency meeting? Indicate the possible outcome(s) of such a meeting. What are the likely consequences of a failure to agree?

RECOMMENDED READING

Farnham, D. (1993). *Employee Relations,* London: Institute of Personnel Management.
Farnham, D. and Pimlott, J. (1990). *Understanding Industrial Relations,* London: Cassell.
Mullins, L. J. (1993). *Management and Organisational Behaviour,* London: Pitman.
Torrington, D. and Hall, L. (1991). *Personnel Management: a new approach,* London: Prentice Hall.

Employee capability in a magistates court

Alan Peacock

This case is based on the author's experience when acting for a Magistrates Courts Committee as a personnel advisor. It focuses on personnel and organisational issues that arise during the employment relationship. In particular it deals with matters relating to an employee's capability to undertake the duties for which he was employed. It links well with legal and behavioural aspects of managerial decision making. It also provides an opportunity to consider the social responsibilities of managers who are required to deal with difficult human relations problems.

BACKGROUND

The Magistrates Courts Committee is a statutory body. It employs staff for magistrates courts and offices in a county in southern England. It is separate from the county council but the two bodies have to work closely together.

Mr French was born on 12 February 1958. At an early age he developed epilepsy. He suffers from temporal lobe epilepsy. This is a common form of epilepsy but it is not a minor condition. A patient with temporal lobe epilepsy may not lose complete consciousness but may have strange warning of an attack. Such warnings are called 'auras'. An aura does not necessarily however herald a recognisable epileptic attack. During the period of the aura concentration is impaired and there may be some disorientation for a short time. An aura, can develop into a general attack, if it spreads across the whole brain. If the aura develops into a full attack, generally known as 'Grand Mal' then the patient loses consciousness for some minutes and during this time he looks blue, jerks his limbs etc. In 1988 Mr French's neurological activity was measured by an electroencephalograph which indicated electrical activity consistent with epilepsy and, apparently, in 1989 he had a Grand Mal.

THE SITUATION

On 15 April 1990 the magistrates committee published an advertisement in *The Times* newspaper for five vacancies for trainee Justices Clerks. The minimum qualification was a law degree and Part 1 of the Solicitors of Bar examinations, and that a successful applicant should in due course pass the final examination. Mr French applied for the post with about 30 others. Fifteen were short-listed and were interviewed. Mr French, who is an LLB. of Southampton University, told the interviewers that he had sat his Bar Final, but they were left with the impression that this was the first time he had done so.

Mr French made a favourable impression and on 5 May 1990 an offer was made to him asking him to complete and return a medical form. This he did on 7 May. An extract of key questions and answers are shown below:

Question 1(g) – *'Have you ever suffered from fits of any kind?'*
Reply – *'Nocturnal occurrence in 1982.'*

Question 3 – *'Have you ever had any mental illness or nervous trouble?'*
Reply – *'No.'*

Question 6 – *'Are you or have you been under medical treatment during the last twelve months? If so, state when and for what reasons.'*
Reply – *'Yes. Mild anti-convulsent therapy.'*

Question 7 – *'Do you ordinarily enjoy good health?'*
Reply – *'Yes.'*

Question 8 – *'Have you any physical disability?'*
Reply – *'No.'*

Then at the bottom of the form the applicant signed the following certificate:

I hereby certify that the above statements are correct and agree that the accuracy of my replies to the questions shall be a condition of any contract of employment which may be offered to me by the Committee. If it is necessary for the County Medical Office to communicate with my doctor or specialist I authorise them to reply to any query concerning my health or medical history.

The Clerk to the Magistrates Courts Committee, Mr Banks, did not appreciate from those answers that Mr French was an epileptic. As a layperson he thought there was no need to worry about the answers on the form.

On 1 July 1990 Mr French started work in a Magistrates Court. He worked in the office, gaining experience in each section, and initially he sat in court as an observer.

At the beginning of July 1990 the results of the Part II Bar Examinations were published. Mr French had failed. The Clerk to the Magistrates had difficulty in getting the true facts from Mr French and eventually in a reply from the Dean of the Council of Legal Education he learnt for the first time that Mr French had now sat, and failed, the final examination three times. The significance of this was that normally an examinee has four chances to pass and so Mr French only had one to go.

In September 1990 Mr French had an attack of Grand Mal in the office. Mr Banks was there. This was the first knowledge the employer had that Mr French was an epileptic. Mr Banks discussed the situation with Mr French who said that he thought with drugs the position could be controlled. Mr Banks decided that the fairest thing to do was to wait and see how matters turned out. Mr Banks said that the knowledge that Mr French had epilepsy was something that could not be ignored, for he had to face the fact that, at worst, Mr French might have a fit in court while proceedings were in progress, or more likely, that his mental alertness might be affected by lesser attacks or by the affects of drug therapy. Mr Banks stressed to Mr French the need to take sensible avoiding action whenever he suspected an impending disturbance was likely to interfere with his work.

Mr Banks discussed the problem with Mrs Oliver, the Chairman of the Bench, and they decided that the other Justices should not be told of Mr French's condition, so as to ensure that reports on his progress would be reliable and to avoid the possibility that some Justices might prematurely lose confidence in his ability to act as a Court Clerk. Mrs Oliver has a medical background, she is a qualified nurse and has been a ward sister and a night sister. Her husband is a doctor and she has helped in his surgery for many years.

Over the next 12 months the magistrates noticed that Mr French had blank periods in court which they could not understand (they were obviously auras, but the magistrates were not aware that he was an epileptic).

Mr French originally intended to sit his finals for the fourth time in May 1992, but he postponed this to September. The results came out in October and again he had failed. So Mr Banks had to report to the Establishment Sub-Committee. Mr French applied to the Council of Legal Education for a dispensation to allow his to take his final examination a fifth time on the ground that the auras which he had suffered from had interfered with his study. The request was granted by the Appeals Committee who informed Mr French that, 'We are strongly of the opinion that on these results you would be throwing away your fifth attempt unless you obtain effective tuition before entering for the examination again.'

On 3 December 1992 Mr Banks reported to the Establishments Committee. His letter reads as follows:

Thank you for your letter of 26 November requesting my observations on Mr French's progress to date as a graduate trainee in this Court. I would submit the following assessment:

1. Performance in Court. For approximately six months Mr French has been acting as Court Clerk in traffic courts once or twice per week without supervision. His handling of the court is inconsistent. He usually operates satisfactorily, if rather slowly, but sometimes he has great difficult in handling the business in an acceptable fashion. I believe that this inconsistency is attributable to his epilepsy which, though controlled, nevertheless causes him to have auras sometimes in court, the effect of which, while falling short of a fit, can seriously interfere with his thought processes. He has suffered one fit in the office but none in court. He does make some mistakes but not to an excessive degree, having regard to the fact that he is a trainee. I am not inclined to allow him to take other courts unsupervised until he shows more confidence and competence in the traffic courts.

2. Reaction of the Magistrates. The general reaction is not favourable. The most common complaint is of slowness. This difficulty should be overcome with experience. There have been misgivings about his competence and it is clear to me that at the moment he does not inspire confidence in court. His manner in handling the court and the Bench is not much liked by the Magistrates.

3. Performance of other duties. When Mr French has taken a court it is his duty to deal with the administrative tasks arising therefrom, with the exception of the routine typing of fine notices and endorsement notices. He carries out these duties satisfactorily. When not taking a court, Mr French observes and assists in all types of courts and committees.

Conclusion. Mr French must learn to take sensible avoiding action so as to prevent his epilepsy from affecting his work as a court clerk. Also he must recognise when he is not sure of himself and when to take advice from myself or his senior colleagues. Further, when he makes mistakes he must accept that fact honestly and philosophically. I think he is beginning to do this now.

In my opinion Mr French could make a useful contribution to the Magistrates Court provided that he improves in the ways mentioned in the preceding paragraph. His performance is improving slowly, but I am not convinced that he has chosen a field that is suited to his personality.

Mr French was asked to reply in person to the committee to Mr Banks' letter. He contended that Mr Banks was prejudiced against him. Mr Banks denied this. He pointed out that it was on his recommendation, at the original interview, that Mr French was appointed and that therefore Mr Banks had a particular interest in ensuring that Mr French made a success of his job. He said that throughout he advised and supported Mr French. The committee decided that the report given by Mr Banks was fair. They found there was no prejudice and, that he was very helpful to Mr French throughout. He knew the problem from the time that Mr French had his attack of Grand Mal in September 1990 and he did his best to help Mr French thereafter.

During 1993 things did not improve. Mrs White, who has been a magistrate for ten years and who for the last 18 months has sat periodically as chairman, remembers occasions when the court got into a muddle, things got out of control and there was a degree of confusion. On a number of occasions, Mr Black, the prosecuting solicitor, had to go to the assistance of Mr French. For example when a defendant was called and came before the court and the Bench were waiting for him to be identified and the charge put to him, nothing happened at all. There was a very long silence that indicated to Mrs White that something had gone wrong. The matter was ended by Mr Black pushing some papers in front of Mr French who appeared then to jolt and start dealing with the case.

Again there were occasions when Mr French appeared unable to comprehend what the Bench wanted or to be able to advise them. During a case in the spring of 1993 there was a long pause which was completely inexplicable during which time nothing happened whatsoever. She remembers a number of occasions when Mr French was acting as Clerk when there had been long pauses in court which bore no relationship to the proceedings. They were not associated with a point of law or a point of difficulty that had arisen, but Mr French appeared to go completely quiet and do absolutely nothing for no apparent reason. At this time she had no knowledge that he suffered from epilepsy, but she felt that there must be something wrong with him. In her ten years experience as a Magistrate she had never known a Clerk so conduct himself.

As a result of these problems Mr Banks arranged to meet Mr French to discuss a way forward and subsequently wrote the following letter to Mr French:

> I have expressed to the Magistrates Courts Committee my view that the difficulties that have arisen in the performance of your duties here are attributable for the most part to the effects of epilepsy. I appreciate that my opinion is that of a layman rather than that of a medical expert, but I am sure you must agree that there is some foundation for this belief and therefore it would appear to be of vital importance to yourself, the Magistrates Courts Committee and any future Magistrates Courts Committee that might consider employing you, to know whether or not your epilepsy prevents you from satisfactorily undertaking the duties of a court clerk or a Justices' Clerk as a full time occupation.
>
> I would suggest that a persuasive opinion could be obtained from the community physician for the county council, if, with your consent, he could consult your own doctor regarding your physical fitness. Do you agree that such a course would be sensible? Would you consent to the community physician consulting your own doctor? I would ask you to respond to this letter as soon as possible.

Mr French was not keen to be examined by the community physician, but after conversation with Mr Banks he agreed to this and he gave his consent in writing asking to have an opportunity to speak with the community physician himself in order to discuss certain intimate matters.

A detailed description of Mr French's job was prepared and sent to the community physician who then obtained from Mr French's own GP a confidential report. As a result, on 29 March 1993, Dr Jenkins, the community physician, reported to Mr Banks as follows:

CONFIDENTIAL

Thank you for your memorandum of 10th March 1993. I have now heard from this man's general practitioner and we are both of the opinion that he would not be a suitable person to be a Justices' Clerk for health reasons. It therefore seems sensible that he should cease to be a trainee in this field. I am not at all sure how he ever came to be taken on in this capacity.

My advice to you is that he should be retired from his present position on grounds of ill health which is likely to be a permanent nature. As an epileptic he could be registered as a disabled person. However, it would seem a pity to waste his legal training and may be if he sought appropriate advice some niche could be found for him in that profession where the responsibilities would not be too great. In view of his relatively young age possibly the county council would consider finding him an alternative position in its own legal department. I would have thought that dealing with day-to-day matters such as conveyancing for a public authority would be his best bet. I notice in the letter from Mr Banks, that Mr French has expressed a desire to meet me in order to discuss certain aspects of his case. Although this would be a departure from our normal practice I would be prepared to see him if he would like to make an appointment with my secretary. However, it is extremely unlikely that anything he will say will influence my opinion that he is not suitable for health reasons to be a Justices' Clerk.

On 13 April Dr. Jenkins saw Mr French, but nothing transpired from the interview which led him to alter the opinion he had already given. On 14 April Mr Banks again reported to the Eastablishment Committee as follows:

Thank you for your letter of 25 February 1993. I understand that you now have the Community Physician's report regarding Mr French. I now submit an addendum to my report of 3 December 1992.

Mr French has continued to take two or three traffic courts per week. Both his performance in court and his relations with magistrates have shown improvement. Only one apparent blank period in court has been reported to me since last December, and while Mr French still conducts the business of the court rather slowly, the Magistrates have more confidence in him than they had in December.

Regarding his duties outside the courtroom, I have made him responsible for the administration of Legal Aid. To date he has carried out this task statisfactorily. It is clear that there has been a general improvement in Mr French's performance, and I feel that he is trying to put himself in order. However, I am not inclined to alter my opinion expressed in the conclusion of my report in December, that he has not chosen a field suited to his personality.

The matter was then considered by the Magistrates Courts Committee and they decided to dismiss Mr French. This was done by letter of 22 April in the following terms:

Further to your meeting with Dr Jenkins, the District Community Physician, I regret to inform you that both Doctor Jenkins and your own General Medical Practitioner advise that you should be retired from your position as Professional Trainee at the Magistrates Court on the grounds of permanent ill health. This advice was considered by the Establishments Sub-Committee of this committee on 15th April 1993 when it was resolved that your appointment should be terminated on the above grounds from 30th June 1993. I should add that when the sub-committee passed this resolution they were acting under delegated powers.

The Establishments Sub-Committee having looked at its own organisation has no suitable alternative employment to offer you at the present time. However, although this forms no part of the sub-committee's resolution, I am prepared to approach the county council with a view to seeing if any suitable employment opportunities do exist with that body or its ancillary organisations. Initially my contact for this purpose would be with the County Personnel Officer, and should you wish me to pursue this aspect of the matter, perhaps you would let me know.

Finally, I would remind you that you have a right of appeal against the resolution mentioned in the first paragraph of this letter, and if you desire to exercise this right you may do so either individually, or through your association, to the Magistrates Courts Committee. Should you be in any doubt about the appeal procedure or with respect to your position generally, I would recommend you to seek advice from your association or other quarter.

ACTIVITY BRIEF

1 *Critically examine the way in which the magistrates court has dealt with the recruitment, selection, performance appraisal and personal development of Mr French. Identify learning points from your examination and recommend improvements to the personnel policies procedures and practices of the Magistrates Courts department.*

2 *In your role as a legal advisor to either the Magistrates Courts Committee or Mr French, prepare a case to present before an industrial tribunal that will either promote or refute the allegation that Mr French has been unfairly dismissed.*

3 *Using information drawn from the case to substantiate your view, consider and debate the contention that the social responsibilities of management should be subordinate to the effective performance of organisational goals.*

RECOMMENDED READING

Legal Aspects
Smith, I. T. and Wood, J. C., (1989). *Industrial Law*, London: Butterworths.
ACAS (1977). *Code of Practice No 1 Disciplinary practice and procedure in employment 1977* – together with handbook on advice on discipline at work first published in 1987.
Employment Protection Consolidation Act 1978 s. 57. (1)(b).

Midshire Association for the Blind – The staffing implications of restructuring

Irene Watson

In these days of economic fluctuations, technological developments and changing markets, few organisations can survive without making adjustments to the size, structure and composition of their workforces. These adjustments happen at the extremes of the employment spectrum (hiring and firing) and during employment (training, transfers, etc). When making these adjustments, organisations must work within the framework of national and European employment legislation.

Redundancy is one adjustment for which there is very extensive, complex and detailed legislation. With the increase in redundancies in the early 1990s, there is a growing body of case law, academic research and practical experience on which to draw.

This case study presents a situation in which external forces have led to redundancies being proposed. Apart from any necessary reference to the appropriate legal background, the case provides opportunities for considering individual and corporate responses to redundancy, for identifying best practice in handling such situations and for assessing strategies for minimising the effects of redundancies on all those concerned.

BACKGROUND

The Midshire Association for the Blind (MAB), a registered charity, is one of the many county associations raising money and providing essential services for people with visual handicaps within their area. MAB does not attempt to compete with the national charities such as the Royal National Institute for the Blind or Guide Dogs for the Blind in terms of services but seeks to complement their activities within the county; indeed, MAB receives grants from these organisations to carry out certain functions. However, all charities are in competition when it comes to raising funds.

History

The origins of MAB date back to Victorian days and Samuel Lewis, a successful manufacturer, whose only child, Thomas, born in 1863, was blind. There were no special schools and few facilities for handicapped children but Lewis was fortunate to engage the services of a remarkable governess, Sylvia Temple, who provided Thomas with an excellent education. On his death in 1893, Samuel Lewis divided his estate between Thomas and a trust fund to provide schooling for blind children.

The Lewis Trust, which numbered Thomas Lewis and Sylvia Temple amongst its trustees, established a small school in the Lewis family home, with Thomas as headmaster and Sylvia Temple as a teacher. The school continued in a small way, surviving Sylvia Temple's death in 1920, until 1933 when Thomas Lewis retired from teaching.

At this time, he reassessed the position of the school. The provision for visually handicapped children was much better by then and there were a number of special schools providing a broad general education. There was little demand for the local, rather limited, facility and the number of enrolments was falling. Perhaps because of his personal experience, Thomas felt that the Trust should do more for visually handicapped people of all ages and he persuaded the other Trustees that the emphasis of the school should be changed from basic education for children to vocational training for young adults.

The Trustees petitioned the Charity Commissioners, changed the name of the Trust to the Midshire Association for the Blind and its terms of reference to encompass financial and practical assistance to blind and partially sighted people of all ages. Thomas Lewis was the first Chairman of the Association and, when he died in 1944, he left his estate, including the house, to the Association 'for the benefit of blind people in Midshire'.

THE SITUATION

The Association is still governed by a board of trustees through two committees, Finance and General Purposes and Operations, which oversee its work. It is managed, on a day-to-day basis, by a chief executive (CE). A new CE, a woman with experience in city institutions, has recently been appointed with the brief of ensuring that MAB meets the needs of the blind and partially sighted people of the county now and into the next century.

Client base

In order to fulfil her brief the CE first commissioned a survey of the population of the county to ascertain what the needs of the visually impaired might be:

(a) there are 42,500 blind or partially sighted people in the county (1.6% of the population) but only 10,500 (25%) are registered;

(b) less than 4,000 (10%) of blind or partially sighted adults were born with this handicap;

(c) 34,000 (80%) of blind or partially sighted people are over retirement age and, of these, 23,000 are over the age of 75;

(d) 66% of blind or partially sighted adults have one or more other serious illnesses or disabilities;

(e) of the 4,000 blind or partially sighted people of working age, only 1,000 are in employment;

(f) there are around 680 blind or partially sighted children in the county and, of these, 360 (53%) go to mainstream schools;

(g) 350 blind or partially sighted children (over 51%) have other physical or mental handicaps.

The results echo national statistics which reflect better ante-natal care reducing the number of children born with visual impairments and greater longevity leading to more elderly people suffering from glaucoma, cataracts, etc.

Financial information

Second, she reviewed the Association's accounts.

INCOME

	Last year £	Previous year £
Grants	500,000	480,000
Donations	410,000	430,000
Investments	350,000	365,000
Fees & Sales	240,000	250,000
Legacies	120,000	120,000
Total	1,620,000	1,645,000

Low interest rates and poor performance on the stock exchange, combined with the recession and increased unemployment in the area had led to disappointing results.

EXPENDITURE

	Last Year £	Previous Year £
Services for:		
– people of working age	550,000	560,000
– the elderly	450,000	440,000
– for children	300,000	300,000
Salaries and administration	500,000	475,000
Total	1,800,000	1,775,000

The figures for expenditure were equally dispiriting and had necessitated dipping into reserves.

Organisation and staffing

Finally, she investigated the Association's organisation and staffing.

The culture of the organisation had changed little over the years and is rather paternalistic with something of the Victorian philanthropist about it. This is quite usual in small charities; the 'caring' nature of the work tends to influence employment policies and attitudes to staff and, as a result, a number of the staff have been with MAB for many years.

Like many other small charities, MAB has traditionally based its terms and conditions of employment on those in local authorities (LAs) and had relied on their local council for advice on personnel and employee relations issues. Now, however, because of staff reductions and competitive tendering, the council can no longer help. Unlike LAs, however, MAB does not recognise any trade union for collective bargaining purposes even though a few of the staff are union members.

There are grievance and discipline procedures, again closely modelled on the LA procedures, and discipline is the one area where unions have been involved, on the odd occasion when such action has been necessary. MAB has not yet adopted policies or procedures covering staff development, appraisal, equal opportunities or security of employment (redundancy).

In addition to its paid staff, MAB relies heavily on voluntary workers particularly for fundraising, where they arrange coffee mornings and jumble sales, carry out street collections, etc. Some voluntary workers visit visually blind and partially handicapped people in their homes, take them shopping, to the doctors, etc. Voluntary workers are also found in schools, where MAB provides people to help visually impaired children in mainstream education. Voluntary workers do not receive any remuneration for their work but those who regularly provide transport for visually impaired people are reimbursed the costs of travel.

The Association had grown in a rather haphazard manner over the years until, by the 1990s, it had 27 staff plus some part-time manual employees and 30–35 voluntary workers. The staff are organised in four main areas – finance, administration, education and social work. The details are shown in Figure 21.1 below.

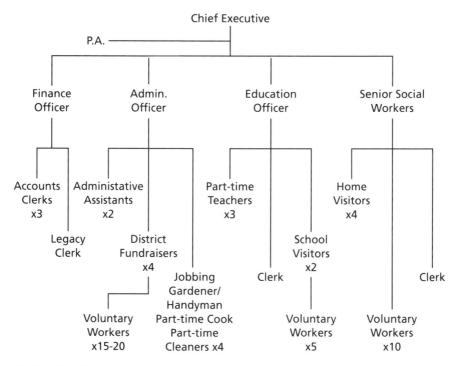

Fig 21.1 Existing structure

Conclusions

The CE analysed the survey data, the financial information and staffing structure, then referred back to the terms of reference of the trust, 'to provide financial and practical assistance to blind and partially sighted people of all ages within the county.' She felt that, on the whole, the Association was not using its resources effectively and was not achieving its stated objectives. The particular areas of concern she identified were:

● The overgenerous resources allocated to the school; although this had been an important training facility in the past, it was now reduced to teaching typing and wordprocessing. Within the school structure, more resources need to be allocated to mobility and life-skills (i.e. dressing, cooking, cleaning, etc.) training to assist people who become visually impaired later in life.

Another area which needs to be enhanced is training for teachers aids. With the majority of visually impaired children now attending mainstream schools, there is an increased demand for people to assist them – the young ones with mobility, work, meals, play, etc., and the older ones with reading and examinations. LAs usually fund teachers aid posts but do not provide professional training.

- The lack of resources devoted to financial and practical assistance for the elderly; this age group constitutes the largest part of the visually impaired population but receives only a small fraction of the resources. More resources need to be allocated to outreach, to visiting visually impaired people in their homes, schools, places of employment and entertainment, identifying the main needs and ensuring they are met.
- The traditional nature of fundraising; too heavy a reliance on flag days, coffee mornings, etc., had resulted in a situation where fundraisers were raising barely enough money to cover their costs. A new style of fundraising needs to be introduced with a more aggressive marketing approach to gain business sponsorship, encourage involvement from local schools and colleges, provide press releases and publicity about events, etc.

The way forward

The CE reported these findings in confidence to the chairman of the board of trustees and gained agreement to develop an outline staffing structure to meet the requirements of the new approach.

The new structure

The CE proposed that the staff should be organised in four departments:

- Education and training
- Client services
- Fundraising
- Finance and administration.

Each would have a manager with clearly defined responsibilities and accountabilities, and there would be radical changes for the staff too.

- Within the Education and Training Department, the demand for mobility and life-skills training is unpredictable and is best carried out on an individual basis in and around the client's home, place of employment, etc. The demand for teachers aid training needed to be more structured and should be carried out once a term in the training school. Training in typing/wordprocessing should be provided through short courses as demand arises.

In the circumstances, these needs might best be met by using the resources to hire specialist consultant trainers as and when necessary, rather than by paying staff who were not fully employed. The existing jobs would disappear and the staff posts be redundant, but a new post of education and training manager would be created and there would be opportunities for self-employed consultant trainers in mobility and life-skills, typing and wordprocessing, and teachers aid training.

- The Client Services Department would be the focus for research into the needs of visually impaired people in the county and for provision to meet these needs through grants and advice; a more proactive approach would be required.

The post of senior social worker would be replaced by that of client services manager to reflect the wider needs of visually impaired people. The home visitor posts would be disbanded and their work, in future, carried out by voluntary workers. Outreach worker positions would be created and people appointed to identify the needs of visually impaired people in the county, at home, school and college, at work and leisure, and to provide advice, guidance and practical assistance on how to make best use of the services provided by the State, county and national charities. There would also be a new post of grants administrator to oversee the allocation of grant aid to applicants.

- The Fundraising Department would be a new, specialist enterprise to give the function the impetus it needs in the current climate; corporate sponsorship and regular support from schools and colleges would be sought and public relations work would increase awareness. This new emphasis would, it was hoped, increase donations through payroll giving, legacies, etc. The traditional activities, e.g. flag days, coffee mornings, etc., would continue but run by volunteers.

The existing posts in administration would be disestablished and new posts of fundraising manager and three positions of fundraiser, each with a particular, specialist function, would be created.

- The Finance and Administration Department would bring together the various support functions, streamlining the central work and providing a more professional financial, personnel and administrative service to the Association.

The new finance and administration manager would take day-to-day control of the department, leading a team consisting of finance officer, admin. officer and personnel officer. The introduction of information technology would facilitate a small reduction in the numbers of support staff and the transfer of clerical positions from education and social work to a central secretariat would make most effective use of the administrative support. Contracting out the gardening, catering and cleaning functions was also proposed.

Details of the proposed new structure is shown in Figure 21.2 over.

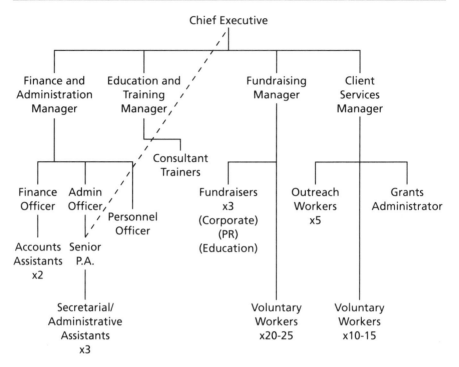

Fig 21.2 Proposed structure

Implementation

The CE had some concerns about her proposals; she was sure that this was the right way forward but knew that a number of staff would have no place in the new structure. There would no longer be positions for part-time teachers, although there would be opportunities for self-employed consultant trainers. Would the home visitors, with their social work orientation, be able to adjust to a more proactive role or be able to train others? The jobs in the new fundraising department were so radically different that the district fundraisers might not have the skills needed for the new roles. The staff in the administration and finance functions were probably the most easily absorbed into the new structure but the manual workers would be without jobs unless they became self-employed and bid for the contracts or were taken on by the successful contractors.

In view of the changes that this new structure would mean for the staff, variations in job content, increased responsibilities for some, decreased responsibilities for others, redundancy a possibility for many, the chief executive thought that it was essential to consult the staff before the proposals became a *fait accompli*.

Before any consultations could start, however, she decided that a focus for human resources issues was necessary. There had not been a personnel officer in the old structure, but the CE's personal assistant (PA) had always dealt with basic personnel administration matters. The PA was aware of the developments and expressed an interest in developing the personnel aspects of her role further. The CE thought that this was an excellent career step for her PA and asked her to take on the role of acting personnel officer, subject to formal appointment procedures in due course. She delegated the first task to the new acting personnel officer – to devise a 'Security of Employment' policy and procedure. The proposed policy and procedure devised by the acting personnel officer is attached at Appendix 1.

The acting personnel officer studied the outline proposals and pointed out that a Security of Employment policy was not the only thing needed before the consultations began. The staff would certainly want to know about how appointments would be made to the new structure, whether they would have to apply for what they might consider to be their own jobs, and what would happen to them if they were not successful. Those whose jobs were disappearing completely, the teaching staff and manual workers in particular, would need information and advice about what opportunities there might be for self-employed contract work. The CE agreed that there should be a procedure for selection and appointment to jobs in the new structure and that it should be given to staff; she asked the acting personnel officer to give the matter some consideration and make recommendations.

The CE was aware that such a radical restructuring, if presented insensitively and without a full explanation of the reasons, could alienate the employees and, through them, the voluntary workers and members of the public. Reorganisations such as the one proposed usually take some time to implement and it would be important to maintain motivation and output during the transition. She had read about the effects of major restructuring on staff and was concerned to ensure that the adverse effects of reorganisation were minimised. She was also aware of the problems sometimes faced by those staff who kept their jobs while others were redundant; steps would have to be taken to maintain morale in the 'staying-ons'. Even more than in a commercial organisation, the whole process needed to be handled with kid gloves to maintain the Association's image.

She started to plan how to make the announcement to the staff.

APPENDIX 1

Security of employment – policy and procedure

Policy

The Midshire Association for the Blind (MAB) strives to offer its employees security of employment by:

- careful management, financial and manpower planning to avoid wide fluctuations in the numbers of staff which need to be employed;
- maintaining a balanced workforce matched, as far as possible, to the present and future needs of the organisation.

There may be situations, however, where it is unavoidable that some positions may have to be declared redundant.

Objective

This procedure has been devised for those situations in order to ensure that employees are dealt with openly, fairly and in a way which will minimise uncertainty and stress.

Procedure

(1) **Prevention**
If it appears that a redundancy or redundancies are likely, MAB will inform the person or group of people concerned as early as possible. The purpose of this first discussion is to identify and, as far as possible, agree on methods of avoiding the need for redundancies.

Compulsory redundancy shall be the last resort and shall not be adopted until all other options, e.g. natural wastage, recruitment freeze, redeployment to other jobs, voluntary severance and short-time working, together with any other suggestions, have been considered.

(2) **Consultation**
MAB is committed to consulting with all staff likely to be affected by redundancy and will commence such consultation as soon as is reasonably practical.

Statutory periods for consultation with recognised trades unions where their members face redundancy are laid down by Parliament. In the case of MAB, this period would be 30 days in the case of 10 or more dismissals in a 30 day period.

MAB accepts these periods as a minimum for all staff, regardless of union membership or numbers involved.

(3) Criteria for Selection

If the measures described in (1) above do not lead to sufficient staff reductions, there will be a trawl for volunteers.

If insufficient volunteers are forthcoming, or if the number of volunteers exceeds the number of posts which must be declared redundant, selection for redundancy will be on the following basis:

- the requirement, subject to prudent financial planning and management, to meet the objectives of the organisation, i.e. 'to provide financial and practical assistance to blind and partially sighted people of all ages within the county.'
- last in, first out (LIFO).

(4) Notice

MAB will give all employees selected for redundancy statutory notice or such notice as stated in the employee's contract of employment, whichever is greater.

Notice will be in writing and will detail statutory redundancy payments and discretionary severance compensation.

Notice will be withdrawn if suitable alternative employment is found within MAB, or if the need for redundancy diminishes or disappears.

(5) Alternative employment

Prior to and during the notice period, MAB will try to find suitable alternative employment for all employees selected for redundancy. Any offer of alternative employment will:

- be made before the notice expires;
- be in writing;
- take effect immediately the current employment ends or within four weeks;
- be suitable for the employee concerned, within the meaning of the Redundancy Payments Act, as amended;
- be subject to a four week trial period during which the employee and manager will determine whether it is suitable or not. If, during this period, either party deems the job not to be suitable, the employee will be entitled to the original redundancy payment and discretionary severance compensation.

An employee who unreasonably refuses an offer of suitable alternative employment may forfeit the right to a redundancy payment and discretionary severance compensation.

(6) Redundancy Payments

In the event of a person or group of people being dismissed due to redundancy, the compensation for dismissal will be as follows.

6.1 *Statutory Redundancy Payment*

Any entitlements due under the statutory redundancy scheme as laid down by the Employment Protection (Consolidation) Act, as amended from time to time.

6.2 *Additional Severance Payment*

For employees with 24 months service or more:

(i)   for the purpose of calculating the redundancy payment, the upper pay limit on statutory redundancy pay, specified in the above Act, will be disregarded;

(ii) The figure resulting from 6.1 and 6.2 (i) above will be doubled to provide the final redundancy payment.

(iii) The total redundancy payment will not be less than 15 weeks pay.

Employees with between 12 and 24 months service will receive 12 weeks pay, those with between 3 and 12 months service will receive 8 weeks pay and those with up to 3 months service will receive 4 weeks pay.

(7) Pensions

The scheme to which MAB contributes on behalf of its employees permits members to retire early in certain circumstances with only limited effects on the resulting pension. Members of the scheme aged 50 or more whose positions are redundant will be treated sympathetically.

ACTIVITY BRIEF

1 *Analyse the redundancy policy and procedure devised by the acting personnel officer of MAB (Appendix 1) identifying its strengths, weaknesses and omissions.*

2 *Imagine you are the chief executive of MAB. Draft an action plan for implementing the reorganisation, bearing in mind the special circumstances and nature of the organisation. Consider the merits and difficulties of announcing proposals which will lead to redundancy:*
(a)   at a mass meeting;
(b)   individually face to face;
(c)   individually in writing.

3 *Identify the possible employee reactions and/or responses to the news of reorganisation and redundancy at MAB and suggest measures that could be taken to deal with them.*

4 *Consider the impact of redundancies on employees who keep their jobs while colleagues lose theirs. If you were the chief executive of MAB, what measures could you take to maintain motivation and morale amongst these employees:*

   (a) during the reorganisation;

   (b) after the reorganisation.

5 *Identify possible methods of making appointments to the new positions in MAB which would be both effective and considered fair by all concerned.*

RECOMMENDED READING

Fowler, A. (1993). *Redundancy (Law & Employment Series),* IPM.

Croner Publications Limited (1986). *A Fresh Start: A Positive Approach to Redundancy,* Croner.

Mullins, L. J. (1993). *Management and Organisational Behaviour,* London: Pitman.

Competence-based recruitment and selection

Marjorie Corbridge and Stephen Pilbeam

This case study considers the concept of competence in work roles and explores a potential application in the area of recruitment and selection. It is not intended to promote competence-based recruitment and selection as the 'one best way', nor is it intended to fully examine the current debate about competence. However, it does aim to promote discussion and develop insight into this area of human resource management as well as offering a practical management application.

The use of competences in recruitment and selection has a number of potential benefits. It focuses activity upon which abilities are necessary to do a job successfully rather than upon factors like age, educational qualifications and traditional stereotypes. This approach presupposes that abilities may be acquired through apparently unrelated work experience and also non-work roles.

Competence is a composite term and various writers define the components in different ways. For our purposes we will recognise that competence includes skill, knowledge and attitudes, and that these components are interdependent. This ensures that competence is viewed as a practical extension of skill development by incorporating the need for underpinning knowledge in order that the individual understands what they are doing, and suggests that skills and knowledge will not be applied effectively in the absence of appropriate attitudes and motivation.

BACKGROUND

Theoretical discussions about the precise definition of competence are extensively covered in a vast range of papers and some reading references are included in the bibliography of this case. Although not making a rigorous attempt at defining competence it is important that we have a working definition which can be that competence is an assessable and consistent ability to perform tasks and work activities to an effective performance standard.

The implication of this working definition for recruitment and selection based on competence assessment is that there is a prerequisite to identify what the individual will have *to be able to do* in a particular job and also determine what performance standards are necessary. It then becomes possible to develop techniques to assess whether the individual is competent for the job. The focus is therefore on job outputs or outcomes – what the individual has to be able to do and whether they can do it, rather than on the qualifications or job experience, or lack of it, of the individual.

One of the fundamental differences about competence-based recruitment and selection that we are trying to establish is that these competences may have been acquired in non-work roles. For example oral communication skills may have been developed through being a parent governor, a role which can involve making presentations at PTA meetings, interviewing candidates for teaching posts and negotiating with suppliers for school equipment.

The competence of decision making requires indicators which would establish whether the individual is able to obtain, analyze and use information in order to make appropriate and logical decisions. This could be evidenced by presenting the candidate with information and scenarios relevant to the job and checking responses against known effective decisions.

This process of defining competences, establishing behavioural indicators and developing assessment techniques is progressive and offers a framework for recruitment and selection which steps outside the traditional approach.

The most important step in the whole process of using a competence-based approach is the identification of the required competences. Systematic recruitment and selection procedures will not be effective unless they are based upon a sound and thorough analysis and expression of what the job holder will need to be able to do.

Within an organisational setting there are a wide range of job analysis techniques available. Job analysis, or more appropriately within our context, competency analysis, is essentially a research activity based upon data collection, analysis and interpretation. The choice of technique will be contingent on the nature of the job, the size of the organisation and the resources available and it is not possible to say that one technique is more appropriate than another. Whatever methods are used the objective is to synthesise an agreed and relevant set of competences, which includes both definition and the identification of behavioural indicators. These agreed standards then provide the framework for systematic recruitment and selection processes.

A summary of the approach.

Stage 1
- Define the target group
- Identify the competences
- Define what may constitute good or bad performance

Stage 2
- Choose the recruitment and selection methods
- Design recruitment material
    Advertising copy
    Application form
- Design selection methods
    Application form
    Short-listing criteria
    Interview structure
    Tests or sampling activities
    Reference enquiries

Stage 3
- Evaluation
    Effectiveness and efficiency
    Predictive validity
    Equal opportunities objectives

In introducing competence-based recruitment and selection it can appear to be complex, complicated and time-consuming. The same can be said of more traditional approaches. In fact competence-related methods can be made relatively simple, cheap to operate and easy to interpret. Students and organisations will have to decide whether the opportunity to respond to demographic changes, promoting equality of opportunity and selecting on merit, thereby contributing to organisational effectiveness, will be enhanced by the competence-based approach.

In undertaking the activities associated with this case it may be necessary

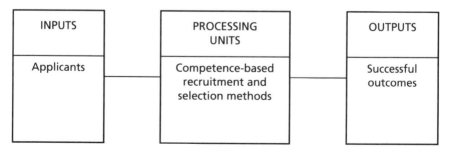

Fig 22.1 The processing unit

for those with experience of more traditional approaches to recruitment and selection to guard against potential negative transfer of learning. If we accept the recruitment and selection process as a system with the applicants as the inputs, the transformation or processing unit as the recruitment and selection approach and methods, and the outputs as successful performers it does require a rethink of the processing unit – in effect starting with an empty box untainted by traditional experiences (*See* Fig 22.1).

THE SITUATION

Recruitment and selection in a retail organisation – an illustration of a competence approach to recruitment and selection

There are an increasing number of organisations that are focusing on competence-based recruitment and selection to supplement their use of the competence approach elsewhere in their human resource management policies, particularly in staff development.

Cobras plc is a chain of supermarkets that is committed to the use of competence as a foundation to the recruitment, selection and development of staff at all levels in the organisation.

Cobras plc is a forward looking and progressive company advanced in its involvement with Management Charter Initiative and who in 1992 considered the further extension of competences in the organisation through the implementation of competence-based recruitment and selection. The following case is an illustration of their approach.

Stage 1:

Deciding on target group
Cobras plc started by identifying the range of jobs that would, in the first instance, be filled using the competency approach. This was predicated on the notion that there may be difficulties in implementation that would be best dealt with prior to this new approach being used at all levels in the organisation. Any problems identified in the pilot stage could be addressed before the method was introduced throughout the organisation. The first group chosen for the pilot study was the first level of management, a group that in the past has been traditionally filled by new graduates. The approach taken was to focus on the production of job descriptions that were written in such a way as to identify the competences required to undertake the job rather than the duties and responsibilities of the postholder.

Job descriptions were drawn up and agreed with the postholder and management. These were to form the basis of the recruitment process. In the past the main criteria for selection had been educational qualifications; the focus now was to be on competence – what the successful postholder was able to do. It was also recognised that performance indicators should be identified so that the appropriate level of competence is defined.

A job profile was produced for all of the posts (see Appendix A) and this was to form the basis for recruitment and selection; it was also appropriate for the identification of individual career development needs.

Identify the competences

The core competences were defined as:

- Managing finance
- Managing people
- Managing assets
- Managing information

These were further subdivided into specific competences:

- Problem solving
- Management control
- Delegation
- Oral communication and presentation skills
- Problem analysis
- Decisiveness
- Leadership
- Written communication

In order to determine good or bad performance, suitable indicators were agreed. These were wherever possible quantitative, although in some cases they were qualitative, but the aim was to reduce subjectivity to a minimum.

Stage 2

Choose the recruitment and selection methods

It was decided to:

- Advertise the posts using a competence focus
- Design an appropriate application form
- Short-list against the defined competence
- Interview
- Provide in tray and group exercises
- Use psychometric tests

Design recruitment material

The next stage was to look at the job advertisement and accompanying company literature to ensure that this also represented a competence approach. The application form was redesigned to ask direct questions about the ability of the applicants, for example 'As an assistant manager – grocery, you will be required to manage stock to ensure that sales and profits are maximised. Can you give an example of when you have had to manage stock in this way?'

The application forms can have a tendency to become very long and complex which may make some potential applicants reluctant to apply. This is not seen as a problem so long as an appropriate number of suitable people are applying.

The application form is both a recruitment and selection tool; its design and structure attracts (or deters) candidates and it also provides information for the selectors.

Design selection methods

It is important that the selection process focuses on the assessment of the competence. Therefore a range of selection tools were used in an attempt to assess as accurately as is possible the competence of the individual to do the job.

Application form

The questions on the application form were weighted and scored to give a structured, less subjective approach which focused on the competences.

Short-listing

The short-listing of applicants for interview was structured according to the priority of competence and in this systematic way an appropriate number of candidates were invited to attend for a selection day. The people involved in the short-listing were the same as those involved in the total selection process to ensure that the criteria were known and understood and there were not managers moving in and out of the process.

Interview

Considerable time was spent in developing an appropriate structure focusing on the core and specific competences.

The assessors were asked to rate the candidates against each of the core and specific competencies using a five-point scale. Adequate time was allocated and all those involved in interviewing were trained and briefed on the approach to take.

Tests

In tray exercise

An in tray exercise was developed by the current first level managers in conjunction with the personnel and training managers to accurately reflect the paper that might 'pass across' the desk in an average week. Priorities were defined and a marking scheme developed.

Group exercise
It was decided to include a short group exercise to test competence that cannot be adequately measured by other methods. This is an excellent way of identifying interpersonal skills and the competences of leadership and decisiveness.

Psychometric tests
It was decided to test for numerical reasoning and computing ability as these competences are best assessed by testing and are difficult to identify in any other way.

At the end of the selection process there was a meeting of all assessors at which each candidate was discussed and ranked according to the points allocated. These rankings were finally agreed and this formed the basis of the job offer.

Assessors were trained in assessment techniques and given definitions of positive and negative behaviours. All the assessors were senior store managers or district managers with extensive experience in Cobras plc in the selection of existing managers and who were well trained in this new approach to selection.

ACTIVITY BRIEF

1 **Either**
   Using either of the traditional job descriptions, in Appendix B identify the competences required for the job, define good and bad performance indicators and write a job profile for the jobs using the competence approach (based on the example in the case study).

   or

   Obtain a job description from an organisation and follow the process outlined above.

2 *Design structured competence-based interview questions for either of the jobs above. Role play an interview with a suitably briefed interviewee.*

3 *Critically evaluate competence-based recruitment and selection through group discussion or written assignments.*

4 *Cobras plc has not as yet undertaken an evaluation of this new approach. In groups, identify and evaluate the criteria that could be used to evaluate this approach to recruitment and selection.*

RECOMMENDED READING

Boam, R. and Sparrow, P. (1992). *Designing and Achieving Competency*, Maidenhead: McGraw-Hill.

Dulewicz, Victor. (1989). 'Assessment Centres as the Route to Competence', *Personnel Management*, November, pp. 56-59.

Employment Service. (1991). *Competency Based Recruitment*.

Fletcher, S. (1991). *NVQ's Standards and Competence*, London: Kogan Page.

APPENDIX A

JOB PROFILE

Title: Assistant Manager - Grocery

Reports to: Store Manager

Organisation chart

```
                        Store Manager
                             |
        +--------------------+-------------------+
  Deputy Manager    AM-Fresh Foods         AM-Grocery
        +-----------+---------+--------------+--------+
  Personnel &   Grocery   Night crew   Beers, wines   Petrol
  training      Mgr       Mgr          & spirits      Mgr
  Mgr                                  Mgr
```

Main purpose

To manage and develop the grocery management team and other store resources (human, physical and financial) as required by the store manager.

To achieve sales and profit objectives while maintaining full compliance policies, procedures and standards in the grocery area in the total store as required.

Major competence	Key result area
Managing people	To manage and develop department managers in grocery departments.
	To ensure a high level of customer service on the grocery departments.
Managing assets	To assist the store manager in the running of the total store.
	To ensure the implementation of legislation, standards, policies and procedures on the grocery departments.
	To manage stock to ensure that sales and profits are maximised.
Managing finance	To control costs within the grocery departments.
Managing information	To maintain effective comminication through the grocery departments and within the total store.

Major competence	Key result areas	Operational competences
Managing people	Management and development of department managers in grocery departments.	1.1 Appraise department managers. 1.2 Set training and development plans for grocery department managers. 1.3 Ensure training and development of grocery staff. 1.4 Recognise and develop potential of grocery department managers. 1.5 Carry out selection interviews for store staff as required. 1.6 Monitor and control company dress and personal hygiene standards. 1.7 Ensure line department managers' implementation of company policies. 1.8 Monitor and control scheduling to maximise productivity. 1.9 Monitor and control manpower shortages. 1.10 Correct implementation of company disciplinary and grievance procedure. 1.11 Minimise staff turnover. 1.12 Chair regular grocery department meetings.
	To ensure a high level of customer service on the grocery departments.	2.1 Deal with customer queries and complaints. 2.2 Attract and retain customers. 2.3 Advise customers on products and services.
Managing assets	To assist the store manager in the running of the total store.	3.1 Monitor the store environment to ensure implementation of Health and Safety legislation. 3.2 Monitor and control security procedures relating to total store operations. 3.3 Ensure the efficient running of the store in the absence of the senior store management.

Major competence	Key result areas	Operational competences	
	To ensure the implementation of all legislation, standards, policies and procedures within the grocery departments.	4.1	Monitor the grocery operation to ensure that all legislation and policies and procedures are adhered to.
		4.2	Monitor the quality and temperature controls and take appropriate action.
		4.3	Monitor and control hygiene standards on the grocery departments.
		4.4	Review standards of presentation and merchandising plans, direct implementation and adjustments.
		4.5	Implement recommendations from company audits and external inspections.
	To manage stock to ensure sales and profits are maximised.	5.1	Control stock loss wastage from grocery departments.
		5.2	Monitor grocery orders to meet sales demands.
		5.3	Monitor the receiving, handling, storing and rotation of stock.
		5.4	Monitor and maintain the grocery departments stocktake procedures.
		5.5	Recognise and take action on sales and profit opportunities within the grocery operation.
Managing finance	To control costs within the grocery departments.	6.1	Monitor and maintain all cash handling procedures for beers, wines and sprits and petrol stations and ensure accuracy of accounting procedures.
		6.2	Analyse and take action on SPS deficiencies in line departments and report to the store manager.
		6.3	Ensure salary costs are within plan.
		6.4	Ensure all controllable costs are kept within plan.

Major competence	Key result areas	Operational competences
Managing information	To maintain effective communication throughout the grocery departments and within the total store.	7.1 Monitor and maintain administration procedures within grocery departments.
		7.2 Process relevant mail and disseminate information to grocery staff.
		7.3 Communicate all policies and procedures in grocery departments.
		7.4 Access, analyse and use relevant information from the computer system and other sources.
		7.5 Supply information required by the company.

APPENDIX B

Job description – Sales Advisor

JOB TITLE: Sales Advisor

DEPARTMENT: Sales Department

RESPONSIBLE TO: Branch Manager/Sales Manager

REPORTING TO: Branch Manager

PURPOSE OF JOB: To offer excellent customer service and so maximise sales profit and minimise losses.

KEY TASKS:

a. *Customer Service*
To use the ability to communicate with customers, offer advice on garment care and accessories and maintain good customer relations at all times.

b. *Selling Skills*
To acquire and use selling skills to select garments, meet the customers' needs and encourage multiple sales.

c. *Product Knowledge*
To acquire and use expert product knowledge to advise customers correctly. To ensure they know the current merchandising floor plan and can find stock easily.

d. *Security*
To be aware of security risks to company stock, cash and property and to reduce the possibility of theft and losses.

e. *Visual Merchandising & Display*
To develop the ability to display and merchandise the sales floor in a commercial manner, to encourage sales.

f. *Professionalism*
To present a smart professional appearance at all times. To be punctual and reliable.

g. *Working Relationships*
To maintain a good working relationship with colleagues.

h. *Other Duties*
To carry out other tasks necessary for the smooth running of the branch e.g. housekeeping, admin.
You are expected to work within the company policies, procedures and staff rules at all times.

JOB DESCRIPTION

JOB TITLE: Checkout Manager

POSITION RESPONSIBLE TO: Store Manager

REF NO: **KEY DUTIES**

1.1 Efficient labour utilisation with the checkout area in order to maximise productivity.

1.2 To foster and maintain the highest level of customer care and service within the department.

1.3 To ensure that all company policies and procedures relating to the handling of cash and checkout operations are adhered to.

1.4 To ensure an even flow of customers at all times through the checkouts.

1.5 To ensure all customers are dealt with in a courteous and pleasant manner and that all queries and complaints are dealt with efficiently, and according to company policy.

1.6 Development and retraining of subordinate staff/trainees in conjunction with instore trainer.

Areas of responsibility

2.1 To assist with instore trainer in interviewing of all Front End staff.

2.2 To ensure that cashier work schedules are planned/updated/followed, together with the accurate recording of actual hours worked for wage purposes.

2.3 To control and schedule meal breaks, ensuring that customers are redirected according to company recommendations from checkouts which are closing.

2.4 To ensure that all baskets and trolleys are cleared according to company guidelines.

2.5 To ensure that all equipment in the department is handled correctly and safely and maintained in good working order.

2.6 To ensure that all cash registers are operated according to company policy.

2.7 To ensure checker tests are carried out according to company policy.

2.8 To ensure that all price checks are dealt with according to company policy.

2.9 To ensure that floats are issued to cash handlers according to company procedures.

3.0 The Lost Property Book should be maintained according to company policy.

3.1 To ensure that the intercom is used within the checkout area according to company policy and that the correct codes are used.

3.2 Ensure that price changes are carried out.

3.3 To carry out regular manpower planning surveys according to company policy.

3.4 To ensure that cashiers are supplied with change as necessary.

3.5 To ensure the accuracy/control of the change float.

3.6 To carry out audit roll checks daily to ensure that all voids over 25p are signed by management, and to collect all used audit rolls.

3.7 Maintain and oversee the record of customers' puchases left within the store.

3.8 Overall authority for authorisation of cheques at checkouts.

3.9 To ensure regular product recognition checks are made on all cashiers.

4.0 To ensure correct documentation of 'No Sales' by cashiers.

4.1 To ensure satisfactory liaison of checkout supervisor and staff with cash office and department managers and store management.

4.2 To assist any cashier, packer or porter in difficulty.

4.3 To conduct regular appraisals in conjunction with instore trainer of all checkout staff.

4.4 To observe cashier/porter/packer performance and carry out regular assessments tests in conjunction with the instore trainer.

4.5 To allocate other duties to cashiers/porters/packers during slack periods.

4.6 To assist with the disciplining of cashiers/porters/packers in conjunction with the store manager.

4.7 To check and maintain the checkout scales daily.

4.8 To ensure that all checkout staff are pleasant and respectful to customers.

4.9 To oversee additional customer services as directed by store manager, e.g. photocare; flowers.

5.0 To maintain the highest standard of cleanliness of the checkouts and the checkout area.

5.1 To ensure that company policy regarding personal hygiene, appearance and dress is upheld by all cashiers/porters/packers.

5.2 To ensure that all aspects of security relating to the operation of the department and the store are implemented and with store management carry out spot checks and till checks in accordance with company policy.

5.3 To ensure that packers/porters operate efficiently within the checkout area.

5.4 To maintain the customer refund box according to company policy.

5.5 To assist with other duties as and when required by senior management.

PART 6

Improving organisational performance

The final group of cases deal with strategic decisions affecting organisational development, management development and organisational effectiveness. *'Halfords – a ten-year programme of organisational renewal 1982–92'* examines the performance of Britain's largest retailer of automobile accessories and bicycles. Organisational development and training policies at Halford's during a period of economic recession are examined, the power, influence and management style of senior staff and their ability to manage difficult interpersonal situations is considered and related to organisational effectiveness. The next case *'The position and contribution of support services to an NHS Trust'*, provides a contrasting view of organisational strategy and how work groups and individuals can be drawn together to contribute towards corporate objectives.

'King Concrete – an analysis of the Bouygues Group' explores the impact of change in a French construction company. A substantial change in leadership style and a new policy of diversification took the company into new and apparently unrelated ventures such as films, frozen food and flour milling. The case examines how the Bouygues group adapted to change and how the culture and climate of the group was affected.

'Experiential learning and the learning organisation' is based on a management development project called Stairway in a financial services company which is subsidary of Next plc. The case examines evidence that training is a strategic activity contributing to organizational effectiveness and considers experiential learning, the evaluation of training and the notion of a learning organisation.

The final case *'Investing in people – Human resource development and organisational change'* explores the contribution which human resource development can make to organisational change. It examines accounts of senior managers from two companies who have implemented the UK Government-sponsored initative 'Investors in People'. The managers express differing views of the experience and demonstrate that although each sought to meet a common set of standards, the problems, issues and outcomes were very different.

Halfords – A ten-year programme of organisational renewal 1982–92

Tom McEwan

This case examines the fluctuating performance of Britain's largest retailer of automobile accessories and bicycles before and during the recent recession. While much of the material provided falls into the area of strategic management, many of the issues that it raises are concerned with organisational change, development and training.

Halfords has undergone a period of considerable upheaval during the past decade. In 1982, it was a fully-owned subsidiary of Burmah Oil plc, but was sold to the Ward White Group in 1984. This holding company was taken over in 1989 by the Boots Company plc.

The main reason for the sale of Halfords to the Ward White Group was the disappointing performance during the early 1980s. Following a profit of £7 million at the height of the 1979 pre-election retail boom, Halfords' performance declined up to 1982 when a small loss was recorded. Profits increased steadily during 1983–84 and further improvements were recorded during the five years of Ward White's ownership.

After Ward White was sold to the Boots Company plc, Halfords' turnover increased from £171 million to £307 million between 1989 and 1992; however profits dropped from £20 million to a loss of £9.5 million. Full-time employees fell from 5,300 to less than 4,000 during this period and the number of stores was reduced from 436 to 425.

BACKGROUND

The first retail division chief executive (1982–1984)

Roger P., a successful senior planning manager at Burmah Oil Group, who had no previous experience of retailing, was appointed chief executive in 1982. He was given a confidential brief to reverse the decline within two years when the parent company would decide whether to retain or sell the Halfords subsidiary.

In view of his lack of retailing expertise, Roger P spent two weeks 'walking the business from top to bottom, soaking it up through my fingertips'. Meanwhile, he asked his financial accountants to prepare a detailed analysis of every company activity, to complement the market research of the company's standing which he had also commissioned and the qualitative assessment of the organisation that was completed within three months of him joining the company. As a result of these analyses, the following business objectives were agreed with the parent company by the end of 1982:

(i)   An annual improvement in store productivity of 20 per cent.
(ii) Refurbishment of existing stores and expansion into superstores.
(iii) Realignment and expansion of the product range, particularly into car servicing accessories.
(iv) The creation of a new management style, which would result in all company activities being broken down into measurable units, so that specific incentives could be set for each manager.
(v)   Individual accountability to be supported through a company-wide management development programme.

Internal reaction to proposed changes

Although all senior managers nominally accepted the new business objectives, it soon became clear to Roger P that his executives could be grouped into two broad coalitions, which he identified as the 'New Halfordians', who genuinely supported the changes, and the 'Old Halfordians' who, although never openly rebellious, were adept at raising plausible objections to most new initiatives. A more telling characteristic of this latter group was their loyalty to Mr H, the managing director of the company, who, unlike Roger P, was not a Burmah Group career manager. Mr H was known to be unenthusiastic about the new business objectives because he feared they would change the culture of the company too rapidly and also result in redundancies for too many loyal managers.

The creation of three new directorates

Mr H had previously held special responsibility for the separate buying and merchandising departments but, by the end of 1982, these two departments were merged under one controller, Ian S, who was transferred from the Burmah Group at the request of Roger P. The new merchandising director was given responsibility for all product groups throughout the company. In parallel with this appointment, Roger P also brought in two more 'outsiders' to fill the new posts of stores development director and finance and systems director.

Roger P saw these appointments as essential to enable the organisational culture to undergo the necessary rapid change during the next 12 to 18 months. His view was that, in such situations: 'Behaviour precedes strategy. The new culture was intended to encourage ideas and release the energy of the 'mavericks' in the organisation but within agreed financial controls. Until the new strategic plan had been tried and tested, the aim was to encourage as much radical change as possible and let the other people catch up with it.'

Roger P and the three new directors soon decided that, in retailing, nothing succeeded in making managers sit up and take notice than more money in the till. What was needed was a rapid 'success story' which would show that the new board knew what they were doing and meant business. In 1983, it was therefore decided to set up a pilot scheme in selected stores based on the new merchandising procedures that had been introduced by Ian S. These changes rationalised the range of products on offer at the point-of-sale and also improved the stock turnover. Only the 'New Halfordian' managers were invited to participate in the pilot scheme which was immediately successful and resulted in 20 per cent more cash being taken in these selected stores. The number of ' New Halfordian' managers increased at an even faster rate, although there was still resistance to the new policy from the majority of area managers, who were unenthusiastic about the pilot scheme and were consequently bypassed by the new directors.

During the next six months, each of the three directors interviewed all the company managers and stressed that 'Halfords had to face up to its history by tackling the necessary rationalisation of the business and developing a strategy for survival and growth'.

The morning of the long knives, 1984

In January 1984, Mr H and Roger P attended a meeting with the main board of the Burmah Group when a new three-year strategic plan was discussed. Mr H was unable to accept an ultimatum that change would have to be pushed through at a faster rate, or else the company would be sold within one year. He resigned under pressure from the main board and Roger P succeeded him as managing director of Halfords. The rate of change was accelerated with the immediate implementation of the following changes:

(i)   The large personnel department at head office was closed down and all personnel functions were regionalised.

(ii) The organisational structure was simplified by removing an entire layer of senior management. In practice, this meant that only nine of the 24 area managers (all 'New Halfordians') were retained and promoted to the new position of regional controllers.

In both cases, outside consultants were used to find jobs for all the redundant employees. Roger P regarded this as 'a costly, but necessary, exercise if the new team were to retain the confidence of the other employees'.

(iii) The formation of four project teams, led by Roger P and the three new directors, who chaired multifunctional teams that were required to convert ideas into concrete proposals within 6 to 8 weeks, which the new controllers were then expected to implement against a weekly audit.

These changes were accompanied by a high-profile training programme, and the entire refurbishment of head office which was completed within one week. According to Roger P, these changes were made 'because all people respond to style. They want to believe the business is going to be successful. Of course, they're concerned about facts, but they are also interested in the image of an organisation'.

Public relations apart, the new changes introduced line accountability for industrial relations (an area of historical aggravation for Halfords); and provided the main board with closer day-by-day links with all operational activities within the company. For example, Roger P and his three directors each spent several days working in different stores. Ostensibly, they were gaining direct experience of the various operational functions, but Roger P had also charged them to identify two projects apiece which, if there were no longer any constraints, would improve the profitability of the business. In practice, nine projects were identified, of which three were implemented during 1984.

The three-year strategic plan (1984-87)

The three-year strategic plan was announced in March 1984 and committed the company to the following objectives, which are relevant to the case study:

(i)   Rationalisation of all high street stores, through refurbishment or closure, as larger edge-of-town superstores were opened.
(ii) Raising productivity by 20 per cent through implementation of the procedures which had been tried and tested during the pilot scheme.
(iii) Increasing store flexibility by changing the full-time/part-time staff from 60:40 to a 40:60 ratio, so that stores could remain open for longer hours, including Sunday mornings.
(iv) The conversion of all stores from conventional cash-points to computerised EPOS (Electronic-point-of-sales) systems, to monitor sales and stock movements, within one year.

Eleven of the proposed fifty superstores were opened across the country during 1984 (and the last of these was opened in 1987) and these were staffed by former highstreet store managers. These stores were financed by progressively selling off the leases of the 400 smaller Halfords stores during the UK property 'boom' between 1986-1987. Operations management consultants were brought in to advise on optimum staffing levels relative to customer flows and, although the total number of employees increased by 12 per cent during the next six months, the new workforce consisted of 31 per cent fewer full-time male staff, compared with increases of 94 per cent part-time males and 28 per cent part-time female staff. These flexible work arrangements were compared to an earth tremor by some employees and, even at this late stage, a dozen senior managers decided that Mr H had been right after all and resigned from the company. Nevertheless, the new productivity targets were achieved and were acknowledged by introducing a generous incentive scheme, which was extended to all full-time and part-time employees.

Roger P commented that 'if flexible work arrangements were regarded as a tremor, then the introduction of new technology was an earthquake; and without doubt, the real cause of attitude change throughout the company'. EPOS computerised tills were introduced in all stores, ahead of target, by November, 1984, and had four immediate effects:

(i)   Controllers could reinforce basic disciplines by including these as rolling daily, weekly, monthly and quarterly 'targets' in the internal managerial systems in all stores.

(ii) EPOS created an 'information explosion' and allowed the more efficient store managers to improve stock control levels and profitability.

(iii) Greater autonomy was given to store managers who were able to provide more accurate sales and stock forecasts rather than having to rely on aggregated data from the merchandising department.

(iv) An increase in what Roger P called 'intelligent questioning' occurred between directors, controllers and store managers. This revealed an alarming 'skills gap' at the managerial level throughout most of the company.

THE SITUATION

The sale of Halfords to Ward White Group, 1984

Unbeknown to all but Roger P, the board of Burmah Group had negotiated the sale of Halfords to the Ward White Group in October, 1984, although this was not formally announced to the Stock Exchange until November. The main board of Ward White had decided to allow the current strategic plan to proceed for a further 13 months, subject to a satisfactory performance, when a decision would be taken about the future direction of the new subsidiary. They also requested Burmah's permission to offer positions to Roger P and Ian S, who were still Burmah Group employees. Permission was given in the case of Ian S, and he accepted the position of retail chief executive until the future of Roger P, who was away on holiday, was resolved. When he returned the Burmah main board informed Ward White that permission would not be given for them to approach Roger P unless, of course, he decided that he wished to leave the company. Roger P took up a senior corporate planning post in the Burmah Group in January, 1985, at the same time as Ian S succeeded him as managing Director of Halfords.

If anything, Ian S was more committed to the three-year strategic plan than Roger P had been, and he described his immediate tasks as follows: 'First, to maintain a sense of stability among staff, without allowing them to lose sight of agreed targets. The Ward White directors were convinced that they had acquired a top class management team with an ability to dominate the market. I was determined to lose no more managers because of the change but, more importantly, none of the new self-belief either, which would have suffered had good people left the company. Secondly, I had to fill the skills gap we had identified, and be quick about it too, so that we could build on the self-confidence of the management team. If that meant a substantial increase in the training budget, then so be it! Third, we had to decentralise as many head office systems as possible to the store level, without dismantling any of the proven 'rolling targets', so that all store managers were encouraged to maximise 'hands-on' control using the new EPOS system. Finally, we had to develop a new type of service-bay superstore to maintain competitive advantage into the 1990s'.

Ian S quickly became known as the 'training champion' of the Ward White Group, after he obtained approval to increase training expenditure to 6.6 per cent of annual profit from 1985 onwards. This expenditure was utilised in the following ways:

(i)   Because such a high proportion of the company's products were automobile accessories, an imaginative training 'package' was negotiated with the Automobile Association. The Association had a surplus training 'capacity', and agreed to train 300 trainee managers as technical specialists at their regional training centres on a part-time basis.

(ii)   Self-learning videotapes on ways of improving customer skills were distributed to each employee through the new regional personnel departments. Employees were also given multi-choice 'test' books which had to be completed with an agreed period for assessment by the store manager as part of the appraisal procedure.

(iii) A problem they were unable to resolve completely during 1985 was the realisation that many of the best high street store managers were unable to run the new service-bay superstores at maximum efficiency. As Ian S noted: 'Here, the 'intelligent questioning' sessions really paid off, because we had built up enough trust for these newly promoted managers to talk about their problems. They admitted that promotion had caused them a lot of stress. The new stores were huge! They couldn't run the business with the old 'hands-on' style; they had to delegate; and the long opening hours meant that they felt they were only 'part-time' managers, no longer in control. So it was a case of the other directors and I getting off our backsides at head office and working alongside three of these managers for a week so that we could appreciate the problem from their standpoint. As a result, the service-bay store management training programme was changed during 1986 to create a 'halfway' position of deputy store manager. This post was held for a six-month period only by each new service-bay store manager so that they could provide support for the incumbent store manager, at the same time as they adjusted themselves to the transition from the high-street store before moving on to take over their own larger unit.' To ensure that these staff increases 'paid their way', Ian S insisted that the new deputy store managers had to master the EPOS system during their six-month stint so that the 'cost' of their training, as salary etc., was met by improvements on the specified target of a 20 per cent productivity increase per annum. This additional target was met in all cases and productivity increased between 26 and 116 per cent in all stores where deputy managers were introduced during 1986.

In 1986, after consultation with the main board of Ward White Group, the decision was taken to leave the original three-year strategic plan unchanged but replace it with a second three-year plan, for the period 1987–90. It was also decided to slow down the superstore programme until after the 1987 General Election, so that the strengths of the existing chain could be fully exploited and the return on investment accelerated. This was to be achieved by stabilising and internalising 'corporate learning' into the management process, which had been gained in the successful launching of the existing 42 superstores. At the same time, current managerial tasks would be redefined, if need be, to stretch the performance of these key employees.

Ward White had built a reputation in the City as a successful holding company which acted rather like an investment bank. That is to say, Halfords, like its other subsidiaries, was set specific financial targets each year then more or less allowed to manage its own affairs on an autonomous basis, subject to strategic decisions taken at the monthly meetings between the Ward White chairman and Ian S, the Halfords, chief executive.

Information on the Halfords performance during 1988–9 is not available, because the Ward White Group, including the Halfords chain, was sold to Boots Company plc in August 1989 for approximately £800 million.

Halfords as a Boots Company plc subsidiary, 1989–1992

The Boots Company plc is a British-based multinational company with subsidiaries in seven EC countries, including France, Germany, Spain and The Netherlands, as well as North America, the Pacific Basin and former British Commonwealth countries.

The group's worldwide trading is conducted through four divisions: pharmaceutical, retailing, Boots the Chemists, and property. The pharmaceutical division's principal activities include the research, manufacturing and marketing of pharmaceutical and related consumer products. The Boots the Chemists division operates 1,085 pharmacies/chemists outlets in the UK and New Zealand and is the largest retailing chemists chain in Britain. The retailing division includes Halfords autoparts (425 outlets), a DIY joint venture with WH Smith, opticians and childrens' merchandising. The Boots property division manages and develops the group's extensive property investments in Britain.

Turnover for The Boots Company plc exceeded £3,655 million in 1992 and profits before taxation amounted to £374.2 million. Turnover for Halfords rose from £170.6 million in 1990 (approximately 8 months trading) to £290.1 million in 1991 and to £306.9 million in 1992. Profits before taxation were £12 million in 1990 and £2.8 million in 1991. A loss of £10.5 million was reported in 1992.

Commenting on the Halfords weak performance in the Boots 1992 Annual Report, the chief executive stated that sales in this retailing subsidiary were affected by the generally gloomy economic climate in Britain and by the decline in motor car sales in particular. As a result, sales of accessories and consumables such as car radios, seat covers, shampoos and polishes were depressed.

In an attempt to reverse the decline, the management structure of Halfords was completely reorganised and divided into three distinct profit centres; namely, car servicing, out-of-town superstores and high street stores. By the end of 1992, these changes were reported as being particularly successful and sales had increased by 8.2 per cent despite a reduction in selling space due to the closure of eleven high street stores. However, the first quarterly report for 1993 indicated only a 3.1 per cent increase in sales, although an improvement in post-Christmas trade was expected with the arrival of the cold weather.

ACTIVITY BRIEF

1 *If you were Ian S what measures would you have introduced to improve relations between the 'new' and 'old Halfordians' following the departure of Roger P and Mr H?*

2 *How have the culture, values and expectations of the principal stakeholders in the Halfords organisation altered between 1982 and 1992; and to what extend have these changes been anticipated by the company's staff development and training policies?*

3 *It is a truism that staff development and training programmes are amongst the first to be cut by companies during periods of economic recession. What arguments would you advance for continuing to invest in these personnel policies in the light of the disappointing performance by Halfords during 1992.*

RECOMMENDED READING

Johnson G. and Scholes K. (1993). *Exploring Corporate Strategy*, 3rd Edition, London: Prentice Hall. Chapter 11.

Mullins L. J. (1993). *Management and Organisational Behaviour*, 3rd Edition, London: Pitman. Chapters 8, 20 and 21.

The position and contribution of support services to an NHS Trust

Jeff Watling and Tony Strike

This case concerns two service organisations within a newly formed NHS Trust providing acute hospital services to its local population in the South of England. It deals, in particular, with personnel and pharmaceutical services. The Trust was formed in April 1993 from two large District General Hospitals, each with approximately 750 beds and 2,200 staff. Although the pharmacies in the Trust provide services direct to patients at ward level and to out-patients, pharmacy is usually seen to be a support service within the organisation. Personnel services are seen by managers to be part of the management structure and support the management of services concerned with patient care. But for many staff, personnel activities relate directly to employees as individuals.

The position of support services within the structure of the two hospitals is examined. Readers will be asked to evaluate two models of experience and approach to date and make proposals to take account of the introduction of clinical directorates.

Issues involved include organisational strategy and how service departments, working groups and individuals can be drawn together to contribute to the objectives of their group, their department and the organisation as a whole.

BACKGROUND

Financial pressures

The setting is the NHS in the early 1990s at a time when there is considerable pressure on public spending. It is Government policy to contract out public sector services to the private sector or, alternatively, to introduce internal markets to encourage efficiency through competition. In 1989 the Government White Paper 'Working for Patients' (Department of Health,

1989) set up an internal market in the NHS and with it came the concepts of: purchasers of services, the District Health Authorities and GP Fundholders; *providers* of services including the *self-governing* hospitals or *NHS Trusts.*

'Working for Patients' and subsequent Government initiatives such as 'The Patients' Charter' (Department of Health, 1991) have increased public awareness of what they can expect from the NHS. The requirement to report waiting time performance twice yearly with deadlines for 'No patients waiting longer than two years for treatment' have set simple, comprehensible targets for which Trusts can be held to account.

The NHS, in common with most Western health care systems, is hard pressed financially. Specifically, the Trust has to find a minimum of £2m in cash-releasing efficiency savings over the next two years equivalent to 1.2 per cent this year and next. This is against a background of Government imposed cash-releasing cost improvements averaging 1.1 per cent per year over the last eight years. There is a feeling within the NHS that there is very little 'fat' left to remove.

Professional issues

The main concern of the hospital consultant is to diagnose and treat disease. The majority wish to be at the cutting edge of their profession using the most up-to-date technology, the most recently developed treatment or the latest drug. Faced with the constant flood of patients through the door of the consulting room, this interest in the newest and best is often compromised. Outside 'interference' from Government, placing pressure to treat patients who have been on the waiting list for a long time, regardless of clinical need, puts considerable pressure on already stretched resources. Management is seen to be concerned with costs, Government targets and budgets and to be unsympathetic to the need to obtain additional resources to treat patients. The real issue is that managers have to be able to sell new ideas which incur cost to purchasers, who have their own agenda in terms of health gain for their resident population.

Management issues

Managers can feel powerless to control revenue expenditure associated with use of new medical technology and prescribing. They are under pressure from Government to reduce waiting lists for in-patient admissions and, more recently, out-patients. Pushing more patients through the system increases costs with little chance of additional income matching up with costs. 'Health Authorities,' according to some managers, 'have changed "personality" from being part of the same management structure and relatively willing to bail out overspendings to *hard nosed negotiators, hell bent on injecting stress into their provider organisations through imposition of contracts which are perceived not to be deliverable at the prices sought.'* Clinicians are seen to have little understanding of this pressure. They carry on writing the cheques (prescriptions) and seeking better qualified staff with little concern for who picks up the tab. Because of this apparent lack of accountability the Government is applying pressure to involve doctors more in management (Disken et al., 1990 and Lyall, 1990).

Pharmacy issues

Pharmacy is concerned with patients and their treatment with medicines. From a pharmacy management perspective there are two main issues:

● provision of pharmaceutical services;
● assisting management and clinicians with controlling expenditure on medicines.

Provision of pharmaceutical services

The professional issues concerned with the provision and development of pharmaceutical services have some similarities to the medical model. Pharmacists, particularly those who have direct patient contact in their work, have a strong desire to develop their services to the patient. This is seen as being particularly significant in work based at ward level rather than in the pharmacy. Pharmacists have identified that doctors are more concerned with diagnosis than treatment except in their own specialist area. Pharmacists with their high level of generalist knowledge about drugs and drug treatment have identified a niche which they can fill as part of the clinical team.

This niche, often called 'clinical pharmacy', takes the pharmacist from the position of 'back room boy' into direct patient care. The aim of the clinical pharmacist is to individualise treatment and obtain the greatest benefit from medicines. Clinical pharmacists have a considerable requirement for information support and have developed techniques for evaluating the use of medicines and devising protocols for their rational use. Clinical pharmacists now spend time checking patients records and pathology results to ensure that drug treatment is producing the desired effect with minimal side effects. The pharmacists also spend time with clinicians on their rounds supporting, in particular, the junior doctors in their prescribing activities.

Involvement at ward level is interesting and demanding and a far cry from the pharmacists traditional dispensing skills. Clinical pharmacists are increasingly being expected to study for postgraduate diplomas in their speciality and are seeing themselves and being seen by others as 'a race apart', closer to their medical colleagues than the rest of pharmacy. These developments are causing a split in the ranks between those who work at ward level and those who staff the purchasing, distribution and dispensing services. This is particularly emphasised when work which has to be done in time for regular late morning and afternoon deliveries is brought back late to the pharmacy, clashing with lunch breaks and the busiest times for out-patient dispensing. Clinical pharmacists do not help their image when they dump the (boring) dispensing and disappear to answer an (interesting) drug information enquiry that they have picked up during their ward visits.

Pharmacy workloads are increasing at a rate higher than the general levels for the Trust as a whole because more patients are being treated with medicines instead of having operations. The drug bill is growing faster than inflation and workloads because of the general pressure to use the latest form of treatment with little regard to cost benefit. These inflationary and workload pressures put further pressure on the pharmaceutical service and funding has not matched workload increases. Managers do not pay for pharmacy services directly as the cost is top sliced before budgets are distributed. Pharmacy managers have had some experience of running trading accounts for traditional support services and have identified a potential benefit in organising the whole pharmaceutical service on a trading basis. The problem is that whilst pharmaceutical products are tangible, information and advice are not. Managers require information on what is being spent and by whom and advice on how costs can be controlled. Pharmacists have responded to this challenge but have rarely been rewarded with additional revenue for intangible services.

In recent years the threat of competitive tendering from an active and, in some cases, voracious pharmaceutical industry has caused pharmacy managers to become more customer orientated. Instead of seeing the patient as the primary customer of the pharmaceutical service, pharmacy managers are identifying more closely with those who could decide that their services are no longer affordable. This trend has been further emphasised by a change in emphasis in quality management programmes.

This has been exemplified by a change in definition of quality from *conformance to specification* to a more customer-orientated *meeting the customers requirements*. Managers have used this simple message as a means of giving pharmacy staff a common sense of purpose. The development of service agreements with customers is seen as a mechanism to raise the profile of the pharmaceutical services within the organisation and tie the customer into the service, reducing the risks from competitive tendering.

Controlling expenditure on medicines

This is a big problem for the Trust. Medicines expenditure is growing at a rate of 12 per cent per year, a rate far greater than the general level of inflation. The medicines budget in 1992/93 was £4.96m, the largest non-staff budget, and the spend was £6.1m. The pharmaceutical service does not hold the medicines budgets. Since 1985 the budgets have been devolved to service managers. The pharmaceutical service supports service managers by providing them with monthly budget statements and information on who is spending what. Pharmacy staff provide advice on how control can be exerted on medicines expenditure by identifying 'best buy' products in each class and advising on protocols for the use of medicines.

Personnel issues

Personnel services are concerned with staff, their employment relationships with the employer and the best utilisation of staff as a resource to deliver patient care.

The three main issues of concern to the function are employee relations, effective employment practices and efficient utilisation of staff.

The function, as it currently exists, is keen to create improved internal customer awareness, service quality and relationships. This is against a background of debate in local government concerning competitive tendering of white collar services and a health service debate concerning moving non-clinical services into internal trading accounts.

Provision of personnel services

For the function to be effective it must do more than offer sound professional advice from well-qualified specialists. These specialists need to be present at the early formation of management thinking and decision making so that they can contribute to and influence policy.

When the two hospitals joined into one organisation designed around large operational reporting structures of a central nature, personnel matched this. As an advisory or executive management service, personnel must match the organisational structure to lock into the decision-making process. If management decision making is to be devolved, it is considered necessary that the personnel function should follow to maintain its influence and its role within each mini-organisation.

The formation of NHS Trusts gives local management the freedom to determine the number and nature of staff employed and the pay and terms and conditions for employment of those staff. Trusts, as employers in their own right and with freedoms delegated from national level, place new burdens on those who have responsibility for the management of staff. At the same time the tendency towards *charters*, quality standards and customer responsiveness place new demands on existing administrative functions, e.g., recruitment activity. The central personnel function is, therefore, under increasing strain, within a cash-limited resource, to deliver a programme of work and to be seen to be contributing to the Trust's business objectives at every level. Managers do not pay for personnel services directly as the cost is top sliced before budgets are distributed. Therefore to each manager, personnel is a free good. Being free and increasingly customer focused means personnel does not always get the resources it needs to perform the task and the managers do not demand value for money. Generalist personnel officers each have between 500 and 800 staff in their 'patch' with a group of managers as their prime customers. These generalists make themselves known as the 'contact' for the managers and staff in their patch. The more glamorous 'specialists' e.g., manpower planning, training and occupational health often act in support of, or are triggered by, the frontline generalists although they also set personnel policy and are the thinking arm of the department. The generalists' objective is, all too often, to get alongside, respond to or influence the specialists' agenda. These generalists are the hard-pushed and visible part of the personnel service and are the answer to the question (as yet unasked by managers) 'What do I get for my money?' It is not expected that the generalists be found in their own offices but should be out with the managers they relate to in their workplaces.

Controlling expenditure on staff

Managers do not always make the link between personnel services and controlling staff costs or improving their unit labour costs against productivity. Staff represent some 75 per cent of the Trust's recurring revenue expenditure annually, excluding capital charges, and are its only means of producing activity to meet contracts for care. Traditionally, staff budgets have been seen as a fixed overhead which inflates annually by the cost of living. Under pressure to compete, staff productivity or efficient utilisation of staff is an important survival issue. Staff costs are being seen as variable; at least at the margins. Personnel staff can offer relevant business information and advice to managers in terms of: unit labour costs, grade and skill mix.

THE SITUATION

Approach to date – pharmacy

As previously stated, pharmacy managers have used quality management as a means to focus the pharmaceutical service on meeting the customer's requirements. A simple, mechanistic approach has been used to focus the organisation. The first step in this process is a cascade system to encourage every department, working group and individual to prepare a single side of A4 paper identifying:

● Their customers, particularly those who can choose to buy or not to buy a particular pharmaceutical service.

- Their purpose: why does the service exist?
- Their principal functions: what has to be done to achieve their purpose and why?

Care was taken throughout to emphasise teamwork by considering the services within pharmacy and the importance of the notion of the internal customer.

This cascade process builds on any quality monitoring that is already going on by asking:

- What quality monitoring is going on to ensure that the service is achieving its purpose?
- What quality assurance measures ought to be in place to monitor its principal functions?
- What quality measures ought to be in place to ensure that we are meeting the customer's requirement?

This final question brings the service into marketing mode, in that, in order to know whether we are meeting the customer's requirement we have to know what the customers require. Pharmacy managers have worked hard to overcome the professional approach to customers, i.e., that customers may know what they want but this is not necessarily what they need, only the professional will know this. Groups were initially encouraged to brainstorm customer requirements from the pharmacy point of view, and then to test these by going out to customers with a blank sheet of paper and asking them what their requirements were. This latter approach developed into a way of negotiating service agreements with customers, and pharmacy managers were happy to allow their frontline staff to go out to customers and identify their needs, but with central co-ordination to ensure a common approach to the documentation of service agreements and calculation of charges for proposed developments.

The 'Customers, Purpose, Principal Functions' approach was extended from departments and groups to individuals in the form of job descriptions set out in the format recommended by Hay Management Consultants: job purpose, key result areas and context of job. These job descriptions took account of departmental and work group role summaries so that they locked into the departmental purpose and principal functions. The job descriptions were also used as a basis for development of work programmes and these were agreed by managers and individuals as part of an active role development programme. Central to this was the notion of ever changing job descriptions, depending on changing customer requirements.

Professional resistance

It is fair to say that this approach did not achieve immediate success. While there was total commitment from the top, enthusiasm was, at best, lukewarm from some managers. Constant pressure through the three-monthly role development meetings and praise for those who took up the challenge has achieved some converts. Initially the pharmacy technicians were the group who committed themselves to the process and subsequently the clinical pharmacists have come into line.

Service agreements

Negotiation of service agreements has proved to be a slow process. It has taken two years and more than three hundred interviews to complete the process in the Trust. By identifying the pharmacy service requirements of service managers, doctors, nurses and others it has been possible to build up a total picture of the service characteristics required by the customers. These include current service characteristics, sometimes with slightly changed emphasis, together with a number of developments which are identified separately and will be subject to negotiation about redeployment of resources or allocation of additional funds by service managers.

Approach to date – personnel

Three generalist teams were created immediately preceding Trust status to match the top structure of the organisation. Three personnel managers were team leaders, each with a group of personnel officers and each had one or more operational directors as prime customers. This structure within the personnel service reflected an internal debate including:

- Personnel needing to reflect the Trust's management structure or reflecting the geography of employees workplaces.
- Personnel as a management function or as an advisory or consultative service.
- The benefit or liability of differing personnel practice or procedure within the Trust for different customers.

The role and agenda of the personnel service was distilled from the Trust's *Statement of Intent, Strategic Directions and Business Plans.* Also various traditional personnel functions, of a maintenance nature were included. The team structure was designed to build in a profound change towards achievement of quality service, customer awareness and a focus on the Trust's business agenda.

The personnel managers met individually with their link directors (and senior managers reporting to that director) following introductory letters. At the next level down the personnel managers attended the management team meetings held within each department by managers reporting to the operational director. It was decided to structure attendance at a cascade of managers meetings with a presentation pack setting out the range of personnel services to take the opportunity to state the function of personnel, the services provided and the commitment to quality and professionalism.

The nature of this initial exercise was to sell the personnel function as a new rather than reorganised service, or at least one that had thought long and hard about its aims and had a new clarity of purpose. The strong link between personnel activity and overall Trust direction and goals was stressed in these sessions.

This agenda was understood by the service director, as prime customer, and the personnel manager, as team leader. It was cascaded through the personnel teams through job descriptions focusing on purpose and accountabilities. Annual objectives were then developed which closely related to the accountabilities, and made specific the timetable for implementation of particular work to quality standards. This cascade of accountabilities aimed to ensure that each personnel team and officer was focused on achieving organisational objectives. Job descriptions and even structure would alter as the strategic direction of the organisation shifted.

As each personnel team leader has integrated with their prime customer the sense of belonging has changed from the human resources directorate as a central function to belonging to the customer. This led to the 'generalists' resenting the ability of their less customer-related specialist colleagues to set the internal agenda for personnel services. Amongst the generalist group a culture shift was visible from a bureaucratic to an entrepreneurial style of working.

Clinical directorates

The main thrust of the *Doctors in Management Initiative* is to involve those who spend resources on patient care, in the operational management of and financial accountability for the organisation. One of the means to this end is to set up a number of *clinical directorates* under the control of a clinical director, who will most likely be a hospital consultant. It has not yet been decided how many clinical directorates will be set up, nor how they will be accountable to the Trust board. It is, however, likely that the directorates will be based on the major medical and surgical specialities, e.g., Dept of Medicine, Dept of Surgery, Trauma and Orthopaedics, etc. Some services may combine together as supporting services, e.g. theatres, which mostly support surgery and orthopaedics, combined with ITU which supports medical and surgical specialities and coronary care which is seen as part of medicine. These clinical support specialities may combine with the more traditional clinical support services such as pathology, diagnostic services (X-ray and ultrasound), physiotherapy and other professions allied to medicine. Alternatively the support services could join together as a single trading organisation providing services for the medical and surgical directorates.

Changing and devolving management to small self-sufficient units is not a short-haul destination. The need exists to consider internal non-medical support services and allow the new directorates to seek internal service agreements, trading contracts or to have their part of any central resource devolved to them. The end result of any management advisory (personnel) or service support (pharmacy) function must be to enhance the clinical directorate's capability to deliver clinical care within the resources available. This end must be desirable to the care providers rather than simply looking to detached central functions to deliver a range of expert and hotel support. Surprisingly, a significant number of managers do not want support services devolved to them. Managers prefer their role as 'customer' to central services and perhaps they fear the responsibility of managing devolved experts. Support functions in a central organisation can be kept at arms length if desired. Managers recognise the economies of scale in centralising expertise to create pools of excellence upon which they can call.

The clinical directorates should, to an extent, self-determine whether to purchase management, clinical and hotel support services from a centralised function or seek fragmentation and devolvement. To decide this each clinical directorate must assess the implications of changes against the capacity and competency of their own management and which model will serve them best.

REFERENCES

Department of Health (1989). *Working for patients: White Paper on the Government's Proposals following its Review of the NHS.* London: HMSO.

Department of Health (1991). *The Patient's Charter,* London: HMSO.

Disken, S. et al. (1990). *Models of Clinical Management,* IHSM.

Lyall, J. (1990). *Visions of Leaders. Resource management experience from the pilot sites,* NHS Training Authority. Page 7.

ACTIVITY BRIEF

1 *Critically appraise the activities of the two departments to date:*
   ● *The pharmacy, which adopted a 'blank sheet of paper' approach to identifying customers needs and building up service agreements from a composite statement of requirements.*
   ● *The personnel approach which had a 'mission focus', looking at strategic objectives of the organisation and organising itself to achieve the organisational purpose.*

2 *With the emergence of clinical directorates what are the strengths and weaknesses of the two alternatives below?*
   ● *A centralised approach based on identifying and meeting customer's needs and 'trading' within the organisation.*

● *Relocating staff to clinical directorates, maintaining only a central core service, providing support.*

3 *If you were a clinical director how would you want pharmaceutical and personnel services organised?*

4 *What are the opportunities and threats of each approach from the clinical director's perspective?*

5 *What activities should be undertaken by pharmacy and personnel in terms of their recruitment criteria and training in the light of the outcome of the clinical director's decisions on structure and provision of support services?*

RECOMMENDED READING

In addition to those mentioned in the References:
Mullins, L. J. (1993). *Management and Organisational Behaviour,* Third Edition, London: Pitman Publishing.

SHREWSBURY COLLEGE
BRIDGNORTH LRC

King Concrete – An analysis of the Bouygues Group

Karen Meudell and Tony Callen

This case concerns a French construction company founded by Francis Bouygues (pronounced 'Bweeg') in 1952. The company was managed in an autocratic style, Bouygues encouraging his employees to feel that they were part of an elite organisation There was a well-defined corporate culture, driven by the personality of Bouygues, a distinctive head office building, known as 'the corporate Versailles' and even a company colour. When he retired in 1989 his son, amid much speculation as to whether his milder management style would be successful, took over the reins and pursued a wide-ranging diversification programme which took the company, among other things, into films, frozen food and flour milling.

The case explores issues of how the group adapted to change from both inside and outside the organisation, the management of culture in a diversified organisation and the implications of the two very different types of management style for the culture and climate of the group.

BACKGROUND

Francis Bouygues, like most top managers in France, was a product of the *Hautes Ecoles*, the prestigious French equivalent of Oxbridge, Yale and Harvard. However it was not his educational background but his determined, dynamic, plain-speaking, proud and charismatic character that provides the usual explanation for his hugely successful business career which includes the creation of one of the largest construction firms in the world. Indeed, his educational background was usually forgotten when he was frequently referred to as 'the bricklayer turned self-made businessman'. Not for nothing was he called *le roi du béton – King Concrete*.

His timing was excellent since, when he founded his building and construction firm in 1952, France, having survived severe post-war deprivations, had embarked on a modernisation plan that made the fifties the most vigorous period of economic growth she had ever known.

Industrial growth rate was 50 per cent compared with 15 per cent in the UK; housing, roads, schools and hospitals were high on the priority list, putting Francis' venture in the front line. Having borrowed the start-up capital from his father, by 1956 his family business was able to create the first of many subsidiaries, which now include companies dealing in real estate, offshore oil platforms, private housing, electricity, water purification and television.

Thus the original family business became the Bouygues Group, a world-wide organisation, employing over 80,000 people. Maintaining an edge over competitors through high quality research and development, it has built some of the best-known Parisian landmarks of modern times: the great arch at *La Défense* , the *Parc des Princes*, the *Forum des Halles* and the *Musée d'Orsay*. Bouygues has also been a leading member of the French consortium building the Channel tunnel, which might not be unconnected with its buying for approximately $193 million, in 1989, a controlling interest in four UK water authorities: Mid-Sussex, West Kent, Mid-southern and Eastbourne.

It has been said that Bouygues' rapid rise was achieved through a combination of personality, drive and his characteristically French exploitation of the 'old boy network'. The choice of Bouygues by the French Government, for example, as controlling stockholder when it privatised the television station TF1 in 1987 was said to be an entirely political decision. However, despite his successful achievements and apparent government patronage, surveys amongst his executive colleagues described him as 'despotic' (56 per cent), 'a megalomaniac' (47 per cent) and a 'boss without scruples' (53 per cent) – the adjective most frequently used about him was 'ruthless'.

Despite an active diversification policy, Francis Bouygues, while leaving specialist managers to get on with their job, maintained control of the overall development of the group; he is described as running it as tightly as the first Henry Ford ran Ford. He is known for his unapologetic use of rousing rhetoric and symbolism for creating and sustaining a vigorous corporate culture. A brochure welcoming new staff, for example, describes the Bouygues approach as being dynamic and modern, with a desire for challenge, hard work and the very highest standards in quality. After a few months the new recruit undergoes integration training which involves a presentation of the group's history, peppered with anecdotes from company folklore. This portrait is amplified in a charter expounding 12 principles, familiarly known by employees as the 12 Commandments: teamwork, people, quality, success, planning, victory, promotion through merit, synergy, adaptability, training, technology and the client are the watchwords. This message is reiterated in the numerous house magazines and bulletins disseminating information throughout the group; the largest one, *Minorange*, is delivered to the home of every single employee. Bulletins, where Francis' style, like a general addressing the troops, are often in evidence: *'Nous sommes des challengers'* a race of men stimulated by challenge, faces turned resolutely toward progress, collaborating in a great adventure, united by the will to be the best.

There are, of course, a company logo and distinctive working clothes. Managers are expected to be stylish (what the French call *b.c.b.g* – *bon chic bon genre*). Then, located appropriately enough near Versailles is a $200,000,000 head office and Francis' personal monument, built like a modern chateau and called *'Challenger'*. It is glass-walled and meant to create a mood of light, space, calm and openness. Visitors are not asked to wear identity tags but access to various areas in the building is controlled by 'smart cards'. The 2,500 employees have full social facilities including hairdressers, a ticket booking agency and gymnasium. There are only 12 small private offices and these are marked only by small brass plaques.

There is also a company colour with its very own name: *minorange*, a reddish hue that is actually the colour of the anti-rust paint a hire firm used on the plant Bouygues rented in the early days of the business. However, the best-known aspect of this cultural symbolism is the existence of a group of elite builders created by Francis in 1963 and called *Les Compagnons du Minorange*.

Building sites have traditional working customs – a consequence partly of the difficulty and danger of some of the operations which require teamwork of a high order. In Britain such customs as 'the cutting of the first turf' and 'topping out' are common as ceremonial events marking the progression of a building's construction. France, of course, puts the emphasis on food and a favourite custom at Bouygues is the *méchoui* – the spit-roasting of a lamb. The idea of *Les Compagnons* builds on this sense of tradition, stressing pride in high quality craftsmanship and fraternal work relations. Although originally created to combat the rapid turnover of staff in the construction industry during a boom period, this order of crack masons (with its own charter, magazine – *Bâtisseurs*, distinctive working clothes, budget for ceremonies, professional awards, initiation rituals, system of ranks, special insurance policy and so on) has been a source of great pride to its creator. In 1987 he even took a thousand of them, with their wives, on a weekend trip to Sardinia – three days of eating, sporting activities, fireworks and famous entertainers to give the event added prestige and sparkle.

Construction work is predominantly a male province. The typical Bouygues manager is male, French, around 35 years old, with a *baccalauréat* ('A' level) and has been with the firm for five or more years. The rhetorical language used by Bouygues has naturally, therefore, spoken mainly of men, and it is said that he prefers his female staff not to wear trousers at work. The familiar form of address using 'tu' is very common in the industry, but respect for the hierarchy is a French tradition firmly maintained in this group where, typically 'vous' is used. In short, Francis Bouygues is a very good example of the powerful, paternalistic boss French business is known for (he has been likened to a combination of Lee Iacocca, Donald Trump and Robert Maxwell). It is rumoured that at one time his practice was to move everyone's desk fortnightly just to keep them on their toes. When it was thought, in 1988, that he had died, the group's shares plummeted, so closely was his personality connected with the success of the firm. Actually, he had a cold.

All this should not be construed, however, as suggesting Bouygues has been backward-looking. Far from it. Unions, despite their relative weakness in France, are recognised. There are carefully designed assessment programmes, recruitment is guided by consultants, training programmes are flourishing (the group spends over three per cent of its wage bill on training, more than twice the legal requirement in France) and employee shareholding is encouraged. After important French employment laws of 1982 required firms to increase worker participation, a major programme of quality circles was put in place. These circles have an annual conference when they share good practice, receive awards for their work and hear their president congratulate them in person.

Francis Bouygues, F.B. to his close collaborators, as well as being a shrewd businessman has clearly been creative in the field of organisational development, leaving a deep imprint on the corporate culture. But what of the climate in the group? Has it adapted well to change? The results of an opinion survey of 7,000 employees in 1987, while endorsing the image of pride in the company and its spectacular construction achievements, appetite for challenge, love for the job, belief in diversification and respect for the client, showed that there was some disquiet. Blame, it was felt, was more typical of the climate at work than praise. Training was harder to get than it should be, and doubt was cast on the level of team spirit and the validity of the promotion by merit claim.

Much of this response is explicable and probably unavoidable if the economic aims of the group are to continue flourishing. Internally, the system of tendering, for example, permits a works or project manager to go outside the group for materials if the *dépôt* is not offering competitive rates. This can be a source of bitterness and conflict. Diversification itself, enhanced by the company's policy of allowing local autonomy and the retention of individual identity, can militate against corporate culture. And in the environment, the state of the economy in general was discouraging.

THE SITUATION

It was at this juncture, in September 1989, that Francis, now aged 67, decided to step down. The question of Bouygues' successor is one which analysts had continued to alternately worry and speculate about; although he had three sons, the issue debated, as with many companies founded and run by a single commanding personality, was not which son was the *Dauphin* but whether *anyone* could effectively succeed him. Nicholas Bouygues, the eldest son and presumed heir apparent, had, after an alleged family row, left the firm altogether and not a few people in the company had their doubts about his successor, the youngest son, Martin, thinking him more 'nice' than business-like. Indeed, Martin himself seems to have had his own doubts and was quoted as saying 'Francis Bouygues is unique. His successor has to find his own style. I have one wish only (and that is) to keep Bouygues in good health and to pursue the principles of management that are dear to us'.

Martin certainly does not have his father's forthright style. He is, for instance, far less talkative, and regards his father as a one-off but his collegiate approach to management – nine other directors and close support from the family (brother Oliver in housing and sister Corinne in publicity) – has worked out well. He had, after all, been well groomed for the post: directing the Forum des Halles project in 1974 at the age of 22; running for many years Maisons Bouygues, France's biggest house-builder; president of a major subsidiary, SAUR, in 1985, and vice-president of the whole group in 1988. His policy, with the core activity in decline, certainly had a clear logic about it: even wider diversification than his father had implemented.

It was not the easiest time to take over the reins. Government was providing less and less support for the kind of major project in which the firm specialised. Recession was hitting the construction industry hard – in Martin's first year road building in France fell off by nearly a half, contributing to a 25 per cent drop in Bouygues' core activity. Similarly affected were the offshore and housing concerns of the company.

Until 1989, mergers, acquisitions and creations had been, more or less, connected with the core business – real estate, water supply, electricity distribution and so on. One of the biggest take-overs, for example, had been *Dragages*, in 1986, a Hong Kong based dredging and public works company. The Bouygues hi-tech, risk-taking style quickly made it one of the top firms in the country by aggressively seeking business in the private sector and introducing industrial prefabrication methods in an overcrowded situation that seemed little suited for them. Martin certainly continued to ensure that the construction side of the firm thrived. The building of the Center Parcs complex at Nottingham for instance, showed that the international aspirations in this domain had not been relinquished. However, the purchase of a controlling interest in TF1, France's leading TV channel, in 1987 had already represented a new direction and this was the one Martin chose to emphasise. He bought into Spain's *Banco Centrale* and Swiss tunnelling expert *Losinger* and, with the purchase, for $22 million, of *Les Moulins de Paris* (after just one month in the job), took the group into the completely new areas of flour milling and frozen food. But he then took the group even further into media activities.

F.B. the Concrete King, however, remained ever present in spirit, a reference point for directors eager to remain an industrial concern and to preserve the culture he had created. He had left the firm in their hands once before, in 1976, when he withdrew to fight lung cancer and develop a passion for cultivating orchids. He returned with only one lung, several more species of orchids and many more ideas. In 1991, he came out of retirement not to take the firm over again this time but to run Martin's most glamorous new subsidiary yet: a film company, Ciby 2000 (theoretically standing for *Cinéma Bouygues* but when pronounced in French sounding very much like C. B. de Mille). F.B. set up his office on Hollywood's Sunset Boulevard and signed up David Lynch to make four films initially, including a spin-off from the massively successful *Twin Peaks*. Directors Wenders and Bertolucci have also been hired in this typically high quality approach, which is further guaranteed by giving these prestigious directors far more control over the final cutting processes than ever they can expect with the Hollywood moguls. 'Francis who?' asked Hollywood . . . of the man who doubled the $40 million the investment had cost.

The Bouygues Group's turnover as a whole was up in 1991 by 8.8 per cent over the previous year.

So, while, during the same recessionary period, the British construction giant, Tarmac, retreated into its three core activities, the Bouygues Group of the nineties forged ahead with a policy of diversification into sectors Martin calls the doors of tomorrow: telematics, video (with 11 per cent of the French market already), teleshopping, music publication, television sport, intelligent tower blocks and refuse collection, including operations in Harrow and Stratford-upon-Avon. Martin has been quoted as saying: 'One is like a hunter – one takes what passes. We are looking for opportunities'. For all that, the King Concrete image holds strong: Bouygues is currently building Hong Kong's national sports' stadium, a dam in Canada, and a town for 800,000 Thailanders. One analyst claims Bouygues has overstretched itself by borrowing too much and at too high an interest rate to succeed in a shrinking construction industry. But this core activity is still the firm's biggest money spinner accounting for nearly a quarter of the turnover. Roads are the most lucrative part and Martin insists they are a consumable item, always in need of repair and replacement. Indeed, one of the first moves made by France's new government in 1993 was to put state funds into building and public works. Martin is now said to be dreaming of a network of motorways *under* the town of Lyons . . .

ACTIVITY BRIEF

1 *Evaluate the differences between the management styles of Martin and his father. What are the implications of these two styles for the culture and climate of the Bouygues Group?*

2 *One analyst suggests that Martin's policy makes Bouygues look more like a holding company than a construction firm. How appropriate is a power culture, typified by F.B., to the type of holding company that Martin appears to be developing? What difficulties might be anticipated and how might they be overcome?*

RECOMMENDED READING

Barsoux, J. L. and Lawrence, P. (1991). *Management in France,* Cassell Educational Ltd.

Handy, C. B. (1993). *Understanding Organisations,* Harmondsworth: Penguin.

Robbins, S. P. (1993) . *Organizational Behavior,* Sixth Edition, New Jersey: Prentice-Hall.

Kransdorff, A. (May 1993). 'Making Acquisitions Work by the Book', *Personnel Management,* pp 40–43.

Hine, B. (April 1993). 'Banking on a Successful Marriage', *Personnel Management,* pp 38 –41.

Mullins, L. J. (1993). *Management of Organisational Behaviour,* London: Pitman.

Experiential learning and the learning organisation

Brian McCormack and Linda McCormack

Towards the end of 1991, the partnership executive of the Human Resource Development Partnership (HRDP) was seeking to encourage local branches of three professional institutes – the Institute of Management, the Institute of Personnel Management and the Institute of Training and Development – and the Industrial Society to support the work of Leeds Training and Enterprise Council. As a result of this initiative, the HRDP was invited to meet the Development Trading Manager at Club 24 (a financial services company whose parent company is Next plc). The partnership executive at this time were intent to prove that good training pays and 'to encourage organisational cultures which were supportive of organisational and people development for their mutual advantage'. In 1991 Club 24 was in crisis and it looked as if they would have to cease trading. A management development project called Stairway had been introduced which had become a central part of the company's recovery strategy. This initiative was of interest to the partnership as it appeared to link in with research work that the partnership was funding into 'The Learning Organisation: A Review of Literature and Practice'.

After interviews with staff, and attendance at a learning event, it appeared to us that their Stairway Experiential Learning Programme was beginning to change the culture of Club 24 and turn it into an embryonic learning organisation. Morale was admittedly at rock-bottom and the department had a bad image with the rest of the company. In addition the recession meant that collecting money – the primary purpose of Club 24 – had become harder; the company had become a growing financial liability and Next had decided to close Club 24 down. However, it is anecdotally reported that at one stage the managing director was called on his car telephone and given a year in which to try to turn the organisation round.

Coincidentally, the HRDP had previously been approached by TV Choice, who were interested in making videos concerned with good training practice. It seemed to make good sense to try and capture the Club 24 experience on celluloid. Frontline business evidence of training as a strategic activity, contributing to improved company performance, had been difficult to find – as the work on the Investors in People programme had shown, so a video was made.

The material presented in this case complements the video and although not focusing on any specific aspect of organisational behaviour, is a vehicle for discussing broad issues such as experiential learning, training evaluation and organisational culture/learning organisation concepts. As such there are few exactly right and wrong answers – the case study is open ended. The case is designed to encourage students to read, gather information, think critically and to build a rich picture of the complexity of the organisational life which may be influenced and within which most people, for good or ill, will spend a good deal of their lives.

BACKGROUND

Club 24 was established in 1977 and is part of Next plc and operates in the financial services sector of the economy and employs approximately 500 staff at a single site at Leeds.

Traditionally the Club 24's core business has been predominantly concerned with retail finance, initially as an in-house facility for Hepworths which subsequently became the retail phenomenon Next. The services of Club 24 are offered to customers who are unable to pay the full purchase price of goods immediately. Typically a deposit is paid and the rest of the payment is financed through a credit arrangement.

Club 24 sustained a rapid growth rate before developing sophisticated technology to support operations and it built and displayed an impressive portfolio of high street retailers. However, the credit boom and subsequent fall in the late eighties coupled with economic and competitive factors resulted in an overall decline of the retail finance market and Club 24's prestigious market share within it. The company entered a period of instability and change which involved consolidating resources and reducing costs. The effects of the changes in the company were unsettling for everyone as the future direction of the business was unknown; even the survival of the company was threatened.

Gradually, the concept of offering a dedicated bureau service to other organisations emerged as the focus of the restructured operation. This has been developed from the recognition of expertise in high volume data processing and telephone operations. The company is currently repositioning itself in the developing market place of support services.

A particular key area and feature of the Club 24 bureau service is the arrears collection operation. It was in this area of the business under the changing circumstances outlined above that the Stairway project and concept evolved.

The collections department

The collections department employs 56 full-time and 49 part-time staff. The management team is headed by a senior manager and two shift managers (one each for the day and evening operation). They are supported by eight supervisors and ten assistant supervisors. The department has an administrator and there are four departmental training instructors with the management team.

The arrears collection department operates from 9 a.m. to 9 p.m. 5 days per week, and 9 a.m. to 1 p.m. at the weekends.

Club 24 operates datapoint powerdialler-assisted telephone calling technology, which improves the efficiency of telephoning, to contact customers directly to negotiate repayments on customer accounts in payment arrears. In addition the operation includes a financial difficulties section, a customer correspondence section and a large telephone support network to deal effectively with incoming calls. Performance and productivity are monitored by supervisors on a daily basis; work planning and scheduling mechanisms are sophisticated as is the supporting information technology. As outlined in the introduction, this area of the business was integral to offering bureau-type services. In April 1991 a new manager, Liz Daykin, was moved into collections from another area of the business and was involved in a new project entitled 'Focus on Collections'. This project had been designed as a motivational/quality intervention which included a small team of telephone collectors and supervisors developing a mission statement and a set of values for the department. A small budget was allocated and a framed mission statement produced with accompanying visual display material.

In addition two further initiatives were launched:

- A departmental newsletter.
- 'Quality Collector' of the month award. The recipient of this award was nominated by another member of the staff for outstanding quality and service to either a customer or to a fellow team member.

The result of this project was the establishment of a small team of dedicated and enthused employees who owned the concept through their involvement with it. However, the rest of the department neither enthused nor criticised, feeling it was a 'one off', 'flash in the pan' and focused their attention specifically into a narrow field of performing day-to-day roles with a high degree of technical competence. They showed little or no ownership of anything to do with improving the overall function which might assist in securing their futures.

The newly appointed manager's observation of this culture in the changing company circumstances were:

- Low commitment/motivation/involvement.
- Minimum communication/positive feedback mechanisms.
- Low team interaction.
- High absenteeism and labour turnover.
- Supervisors had low accountability for the work of their staff.

It was at this stage a training intervention was considered in order to develop the departmental culture.

THE SITUATION

The situation facing the collections department is sketched through the following extracts from interviews collected by Duncan Clark of TV Choice, London. These provide an insight into the views of staff involved in the project and their perceptions of the nature of the work and of the Stairway initiative itself.

The sales and marketing director

Ian Kendall, Club 24's sales and marketing director, has been with the company for 13 years. The following extracts from an interview with Ian explains the background which led to the implementation of the Stairway programme.

'The growth of Club 24's debt to something like £4m was beginning to pose significant strains on Next's (Club 24's parent company) balance sheet. The decision was taken in the light of this, first of all, to try to sell the company, and of course back in 1990 there were many finance houses for sale and very few were sold. Ultimately the decision was taken to run out the debt at Club 24 and possibly close the doors on business around the 1992/93 line.'

'The company was in a crisis situation; we were basically faced with closure. The requirement of the parent company was to run the debt out with maximum efficiency, and obviously this meant minimum loss to them. Club 24 at the end of 1990 was effectively faced with a closure situation.'

'Next took the view, quite rightly, that they could no longer afford this subsidiary. It was posing too much of a strain on their resources in terms of manpower and finance. Basically, our task as management team was to run out the existing debt as quickly and efficiently as possible.'

'As a management team we took stock of the situation and we said – let's not take this lying down. There is tremendous potential here.'

The departmental manager

Liz Daykin is the senior collections manager at Club 24. She was a prime mover behind the Stairway programme. The following extracts from an interview with Liz provides an insight into her views of staff attitudes before the Stairway project and some initiatives introduced to promote ownership of the stairway project.

'The staff in collections were exceptionally negative, criticised the supervisors, the management team, the way they worked and information they were given, and they didn't know how they were performing. Collections was a separate entity, their morale was very low; it felt a bit like Colditz.'

'I saw the job as a challenge. I thought it important we should improve collections so we could give the marketing people time to look for new business, because I still believed in Club 24.'

'I had a clear set of objectives and I wanted my supervisors to own those objectives, but to own them willingly. So we went away on an experiential learning course and got to know each other, and at the end of that session I asked them what were their objectives for the next six months and they asked me to do the same, and at the end of that course we actually had the same objectives and we trusted each other and we knew each other better. That bought me six months.'

'The key action plan was how to improve staff morale and how to make things happen and to make staff committed to taking this department forward; to make the best department in Club 24.'

'I had clear directions and I knew where I wanted to be and I expected the people to be there with me immediately and life isn't like that. You've got to allow people to develop and grow and take responsibility for themselves, and this allowed me to come to terms with that and pointed me in the right direction.'

'Liz Wray, the training manager, and I work exceptionally well together in so much as we spark off each other and it just flowed, I think we tired each other out!'

'Every customer is an individual, and while some people don't care about being in arrears, the majority of people are upset or embarrassed and we are in hard times, and so staff have to be able to respect that customer, empathise and yet negotiate a solution which is acceptable to Club 24.'

'I think it was perceived that collection staff should be aggressive people, not assertive people, and not people with counselling skills.'

The development training manager

Liz Wray is the development training manager. She has been with Club 24 for three years.

'. . . Liz Daykin and I put together the concept of the Stairway training programme to help manage the change that was coming to the business and looking at it as an opportunity rather than a threat. [We felt that] there was nothing to lose by trying this. We found that we didn't have to sell the idea too strongly as it wasn't going to cost very much.'

'I think now collections sees itself as providing that customer service and that advisory service as well. And customer care is very important in a department like Collections.'

'There was a need for all the line managers' commitment.'

'. . . training and personnel functions will become more advisory functions, working very closely with managers, because for far too long in British companies the management of the people issue has been delegated off to other people.'

'I think the coaching element that's happening in the department now is a natural development from the Stairway process. Learning the development isn't just about Stairway. That's not the end of it. It's a continuous process and we're always looking to develop and improve everybody's performance. It's very much a negotiated process, not a 'telling' process, and certainly not a corrective process. Stairway is a journey which has to be checked for its progress in terms of business.'

The assistant supervisor

Luke Walwyn, an assistant supervisor at Club 24 expressed his views as follows:

'Before Stairway? . . . People would come to work not knowing what they were doing. Nothing was totally structured and it was a case of 'Them versus Us' as far as staff were concerned. Whereas now they're prepared to ask questions of supervisors, managers . . . and consequently the department is running on a smoother level than it was prior to Stairway.'

'[Now] we're able to plan and meet deadlines more efficiently. We work more as a team. Moreover, we involve the staff more.'

'When I first started working with the company, we used to send out telemessages – like the old telegrams, and what they actually stated was: 'Urgent, please contact'. And we gave a pseudonym. It was up to the customer to contact us – and we'd establish we were speaking to the right person, and what we would do is tell them about their account being behind. And one particular individual said he had flown back from the Falklands basically, just to answer the telemessage. And he was threatening blue murder and everything else.'

The collector

It is argued that most successful training interventions have been carried out in a 'nice' environment. This interview with the collector gives an indication of the nature of the job and the nature of the clients dealt with by the collections department. Mr P, a difficult client, seemed to have a number of unlikely reasons for his inability to pay his dues. His first excuse was related to the death of his wife.

> 'His wife didn't die in a car accident. The following call we got – she was them in a mental home. When he used to come through on the phone, we used to go: 'We've got Mr P'. And we used to all want to know what's the latest development Mr P?'

> 'Well his wife's been committed to a psychiatric hospital. His sons, both of them now, are dead! One in a car accident, one with an overdose of drugs. And his social worker's been killed, and the social worker seeing him at the moment was just about to top himself! I mean, in real terms I suppose, he was just a compulsive liar, or he was sick. But you couldn't help but laugh, when he came on the telephone.'

Sometimes the story took a different turn.

> ' This young chap, he was only 23, and he'd got cancer of his chest, and he'd rung up to say that his mum and dad were looking after him and he'd only so many weeks to live. You tend to think – another Mr P, don't you? But as it happens, this chap was genuine. He's since died and the debt's been written off because we did monitor that account. We often get abuse in this job, it's not easy to shrug off; it still hurts your feelings when people call you names.'

> 'It's a job though there's a sense of satisfaction when you've solved a problem.'

ACTIVITY BRIEF

1 *Consider what an experiential learning programme like 'Stairway' would look like if you were designing it on the basis of the information given.*

2 *How would you evaluate the programme?*

3 *Outline the kinds of parameters and frameworks you would use to decide to what extent the Collection's Department had become a 'Learning Organisation'.*

RECOMMENDED READING

Jones and Hendry(1992). *'The Learning Organisation: A Review of Literature and Practice'*, London: HRD Partnership.

Pedler, M., Burgoyne, J., and Boydell, J. (1991). *'The Learning Company: a strategy for sustainable development'*, Maidenhead: McGraw Hill.

Hall, D. and Pedler, M. (1989).'Creating Good Business Through the Learning Company', Unpublished paper from David Hall Partnership (Paisley).

Mant Devereux (1992). *'UK Management Consultants and the Small/Medium Firm'*, London: HRD Partnership,

Investing in people: Human resource development and organisational change

David Goss

The UK government-sponsored initiative Investors in People (IIP) is based on a commitment to the benefits organisations can gain from a rigorous approach to human resource development (HRD). However, although IIP provides a common set of standards, its effects can be very variable. This case looks at the experiences of two companies – one small, the other large – as a basis for the exploration of the contribution which HRD can make to organisational development.

BACKGROUND

Investors in people

In response to internationally uncompetitive levels of employee training and emerging skill shortages that became increasingly apparent during the 1980s, the UK government has increasingly exhorted employers to invest more in training. To facilitate this process it has established a 'dual process' of setting national standards for training provision and vocational education but devolving responsibility for administering these to local level through the regional Training and Enterprise Councils (TECs). A key development in this field has been the Investors in People (IIP) initiative, introduced in late 1990. This scheme focuses, in particular, on the need to link training and development to business strategy.

The rationale behind IIP reflects the well-established view that the key to business success lies in the effective development of human resources. What is more apparent than in many previous exhortations to train, however, is the deliberate emphasis which IIP puts upon the need to link training provision for all staff directly to business strategy and objectives. It is thus not sufficient to provide staff with *ad hoc* training to be a 'good trainer'; there must be a strategic focus.

To achieve this strategic focus IIP provides a planning framework to allow organisations to develop systematically their own training provision to a standard that is nationally recognised. In this respect the emphasis is on encouraging organisations to assess the process, relevance and adequacy of training requirements in the light of their own business strategies, rather than upon detailed prescriptions of what any particular training course should involve, how it should be organised or to whom it should be provided. In this respect the IIP 'national standard' involves a set of general principles, thus:

- 'An Investor in People makes a public commitment from the top to develop all employees to achieve its business objectives.' (This involves providing a written but flexible plan of business goals and how employees will contribute to achieving these. The essence of this plan and the role of employees within it should also be communicated to all staff.)
- 'An Investor in People regularly reviews the training and development needs of all employees.' (Here it is necessary to identify the resources that will be allocated to training, and the managerial responsibility for determining and providing training opportunities).
- 'An Investor in People takes action to train and develop individuals on recruitment and throughout their employment.' (This requires the ability to determine training needs on a regular and ongoing basis and to act upon these.)
- 'An Investor in People evaluates the investment in training and development to assess achievement and improve effectiveness.' (Evaluation returns the training process to the initial objective: its continuing relevance to the business objectives of the organisation.)

The process of becoming a recognised IIP involves careful planning and assessment of evidence of achievement. Thus, an organisation will first have to audit its current training provision (with the assistance of survey instruments available through the scheme) and take appropriate action to meet the standards where necessary. When this is done, it can apply to its local TEC for recognition, at which point it will need to provide evidence of its achievements for assessment and be visited by an assessor nominated by the TEC. Following a report and recommendations a TEC committee will make a decision on recognition.

The following cases are based on accounts of implementing IIP provided by senior managers of two companies.

THE SITUATION

Case One

This case concerns a manufacturing company producing highly specialised components for petro-chemical refining employing approximately 1,000 staff, almost all full-time. The company has been established for forty years and has a 'traditional' manufacturing culture and a very stable workforce. About 60 per cent of employees are (male) manual workers, the vast majority of these being multi-skilled craftsmen. The remaining staff are technical, professional and managerial grades and clerical workers.

The major challenge now facing the company is to produce products of a consistently high quality at an internationally competitive price. Most of its major competitors are now based outside the UK, especially in the Far East. Until 1989 the company had manufactured many of its own basic sub-components but has now moved towards greater use of contractors. It has, however, endeavoured to retrain and reskill most of its manufacturing workforce (driven by a sense of 'paternalistic' responsibility and 'duty' to the local community). Thus, human resource development (HRD) has primarily involved the upgrading of existing skills and the retraining of employees to create a flexible multi-skilled workforce. Now virtually all manual employees have at least two craft capabilities.

The company had established a strong local reputation as a 'good trainer' built upon a close involvement with the (then) Engineering Industries Training Board and, more recently, with the local TEC. Indeed, it has its own training department and an on-site training centre, under the direction of the personnel department. There is an overall training budget set at board level and based on the competing claims of department managers. Department allocations are 'activated' by the training centre manager through in-house and external provision (generally the former). This system is proudly (and somewhat jealously) guarded by the personnel department which has resisted suggestions that full responsibility for arranging departmental training needs should be devolved to line managers.

The company committed to IIP on the instigation of the personnel director and marketing director and was aiming for accreditation within two years. Although the formal commitment to IIP was made at board level, it was understood from the outset that operational responsibility for the initiative would rest with the personnel manager and the training manager. Both these managers had expressed reservations about IIP which they viewed, somewhat cynically, as an example of government bureaucrats 'trying to teach grandmothers to suck eggs' and an unnecessary intrusion into their established and, in their view, highly effective, training regime. But they also appreciated that the company's decision to commit to IIP was motivated by factors other than training *per se*. In particular, there was the view that without IIP accreditation, the company would be disadvantaged in bidding for the potentially lucrative training contracts administered by TEC and tendering for government contracts (i.e., it was assumed that IIP accreditation could become an issue of contract compliance for government-sponsored work).

Perhaps not surprisingly, the experience of IIP reflected these initial misgivings. In practice, none of the company's systems of appraisal, communication and training allocation were changed other than in terms of the ways in which they were recorded and reported. Indeed, the main work which IIP created for the personnel department was in the production of reports, action plans and paperwork.

On the basis of this experience, there were seen to be three main problem areas associated with IIP: systemic, financial, and human. The systemic problems were related first to the formal requirements of the IIP documentation process: too much effort had to be put into 'translating' the perfectly workable systems which the company already had into a form acceptable to the 'bureaucratised' strictures of IIP. Second, there were felt to be problems with the assessment process; in particular, there was a concern that the full range of evidence required to gain IIP accreditation was just too daunting to justify the benefits other than for a very small (or very rich) organisation. This was experienced as doubly galling because IIP seemed to demand assessment on the basis of good 'form-filling' rather than on the basis of practical demonstrations of success.

In terms of financial problems there was a perception that IIP was very costly in a number of ways such as the time necessary to plan the programme, that spent in committees, meetings and interviews, the cost of assembling the assessment portfolios, and the general nuisance of people having to do things differently just to meet IIP 'dictates'. In summary there was a concern that the amount of money allocated to getting IIP accreditation could be better spent on providing direct training and, even, job creation.

The human problems were mainly in the form of workforce apathy and cynicism. The decision to adopt IIP was communicated to employees via the established team-briefing sessions and an article in the company newspaper. The response was claimed to be 'underwhelming'; it was viewed either as a waste of time (a view shared by most of the line managers), or, more damagingly, as an underhand management scheme to engineer job losses and redundancies. In short, managers had had to spend a great deal of valuable time convincing employees that IIP was not going to effect their position adversely. It was widely felt that winning the commitment of the employees would be an uphill struggle. Indeed, many managers felt that IIP would be 'dropped' on the grounds of impracticality well before the planned accreditation date.

Case Two

This company commenced trading in 1979; it produces hydraulic valves for a wide range of major manufacturers of industrial and domestic products. There are 56 people employed, 26 of whom are white collar and professional workers. There is no specialised personnel department and human resource matters are dealt with either by line managers or by the board. The company has performed well, even during recession, and both profitability and turnover have grown year on year for the last five years. This has been achieved in a competitive market offering low margins and has involved the company in cost reductions complemented by greater quality awareness. In turn, this has necessitated more effective business planning and human resource development.

The managing director first heard of IIP at a 'business breakfast' organised by the local TEC. It made an immediate impression because it seemed to address two problems which he anticipated would face his growing business. The first was the need to have a system of HRD that would support the company's bid to achieve BS 5750. IIP appeared to provide a systematic method of reviewing activity, measuring performance and generally assisting the quality monitoring process. The second reason was the realisation that managing a dynamic and expanding organisation required a more sophisticated and consistent approach to human resource management than had been the case hitherto. On this basis the company moved from commitment to accreditation within twelve months.

Prior to IIP the management style was described as being based on consensus with *ad hoc* autocracy'; this, however, had led to inconsistencies in downward communications and the existence of a 'permafrost' below middle management level. It also meant that the organisation was 'politicised' to the extent that a number of 'empires' had developed, further disrupting communication by sparking negative rumours fuelled by vested interests.

Under these conditions, committing to IIP was a large and not always easy step. A number of obstacles had to be overcome, the first of which was gaining the commitment of all senior managers. In this respect the key issues were those of 'lip-service' (people who, in meetings, agreed that IIP was a good idea but were unprepared to follow through in practice) and breaking down the internal 'empires'. For IIP really to work it was felt necessary for everyone to be fully committed to the idea in theory and practice, a commitment which had to start at the top. To this end IIP was made a part of all senior managers' objectives against which their performance was assessed. In this respect the 'championing' of IIP by the managing director was crucial in convincing other organisation members that this was a scheme that *had* to work and which could not be 'played at'. However, it was not only top managers who had to be convinced; in the past the company had had a tendency to take on 'fashionable' schemes and then let them lapse, and one concern of employees was that they would not get the training and development promised in the IIP action plan. To overcome this scepticism a great deal of effort was put into convincing staff that IIP was not a one-off process but a continuous activity covering everyone in the organisation. This involved the managing director acting as an 'IIP disciple', 'spreading the gospel' anywhere and everywhere within the organisation. Once the initial message had been got across the whole company was taken on an 'away-day' to a local hotel where this new company initiative was explained and discussed.

The key change initiated by the commitment to IIP was a greater sense of consistency, both in terms of linking employee development to business needs and in making sure that individual needs were taken account of in a fair and positive manner. To achieve the latter the company instigated a Performance Management System (PMS) through which everyone in the organisation was made aware of the company's objectives and of how they, as individuals, could contribute to them. As a result it is now common for employees at any level to approach top managers with suggestions and plans for improving their job efficiency, knowing that they will be listened to and taken seriously. By the same token the suggestions they present, because of the relevant company information upon which they are based, are usually realistic and practicable.

To support individual development the company introduced a regular appraisal and review system for all employees. Whereas the PMS dealt with issues relating to general organisation performance, the appraisal and review system focused more on staff development based on the quarterly review of performance which every employee receives. On the basis of this system every employee has a personal development plan which, in turn, allows for the construction of training plans at department and company levels which can then be costed, budgeted for and prioritised.

Establishing IIP was not without costs. In addition to the problem of gaining commitment, the main cost was in terms of time, especially management time. Initially this was very heavy and there was a temptation to 'sideline' IIP activities when unforeseen business demands arose. Persistence, however, paid off and, as the initiative became integrated into the company's normal operating procedures, the time-loading reduced. Indeed, the processes established by IIP are now claimed to be virtually 'self-managing', driven by staff involvement and commitment.

Overall, the top managers of the company are convinced that IIP has created a new 'can do' climate and has contributed in very real terms to the organisation's continuing success and vitality. Not only has it motivated employees at all levels but it has provided a systematic and 'open' human resource management system without the need for personnel specialists.

ACTIVITY BRIEF

1 *What do you think accounts for the difference in experience of IIP between the two cases?*

2 *What do the cases reveal about the role of top managers in change processes?*

3 *Does IIP point the way towards a system of human resource management without personnel specialists?*

4 *Both cases are based on the views of senior managers. What cautions should this suggest when it comes to interpreting their views?*

RECOMMENDED READING

IDS study 530 'Setting a Standard for Training', May 1993.
Goss, D. (1994). *Principles of Human Resource Management*, London: Routledge.
Mullins, L. J. (1993). *Management and Organisational Behaviour*, London: Pitmans, Chapter 20; Chapter 21, Chapter 9.

INDEX TO THE INTRODUCTION

Also available from Pitman Publishing

HUMAN RESOURCE MANAGEMENT
A Contemporary Perspective

Ian Beardwell and Len Holden

This exciting new text gives a fresh and up-to-date analysis of human resource management with particular regard to European and international debate. It presents a balance between the conceptual issues surrounding the HRM debate and the theoretical and practical issues and highlights the complexities of the transition from personnel management to human resource management. It provides a user-friendly overview of this complex subject and focuses on current controversial issues.

Human Resource Management:
- is printed in an attractive 2-colour design
- provides lecturers with a much-needed alternative to existing HRM texts
- progresses the debate on HRM versus personnel management, and areas of current and future development for the discipline
- continually makes reference to European and international issues
- is written by established authors from a leading teaching and research human resource management department
- contains in each chapter, objectives, cases, summaries, exercises, tasks, self-checks, discussion questions and references for further reading

Human Resource Management takes an analytical and practical approach to a complex subject. Its student-orientated approach ensures a clear and comprehensive analysis of all aspects of this field.

The text is ideal for undergraduate business studies students taking units in human resource management. It is also suitable for IPM, DMS and MBA students.

Ian Beardwell is Head of Department of Human Resource Management and Len Holden is Senior Lecturer, Department of Human Resource Management, both at Leicester Business School, De Montfort University.

ISBN: 0 273 60244 6

MANAGEMENT AND ORGANISATIONAL BEHAVIOUR
Third Edition

Laurie J Mullins

'A significant British Management text aimed at improving work performance through better understanding of human resources. Emphasising the management rather than the sociological perspectives throughout . . . The information is very well presented and there are strong interactive components.'
– Journal of the Institute of Health Education

This best selling book presents a managerial approach to the study of organisational behaviour with an emphasis on improving work performance through a better understanding of human resources. It is concerned with interactions within the structure and operations of organisations, the process of management and the behaviour of people at work. The central theme is the need for organisational effectiveness and the importance of the role of management as an integrating activity.

Management and Organisational Behaviour is written with the minimum of technical terminology and the format is clearly structured. The concepts and ideas presented provide a basis on which to formulate a critical appraisal of different perspectives on the structure, organisation and management of organisations, and interactions among the people who work in them.

Management and Organisational Behaviour:
- is in 2-colour text throughout
- contains end of chapter exercises and case studies for practical assignments and group work
- is written in a clear and accessible student-orientated style
- emphasises a managerial rather than a sociological approach to organisational behaviour

The text is ideal for first year undergraduates of organisational behaviour as well as those on DMA and MBA courses.

Laurie J Mullins is Principal Lecturer, Department of Human Resource Management, The Business School, University of Portsmouth.

ISBN: 0 273 60039 7

WORK PSYCHOLOGY
Understanding Human Behaviour in the Workplace

Derek Adam-Smith, Professor Cary L Cooper and Dr Ivan T Robertson

This major text for students of management and applied psychology shows the reader how psychology contributes to the understanding of human behaviour at work. Part One deals with the theory and issues, Part Two with techniques for assessing people in the workplace, Part Three covers the day-to-day interaction of people at work and Part Four focuses on strength, development and well-being.

'This is a valuable text for the specific group of undergraduate students at which it is targeted. The psychological content is more explicit than in some organisational behaviour textbooks.'
– Times Higher Educational Supplement

The text is suitable for undergraduates studying work psychology on business studies, management and related degrees. Students of occupational psychology will find this book invaluable.

ISBN: 0 273 03329 8

ORGANISATIONAL BEHAVIOUR
Second Edition

Roger Bennett

This M + E Handbook summarises the extensive literature in this field, concentrating on principles and methods rather than on particular empirical studies or organisational techniques. It covers scientific methodology and the role of the behavioural sciences in the analysis of organisations; conventional topics such as motivation, groups and leadership theories; principles and methods for structuring organisations and recent developments in the practice of organisational design. It includes an account of the Japanese approach to management and refers to pioneering research studies in the field of organisational behaviour.

Organisational Behaviour provides a concise but comprehensive treatment of this subject. It is suitable for business studies undergraduates and for students taking the exams of ICSA, IAM, IMS and IPS.

ISBN: 0 7121 1549 8

THE MANAGER AS COACH
Developing Your Team for Maximum Performance

Jim Durcan and David Oates

A key task for many managers has become that of developing the potential and performance of their teams to achieve standards and levels not previously dreamt of. Such developmental activity – coaching – poses new demands on managers and teams.

This book shows how managers can develop themselves to meet these challenges. Based on extensive case studies at companies including ICI and Nuclear Electric, the book covers changing management styles, coaching in a crisis and maintaining team spirit.

It shows how to combine empowerment, motivation and delegation to create super-effective teams.

ISBN: 0 273 60464 3

EMPOWERING PEOPLE

Aileen Mitchell Stewart

This book provides managers with a step-by-step guide on how to achieve empowerment in their organisation.

It looks at the organisation as an inverted pyramid with managers leading from behind, becoming facilitators, sharing visions and breaking down traditional barriers instead of leading from the front without keeping an eye on what employees are really doing.

It provides a sound understanding of what empowerment is and its benefits. It also provides the practical skills needed in planning and implementing empowerment strategies.

ISBN: 0 273 60344 2

Other related titles include:

RETHINKING THE COMPANY
Thomas Clarke ISBN: 0 273 60713 8 *Financial Times/Pitman Publishing*

RE-EDUCATING THE CORPORATION
Daniel R Tobin ISBN: 0 939246 48 1 *Oliver Wight omneo*

For further information contact:

The Marketing Department
Pitman Publishing
128 Long Acre
London WC2E 9AN
(Telephone 071-3797383).